John Debrett, William Felton

A treatise on carriages : comprehending coaches, chariots and phaetons

John Debrett, William Felton

A treatise on carriages : comprehending coaches, chariots and phaetons

ISBN/EAN: 9783337102555

Printed in Europe, USA, Canada, Australia, Japan

Cover: Foto ©Andreas Hilbeck / pixelio.de

More available books at **www.hansebooks.com**

A

TREATISE

ON

CARRIAGES.

IN TWO VOLUMES.

———

VOLUME II.

———

SECOND EDITION.

Entered at Stationer's-Hall.

A

TREATISE

ON

CARRIAGES;

COMPREHENDING

COACHES, CHARIOTS, PHAETONS, CURRICLES, WHISKIES, &c.

TOGETHER WITH THEIR PROPER

HARNESS.

IN WHICH

THE FAIR PRICES OF EVERY ARTICLE
ARE ACCURATELY STATED.

By WILLIAM FELTON, Coachmaker,

No. 36, LEATHER-LANE, HOLBORN.

LONDON:

PRINTED FOR AND SOLD BY J. DEBRETT, PICCADILLY;
R. FAULDER, NEW BOND-STREET; J. EGERTON, WHITE-
HALL; J. WHITE, FLEET-STREET; W. RICHARDSON,
CORNHILL; A. JAMESON, LONG-ACRE; AND ALL OTHER
BOOKSELLERS IN GREAT BRITAIN AND IRELAND.

1796.

ADVERTISEMENT.

THE very flattering encouragement, already received by W. FELTON from a candid and liberal public, even exceeds his expectations, and demands his grateful acknowledgments. As he at firſt premiſed, ſo it has ſince occurred, that ſome oppoſition to the work has been experienced from the illiberal part of the trade, by whom it has been inſinuated, with a deſign to prejudice, that many of the prices are erroneous: to this

       it

*it may be obferved, that, in a manufactory,
where the articles are numerous, tradefmen
will vary fomething in their charges, according to their feveral ideas of the profit;
but it has been the author's ftudy, uniformly,
to make his calcultions and ftatements with
an accuracy and fairnefs, that may render
the whole a juft ftandard, as well on the part
of the purchafer as the tradefman; and fuch
as he ever intends to abide by, for work executed in the beft manner, as alfo do many
others of the trade; it may therefore be pre-
fumed, whoever objects to them as unfair,
have only their views to miflead and impofe on their employers.*

*As a proof of the utility, and as a further
recommendation of this work, it has been
honoured with the encomiums and approba-
tion of fome of the moft independent and ingenious part of the trade, and, in feveral
inftances, it has been introduced as a fuccefs-*

3   *ful*

*ful arbitrator, under contending circum-
stances; having thus far succeeded, and
discharged his duty to the public, and that
with strict justice to the trade,*

He remains, with grateful respect,

Their most obedient servant,

W. FELTON.

CONTENTS.

CHAP.

The

CONTENTS.

INTRODUCTION.

THE former volume explains the method of building the various kinds
of carriages in general ufe, and defcribes
alfo the different component parts, in
their feparate ftates, and the various
purpofes to which they are applied :—
their feveral prices are alfo ftated according to the different manners in which they
are finifhed, fo that any of them may
eafily be felected, and added to either
old or new carriages, agreeable to the
fancy of the proprietor, and the prices
thereby eafily known.

In

In order to render the information of the price for carriages more correct, the feveral parts which are neceffary, and which conftitute the plain-finifhed carriage of each fort, will be felected, and the prices to each article ftated, which, when added, the fum total thereof will be the firft charge for each carriage of the kind; and whatever more is required to be added, or whatever materials are greater in expence than thofe mentioned in the tables of the firft cofts, they will be ftated in feparate tables, under the title of extras; fo that, by obferving this rule, the price of every carriage, however finifhed, may be readily obtained. As the reprefentation of finifhed carriages will convey a better idea of their feveral properties, two of each fort will be reprefented, the one finifhed in a plain, but modern, ftyle; the other to the extreme of fafhion, with the prices for

each,

each, ftated agreeable to the above rule, the value of thefe two being given, thofe of the intermediate pattern will be regu- lated by the different degrees of ornament the proprietor's fancy may lead him to.

It has been an uniform practice throughout the trade, to make a firft charge, and alfo to add feveral things as extras, which they conceive are not com- prifed in the meaning thereof; and it is not uncommon to find the amount for extras exceed the firft price. Many ad- here to their old rule, making the fame firft charge now as they did 30 or 40 years fince, adding thereto, as extras, all the improvements which, fince that time, have been made, which confounds the bill, even for a plain carriage, with fuch numbers of charges as would lead a per- fon to fufpect them as impofitions, The moft explicit method would be, to abide

c by

by one general rule, ftating to what extent the firft coft is made up to, and then add the feveral additions as extras, the fame as here obferved.

The harnefs neceffary to be ufed with carriages is treated on in this volume and the fupplement only ; in this a minute defcription of every part of a harnefs is given, defcribing what parts are neceffary for ufe, and what for ornament only : alfo the particular kind of harnefs to be ufed for each particular purpofe, the prices of each harnefs finifhed to the extent of what is alone neceffary, are ftated in feparate tables as a firft coft, and thofe parts, which are neceffary for ornament, are made extras of, agreeable to the fame rule obferved in the ftatement of finifhed carriages, whereby the price of any harnefs, however much or little ornamented, may be afcertained

2   with

with accuracy. The prices for the separate parts of a harneſs, except thoſe
which are compriſed under the title of
ornaments, are ſtated in the ſupplement,
being conſidered as under the deſcription
of repairs.

TABLES

TABLES OF PRICES

FOR

PLAIN CARRIAGES,

FINISHED IN THE MODERN STYLE.

CHAP. I.

SECT. 1.

DESCRIPTION OF THE EXTENT TO WHICH A COACH, A LANDAU, A POST-CHAISE, AND DEMI-LANDAU ARE FINISHED,

TO REGULATE THE FIRST COST OF EACH BY.

THE Bodies are to be confidered as plain, lined with fecond cloth, and trimmed with a two-inch lace, and two and a half ditto for the holders, pleated feat-falls, double folding-fteps, infide feat-boxes, the bottoms carpeted, plate glaffes, the frames covered with cloth, mahogany

VOL. II.   B   fhutters,

fhutters, octagon back-lights, plated door-handles, but no plated mouldings or frames.

The Carriages plain, with S-formed fprings, common axletrees and pipe-boxes, the wheels of the common height, twelve and fourteen fpokes, ftraked tyre, main check and collar-braces, with Englifh pole-pieces, the main and check-braces with plated buckles. The body and carriage painted any plain colour, without picking out, or ornaments, the body varnifhed and japanned.

Neither boots, coach-boxes, raifed hind or fore ends, are included in the firft coft; for, being of various patterns, their different prices are ftated in the tables of extras.

PRICE

PRICE or FIRST COST of A COACH, LANDAU, POST-CHAISE, and D..LANDAU.

[The prices of the separate articles of which a carriage is composed, are here collected from the statements in the first Volume, to which all other charges are to be added, and constitute the first charge.]

Vol. I.

Page		Coach. £. s. d.	Landau. £. s. d.	Post-Chaise. £. s. d.	D.-Landau. £. s. d.
35.	Bodies	30 0 0	46 0 0	25 0 0	40 0 0
67.	Carriages	24 15 0	24 15 0	22 0 0	22 0 0
114.	Wheels	7 10 0	7 10 0	6 16 6	6 10 6
151.	Linings	15 10 0	17 1 0	12 0 0	13 1 0
152.	Glasses and frames	6 10 0	6 10 0	6 15 0	6 15 0
163.	Glass rollers	0 10 6	0 10 6	0 10 6	0 10 6
152.	Shutters	1 15 0	1 15 0	1 15 0	1 15 0
	Carpet	0 10 6	0 10 6	0 10 6	0 10 6
	Sliding seat-boxes	1 10 0	1 10 0	1 10 0	1 10 0
190.	Steps	3 0 0	3 0 0	3 0 0	3 0 0
200.	Painting, japanning, and varnishing body & carriage	7 12 0	5 2 6	3 6 0	4 12 0
214.	Main braces	4 4 0	4 4 0	3 13 6	3 13 6
	Check braces	0 10 0	0 10 0	0 10 0	0 10 0
	Collar braces	0 12 0	0 12 0	0 12 0	0 12 0
	Pole pieces	1 0 0	1 0 0	0 18 0	0 18 0
	Sum total for plain perch carriages	105 9 0	120 11 0	93 1 6	107 2 6
67.	Addition for crane instead of perch carriage	16 5 0	16 5 0	14 13 0	14 13 0
	Sum total for crane-neck carriages	121 14 0	136 16 0	107 14 6	121 15 6

B 2

SECT.

SECT. 2.

PHAETONS.

THE various patterns and fizes of phaetons, make it more difficult to afcertain a regular ſtandard of prices for them than for other carriages; but to proportion them to three fizes, all one way finiſhed, and omitting thoſe things which make the variety, a tolerable perfect ſtatement may be made.

———

DESCRIPTION OF THE EXTENT TO WHICH PHAETONS, OF A LARGE, MIDDLE, AND SMALL SIZE, ARE FINISHED, TO REGULATE THE FIRST COST OF EACH BY.

THE Bodies plain, lined with a fecond cloth, and trimmed with a two-inch broad lace, a carpet and feat-box. The heads, wings, and knee-boots are omitted.

The Carriages are perch, with ſtraked wheels, having twelve and fourteen ſpokes for the large, ten and twelve for the middle, eight and ten for the ſmall phaeton; common axletrees and boxes, long tail ſprings behind, ſingle elbow ſprings before, main braces only behind, five feet long, and two inches and a half wide for large; four feet long, and two inches and a quarter wide for middle; three feet and a half long, and two inches wide for ſmall; a pair of check-braces, pole, and pole-pieces, or ſhafts for one horſe.—The paint-

ing

ing of any colour, and plain varnifhcd; neither blocks, boots, nor budgets are included.

[The prices collected as in the former table.]

Vol. I. Page	Large. £. s. d.	Middle. £. s. d.	Small. £. s. d.
35. Bodies plain -	8 10 0	7 0 0	6 10 0
67. Carriages -	20 0 0	18 0 0	16 4 0
114. Wheels ftraked :	6 12 0	5 11· 0	4 10 0
151. Linings -	4 14 6	4 14 6	4 14 6
152. Carpet or oil-cloth	0 7 6	0 7 6	0 7 6
Seat-box -	0 15 0	0 15 0	0 15 0
200. Painting and varnifhing -	3 15 0	2 19 6	1 19 6
214. Main braces -	2 0 0	1 15 0	1 2 0
Check ditto -	0 7 6	0 7 ·6	0 7 6
Pole-pieces -	0 18 0	0 18 0	0 18 0
Total for perch phaetons	47 19 6	42 8 0	37 8 0
67. Cranes in addition	13 10 0	11 18 0	10 14 0
Total for crane-neck phaetons - -	61 9 6	54 6 0	48 2 0

SECT. 3.

TWO-WHEELED CARRIAGES.

THOSE, like the phaetons, are finifhed in various fanciful ways, and can only be regulated in their prices by reducing each defcription of them to a plain fimple rule, omitting thofe things, however neceffary, which differ in their patterns, to be valued by themfelves, and added as fancy may direct the choice in finifhing.

B 3   DESCRIPTION

THE Bodies plain, lined with fecond cloth, and trimmed with a two-inch broad lace, carpet and feat-box to the curricle and gig, and carpet only to the whiſkies.

The curricle carriage, plain, with ſtraked wheels, fourteen fpokes, whip-fprings behind, French-horn fprings before, long main-braces to go round the hind fprings, feven feet long, two inches wide, with jacks ; ſhort braces, with a lug-plate in front ; common axletrees and boxes.

The gig carriage plain, with ſtraked wheels, twelve fpokes ; whip-fprings behind, main-braces, with buckles, four feet long, two inches and a quarter wide ; fmall fingle elbow-fprings in front, with loops to the body ; common axletrees and boxes.

The whiſkey carriage, plain, with ſtraked wheels, ten fpokes, grafshopper fprings, with loops ; common axletrees and boxes.

The draught of each of the carriages to be taken from a fplinter-bar.

Heads, wings, and knee-boots are omitted in all.

PRICE

PRICE OF TWO-WHEELED CARRIAGES.

[Collected as before.]

Vol. I. Page		Curricle.			Gig.			Whiskies. Pannels.			Whiskies. Cane.		
		£.	s.	d.	£.	s.	d.	£.	s.	d.	£.	s.	d.
35.	Bodies	7	0	0	0	7	0	0	5	0	0	5	0
67.	Carriages	15	0	0	11	11	0	9	9	0	9	9	0
114.	Wheels, flaked	3	10	0	3	2	0	2	11	0	2	11	0
151.	Linings	4	14	6	4	14	0	4	14	6	3	10	0
152.	Carpet or oil-cloth	0	7	6	0	7	6	0	7	6	0	7	6
	Seat-box	0	15	0	0	15	0	—	—	—	—	—	—
200.	Painting and varnishing	3	2	6	3	3	6	2	11	0	1	19	0
214.	Pair of main-braces	1	8	0	1	2	0	—	—	—	—	—	—
	Pair of pole-pieces	0	18	0	—	—	—	—	—	—	—	—	—
80.	Pair of jacks for main-braces	0	15	0	—	—	—	—	—	—	—	—	—
	Total	37	10	6	31	14	6	24	9	6	22	12	6
67.	The curricle made gig, the gig and whiskey made curricle	2	3	0	4	9	0	4	0	0	4	0	0
	Total for curricle, gig, or whiskey	39	13	6	36	3	6	28	9	6	26	12	6

The

The fums total for the feveral carriages, finifhed to the extent defcribed, are here colleĉted,
whereby ready information is obtained of the firſt
coſt of each. Whatever ornaments or conveniencies it may be thought proper to add for completing them, according to any pattern, the prices
of them will be found ſtated in the following
tables of extras:

ſ━━━ˈ

SUMS TOTAL, OR FIRST CHARGE, FOR EACH
CARRIAGE.

		Perch.			Crane neck.		
		£.	s.	d	£.	s.	d.
Coaches, &c.	Coach	105	9	0	121	14	0
	Landau	120	11	0	136	16	0
	Poſt-Chaife	93	1	6	107	4	6
	Demi-Landau	107	2	6	121	15	6
Phaetons	Large	47	19	6	61	9	6
	Middle	42	8	0	54	6	6
	Small	37	8	0	48	2	0
		For one horfe as gig and curricle.			or twohorfes as curricle.		
Two-wheeled carriages	Curricle	39	13	6	37	10	6
	Gig	31	14	6	36	3	6
	Whiſkey, pannel-ed	24	9	0	28	9	0
	Ditto, caned	22	12	6	26	12	6

CHAP.

CHAP. II.

ON EXTRAS.

THE fums total may be confidered as a rule to proceed upon for the firft charge of the different kinds of carriages now generally in ufe, and, by adding the amount of other conveniencies, with the increafed difference of thofe articles which are finifhed in a fuperior manner from thofe already ftated, a perfect knowledge of the value of carriages, every way completed, is eafy to be obtained ; to do which, without the trouble of referring to the former work; feparate tables, containing the prices of the various articles which are to be added, and the difference of thofe, which are fuperior to what have already been given, are ftated in regular order agreeable to the plan of the former work ; fo that by adding the feveral Extras, which are hereafter mentioned to the Sum Total, the value of all carriages, however finifhed, may be eafily known.

TABLES OF PRICES FOR EXTRAS,

WHICH ARE TO BE ADDED TO THE SUMS TOTAL, OR FIRST
COST, OF EACH SORT OF CARRIAGE.

FOR BODIES.

FROM PAGE 35, 36, 37, AND 38, VOL. 1.

	Coach.	P. Chaife or Chariot	Landau.	Demi-Landau.
	£. s. d.	£. s. d.	£. s. d	£. s. d.
Door-lights contracted on the fides	— —	2 0 0	— —	— —
Round fides	2 0 0	1 0 0	2 0 0	1 0 0
Sword-cafe, or boodge	2 10 0	2 10 0	2 10 0	2 10 0
Side-lights for glaffes and fhutters	7 0 0	3 10 0	— —	— —
A large back-light for ditto	2 0 0	2 0 0	— —	— —
A ditto divided for ditto	2 15 0	2 15 0	— —	— —

	Phaetons or Chaife Bodies.
Real doors, to open on the fides, to gig, whifkey, phaeton, or curricle	2 0 0
Sham ditto, to imitate doors	0 15 0
A fword-cafe, or boodge	1 10 0
A drop feat-box fixed on the feat-rails	0 7 6

SECT.

SECT. 2.

EXTRAS TO CARRIAGES.

FROM PAGE 67, VOL. 1.

	Coach or Landau.	Chariot, PostCha- riot,or D. Landau.	Phaetons.		
			Large.	Middle.	Small.
	£. s. d.	£. s. d.	£. s. d.	£. s. d.	£. s. d.
A bent or compass perch —	1 1 0	1 1 0	1 1 0	0 18 0	0 16 0
The sides of the compass or straight perch plated with iron —	3 3 0	2 15 0	2 10 0	2 2 0	1 16 0
A whole wheel front to the perch carriage -	2 10 0	2 5 0	2 0 0	1 15 0	1 10 0
A half ditto to ditto -	1 5 0	1 3 0	1 0 0	0 8 0	0 15 0
Double bows to the cranes of a crane-neck carriage —	3 3 0	2 15 0	2 10 0	2 2 0	1 16 0

SECT. 3.

EXTRAS TO SPRINGS.

FROM PAGE 79 AND 80, VOL. 1.

THE springs, which are included in the original price of carriages, are, for the Coach and Chariot, the S-formed spring all round; for the Curricle, the large whip; and for the Gig and Phaeton, the small L flap hind springs, with Frenchhorn or single elbow fore springs and loops; for

2   the

the Whiſkey, the double elbow or graſshopper
ſpring; the following prices to be added, if any
of the other patterns are uſed.

	Coach or Landau.			Chariot, Poſt-Chaiſe, or Demi-Landau.		
	£.	s.	d.	£.	s.	d.
A ſet of double ſprings to carry body and boot —— ——	5	4	0	4	8	0
A ſet of large ſcroll ſprings for heavy travelling carriages ——	4	16	0	3	4	0
A ſet of ſpring body loops inſtead of iron ones, as included with the body	2	5	0	2	0	0
A ſet of ſpiral or worm ſprings —	2	10	0	2	10	0

	Large Phaeton.			Small Phaeton or Chaiſe.		
A pair of ſpring jacks — —	0	18	0	0	15	0
A pair of worm ſprings ——	1	5	0	1	4	0

SECT. 4.

EXTRAS FOR THE PATENT AXLETREES.

FROM PAGE 93, VOL. I.

	Coach, &c.			Chariots, &c.			Phaeton, large, middle and ſmall.			Gig and Whiſkey, or Curricle.		
	£.	s.	d.	£.	s.	d.	£.	s.	d.	£.	s.	d.
Patent anti-attrition	15	14	0	15	5	0	14	19	6	7	7	0
Patent cylinder —	22	10	0	21	10	0	22	4	6	10	12	0
New pattern ditto -	17	14	0	17	15	0	17	13	0	8	10	0
New patent axletrees, with double box -	21	4	0	21	15	0	20	3	0	9	4	0

SECT.

SECT. 5.

Common-fized Wheels are ufed for the Coach, the Chariot, and large Phaeton, but light Wheels for the middle and fmall-fized Phaetons, Gigs, Whifkies, and Curricles.

EXTRAS TO WHEELS.

FROM PAGE 114, VOL. I.

	Phaetons				Two-Wheeled Carriages		
Number of fpokes.	Coach and Chariot.	Large.	Middle.	Small.	Curricle.	Gig.	Whifkey.
	12 and 14.	12 and 14.	10 and 12.	8 and 10.			
	£. s. d.	£. s. d.	£. s. d.	£. s. d.	£. s. d.	£. s. d.	£. s. d.
Hooped tyre	1 0 0	1 0 0	1 5 0	1 5 0	0 14 0	0 12 0	0 10 0
Patent ditto	—	—	0 0 0	2 10 0	0 14 0	0 12 0	0 10 0
Moulded fellies	3 0 0	3 0 0	3 5 0	0 0 0	0 0 0	0 0 0	0 0 0
	0 19 0	0 19 0	0 17 0	0 15 0	0 10 0	0 9 0	0 8 0

Very heavy wheels for a travelling Coach or Chariot, £.1 10s. each fet.

SECT. 6.

BOOTS AND BUDGETS.

FROM PAGE 119, VOL. I.

	Coach, Chariot, and large Phaeton £. s. d.	Middle-sized Phaeton. £. s. d.	Small ditto, or Curricle, Gig, &c. £. s. d.
A platform, or luggage-boot — —	8 0 0	6 0 0	4 0 0
A trunk boot —	5 0 0	3 10 0	2 10 0
A framed boot, for an iron coach-box —	6 0 0	4 6 0	3 3 0
A ditto, with a concealed coach-box —	10 0 0	9 0 0	— —

SECT. 7.

PLATFORMS, or raised hind and fore ends, and blocks, for Coach and Chariot.

FROM PAGE 124, VOL. I.

	Plain. £. s. d.	Middling, or neat. £. s. d.	Much ornamented. £. s. d.
A pair of pump, plow, or guard-handles, and foot-board — —	2 0 0	3 0 0	4 0 0
Ditto short blocks and foot-board for post-chaise or hind standards —	1 10 0	2 5 0	3 0 0
Raised fore ends, or budget blocks — —	1 10 0	2 10 0	3 10 0

CUSHIONS.	Plain.	With a plated top frame.	Plated top and bottom frame.
A footman's cushion —	2 2 0	2 18 0	3 16 0
A ditto with carved hind standard — —	6 0 0	6 18 0	7 18 0

SECT.

SECT. 8.

BLOCKS FOR PHAETONS, CURRICLES, OR GIGS.

FROM PAGE 124, VOL. I.

	Large.			Middle.			Small.		
	£.	s.	d.	£.	s.	d.	£.	s.	d.
Hind fpring blocks —	4	4	0	5	3	0	2	2	0
Fore fpring blocks —	1	0	0	0	15	0	0	10	0
Hind platforms, raifed with blocks — —	1	10	0	1	5	0	1	0	0

If thofe fpring blocks are more or lefs orna-mented than what is defcribed in Plate xiii. an allowance of one-third muft be added to, or re-duced from the above ftatement, which are for blocks carved in a neat, but not extravagant manner.

SECT. 9.

COACH - BOXES, INCLUDING THE SEATS AND CRADLES TO EACH.

FROM PAGE 131, VOL. I.

	£.	s.	d.
The common ftandard coach-box — —	5	5	0
The Salifbury boot or budget ditto —	10	5	0
The iron coach-box — — —	10	0	0
The iron coach-box and trunk-boot — —	16	6	0
The iron coach-box and carved blocks —	18	8	0
The budget and concealed coach-box — —	10	0	0
The chair, or chaife coach-box to fix on the boot —	10	0	0
The travelling feat, for either common or Salifbury coach-box, in addition to the former price · —	2	3	6
Ditto, hung with fprings — —	5	17	0

TRIM-

T R I M M I N G S.

FROM PAGE 132, VOL. I.

FOR the Lace and Fringes, of different widths and qualities, reference muſt be had to the former ſtatements, as the variety is ſo great, and the quantities ſo uncertain, that are uſed; however, the amount is eaſily known, by adding the difference of price for quality and quantity above what is ſtated in the following table of prices for linings.

SECT. 10.

EXTRAS FOR THE LININGS.

FROM PAGE 151, VOL. I.

	Coach or Landau.			Chariot or Landaulet.			Phaeton or Chaise With Head.			Phaeton or Chaise With Wings.		
	£.	s.	d.	£.	s.	d.	£.	s.	d.	£.	s.	d.
The cloth ſuperfine	4	0	0	3	0	0	2	0	0	1	0	0
Morocco leather, inſtead of ſecond cloth	8	0	0	6	0	0	4	0	0	2	0	0
Quilting the lining with ſmall tufts	1	1	0	0	10	6	0	10	6	0	10	6
Swinging holders, and the other laces, 2½ inches broad, inſtead of 2 inches	1	11	0	0	18	0	0	2	6	0	3	6
Ditto, 3 inches	2	7	0	1	2	0	0	5	0	0	7	0
Ditto, 3½ inches	3	3	0	1	18	0	0	7	6	0	10	6
Ditto, 4 inches	3	18	0	2	3	0	0	10	0	0	14	0
A falſe lining, made of printed cotton	3	10	0	2	15	0	2	2	0	1	4	0
Ditto, if the roof is covered	4	0	0	3	3	0	—	—	—	—	—	—
Ditto, if the lining is trimmed with bordering	5	5	0	4	10	0	2	10	0	1	8	0

SECT.

SECT. 11.

EXTRAS TO THE INSIDE FURNITURE FOR BODIES.

FROM PAGE 152, VOL. I.

	Coach.			Chariot.		
	£.	s.	d.	£.	s.	d.
A set of silk squabs, with half backs, faced on one side with silk —	4	0	0	2	12	6
Ditto with Morocco leather —	4	15	0	3	3	0
Ditto, faced with silk on one side, and Morocco leather on the other —	5	15	6	3	13	6
A set of silk spring curtains —	3	3	0	3	0	0
A set of festoon ditto, tops only —	2	12	6	2	12	6
A set of ditto with side drapery –	3	13	6	3	13	6
The outsides of the glass frames covered with two-inch lace instead of cloth	1	7	0	1	10	0
Venetian blinds instead of mahogany shutters — — —	2	15	0	2	15	0
A net for the roof — —	0	10	6	0	10	6

———

SECT. 12.

HAMMERCLOTHS.

FROM PAGE 158, VOL. I.

	Livery.			Second.			Superfine.		
	£.	s.	d.	£.	s.	d	£.	s.	d.
To a six-breadth hammercloth without any trimmings —	4	10	0	5	10	0	6	10	0
Ditto with top and bottom row of two-inch lace —	5	5	0	6	5	0	7	5	0
Ditto with a top row, and two bottom rows of 2½ inch lace	6	6	0	7	7	0	8	8	0
Ditto with a row of five-inch fringe at top and bottom —	8	1	0	9	2	c	10	3	0

	Plain oiled Linen.			Painted.			Patent.		
An oil-skin cover —	1	16	0	2	2	0	3	13	6

C   To

To know the amount of every other hammer-cloth, is only to add the quantity of trimmings with which they are trimmed : every row of trimmings is nine yards, except the top feat, which is only four.

———

SECT. 13.

OCCASIONAL REQUISITES.

FROM PAGE 163, VOL. I.

	£. s. d	£. s. d.
A fet of private locks with bolts on the fhutters	— —	1 1 0
		Large.	Small.
Silvered ftuds, each —	—	0 0 8	0 0 4
Plated ftuds, each —	—	0 1 0	0 0 8

———

SECT. 14.

PLATED FURNITURE.

FROM PAGE 164, VOL. I.

THERE are three forts of plated furniture, beft, middling, and inferior; what is here ftated is the beft, the difference of price, for either middling or inferior, is known by referring to the former volume; the compofition and brafs metal furniture are here alfo regularly ftated.   As it is

impoffible

impossible to ascertain the certain quantity of moulding used to each carriage, the different widths only, at the price per foot, is here stated.

Parts of an Inch.	Best silver plated. £. s. d.	Composition Metal. £. s. d.	Brass. £. s. d.
Mouldings { 2-8ths	0 1 3	0 0 10	0 0 8
3-8	0 1 9	0 1 2	0 0 10½
4-8	0 2 3	0 1 6	0 1 1¼
5-8	0 2 9	0 1 10	0 1 4½
6-8	0 3 3	0 2 2	0 1 9½
Scroll ornaments, the pair —	0 8 0	0 4 0	0 3 0
Tip ditto, ditto —	0 6 0	0 2 8	0 2 0

FRAMES.

	Best silver plated.	Composition Metal.	Brass.
An octagon back-light ——	0 10 0	0 7 8	0 5 0
Pair of whole sword-cases for coach or chariot ——	0 11 0	0 8 4	0 5 6
Ditto, for chaise or phaeton —	0 9 0	0 6 0	0 4 6
Pair of half do. for coach or chariot	0 8 0	0 5 4	0 4 0
Ditto, for chaise or phaeton —	0 6 0	0 4 0	0 3 0
A pair of wing frames for phaeton or chaise — ——	1 15 0	1 4 0	0 18 0

HEAD-PLATES, the set.

Coach, twelve.

	Silver. £. s. d.	Best silver plated.	Composition Metal.	Brass.
Fancy device, middle size — —		2 10 0	1 13 0	1 5 0
Crest embossed ——	4 4 0	3 0 0	2 0 0	1 10 0
Circles to contain ditto —	1 16 0	1 4 0	1 5 0	1 0 0

Chariot, six.

	Silver.	Best silver plated.	Composition Metal.	Brass.
Fancy device — —		1 5 0	0 16 6	0 12 6
Crests embossed —	2 2 0	1 10 0	1 0 0	0 15 0
Circles to contain ditto —	0 18 0	0 10 0	0 10 0	0 7 0

Phaeton, or Chaise.

	Silver.	Best silver plated.	Composition Metal.	Brass.
Fancy device — —		1 5 0	0 16 6	0 12 6
Crests embossed —	2 2 0	1 10 0	1 0 0	0 15 0
Circles for ditto —	0 18 0	0 10 0	0 12 0	0 9 0

N. B. For each flat pierced crest head-plate, of plated metal, in a circle, or fancy pattern, add ninepence to the prices stated for the fancy device.

JOINTS.	Beſt ſilver plated.			Compoſition Metal.			Braſs.		
Real.	£.	s.	d.	£.	s.	d.	£.	s.	d.
A ſet for a landau ———	12	12	0	8	8	c	6	6	0
A pair for a demi-landau ——	6	6	0	4	4	0	3	3	0
A ſet for a chaiſe or phaeton –	8	8	0	5	5	c	4	4	0
Sham.									
A ſet for a coach, thick ———	7	0	0	4	12	0	3	10	0
Ditto for ditto, thin ———	6	0	0	4	0	0	3	0	0
A pair for a chariot, thick –	3	10	0	2	6	6	1	15	0
A ditto for ditto, thin ——	3	0	c	2	0	0	1	10	0
Four barrel props with caps, for a pair — ———	1	4	0	0	16	c	0	12	0
PLATING the BODY-LOOPS.									
The whole outſide ſurface —	3	13	6	2	6	0	1	12	0
The four flat-heads ditto ——	0	10	c	0	6	6	0	5	0
The four plain heads ditto ——	0	8	0	0	5	4	0	4	0
The four top outſide edges ditto	0	6	0	0	4	0	0	3	0
POLE-HOOKS.									
For a coach — ———	2	10	0	1	15	c	1	5	0
...	2	2	0	1	8	0	1	1	0
...	1	18	0	1	5	8	0	19	0

...JOINTS, per pair.	Inch.									
	2¼	0	11	c	0	7	4	0	5	6
	2½	0	9	c	0	6	0	0	4	6
	2¾	0	7	6	0	5	0	0	3	9
	2	0	6	0	0	4	0	0	3	0
	3	0	4	c	0	2	8	0	2	0
	1½	0	3	0	0	2	0	0	1	6
		0	7	0	0	4	8	0	3	6
		0	6	c	0	4	0	0	3	0
		0	5	0	0	3	4	0	2	0
		0	4	c	0	2	8	0	2	0
		0	3	c	0	2	0	0	1	6
		0	2	c	0	1	4	0	1	0
		0	0	0	0	0	0	0	4	0

WHEEL-

WHEEL-HOOPS, per pair.	Beft filver plated.			Cafed with filver plated metal.			Compofition Metal.			Brafs.		
	£.	s.	d.	£.	s.	d.	£.	s.	d.	£.	s.	d.
Coach — —	3	3	0	1	15	0	1	2	0	0	17	6
Chariot or large phaeton — —	2	16	6	1	10	0	1	0	0	0	15	0
Small phaeton, curricle, or chaife —	2	2	0	1	5	0	0	10	3	0	12	6

Seldom any other plated hoops are ufed, than thofe cafed with filver plated metal.

—————

SPIRAL OR WORM SPRINGS, PLATED.

	Beft filver plated.			Compofition Metal.			Brafs.		
	£.	s.	d.	£.	s.	d.	£.	s.	d.
A fet for a coach or chariot complete — —	6	10	0	5	5	0	4	4	0
A pair for phaeton or chaife do.	3	0	0	2	5	0	1	16	0
The plates and fcrews only, for a plain fet to a coach or chariot	2	5	0	1	15	0	1	10	0
Ditto for a pair to a phaeton or chaife — —	1	1	0	0	15	0	0	12	0

In the above price for plating, the value of the worm-fprings are alfo included; but, if the old ones are plated, deduct the price of them from the prices here ftated.

C 3 SECT.

SECT. 15.

LAMPS, PER PAIR.

FROM PAGE 184, VOL. I.

GLOBES.	Coach.			Chariot.			Phaeton or chaife.		
	£.	s.	d.	£.	s.	d.	£.	s.	d.
Common plated backs —	1	18	c	1	15	0	1	12	0
Glafs reflector backs —	2	2	c	1	18	c	1	16	0
Ditto with plated heads and barrels — —	2	10	c	2	6	0	2	0	0
ITALIAN.									
Common, with flat fides —	1	15	c	1	12	0	1	10	0
Round fides — —	2	4	c	2	0	0	2	6	0
Plated heads and barrels —	2	12	0	2	8	0	2	2	0
OVAL, or SQUARE PATTERN.									
Plain, with glafs backs —	2	6	c	2	2	0	1	18	0
Plated heads and barrels —	2	10	c	2	8	0	2	6	0
Extra large plated heads and barrels —	3	3	0	2	16	c	2	10	0

The lamps are of the fame expence, whether plated with brafs or filver.

SECT. 16.

STEPS.

FROM PAGE 190, VOL. I.

	£.	s.	d	£.	s.	d	£.	s.	d.
Extra for a pair of treble folding fteps to either coach or chariot — —	—	—		—	—		2	10	0
	Single.			Double.			Treble.		
̄or a pair of chaife fteps —	—	—		0	14	0	—	—	
or a hanging-ftep to a phaeton	1	1	0	2	2	0	3	3	0

SECT.

SECT. 17.

EXTRAS TO THE PAINTING OF BODIES.

FROM PAGE 200, VOL. I.

	Coach.			Chariot.			Phaetons.									Pannels.			Whiskies, with Cane.		
							Large.			Middle.			Small and Gig.								
	£.	s.	d.	£.	s.	d.	£.	s.	d.	£.	s.	d.	£.	s.	d.	£.	s.	d.	£.	s.	d.
Picking out the mouldings	0	10	6	0	10	6	0	7	6	0	7	6	0	7	6	0	7	6	0	7	6
Polishing the pannels	2	10	0	2	0	0	1	5	0	1	5	0	1	5	0	1	1	0	—		
High varnishing ditto	5	15	6	6	4	4	0	3	3	0	3	3	0	3	3	2	10	0	—		
Japanning the doors and sword-case of phaeton or chaise	—			—			0	10	6	0	10	6	0	10	6	0	10	6	—		

EXTRAS

C 4

EXTRAS TO PAINTING OF CARRIAGES, AND JAPANNING THE BOOTS.

	Coach.			Chariot.			Phaetons.									Whiskies, with Pannels.			Whiskies, with Cane.		
							Large.			Middle.			Small and Gig.								
	£.	s.	d.	£.	s.	d.	£.	s.	d.	£.	s.	d.	£.	s.	d.	£.	s.	d.	£.	s.	d.
Picking out the mouldings with one colour	1	1	0	1	1	0	0	18	0	0	15	0	0	12	0	0	10	0	0	10	0
Picking out and lining ditto with two colours	1	15	0	1	15	0	1	11	6	1	10	0	1	4	0	0	18	0	0	18	0
Ditto three colours and pannel-ing	2	10	0	2	10	0	2	5	0	2	0	0	0	10	0	0	15	0	0	15	0
Oil varnishing the carriages after painting	0	15	0	0	15	0	0	15	0	0	15	0	0	10	6	0	10	0	0	10	0

SECT.

SECT. 18.

FOR HERALD AND ORNAMENT PAINTING.

FROM PAGE 201, VOL. 1.

ARMS AND CRESTS.	SIZES.		
	Large. £. s. d.	Middling. £. s. d.	Small. £. s. d.
The arms painted in a circle, an oval shield, or a lozenge	0 10 0	0 7 0	0 5 0
Ditto, with supporters and crests	2 12 0	1 18 6	1 6 0
The crest of a private gentleman	0 5 0	0 4 0	0 3 0
Ditto of a nobleman with coronet ———	0 10 0	0 8 0	0 6 0
CYPHERS.			
The single initial of a person's name ———	0 3 0	0 2 6	0 2 0
The double ditto ———	0 4 6	0 3 6	0 2 6
The treble ditto ———	0 5 0	0 4 0	0 3 0
MANTLES.			
A mantle plain ———	0 10 6	0 7 6	0 5 0
Ditto, much furled or folded	0 15 0	0 12 0	0 10 0

	Inches wide.	Rich.		Plain.		
Borders for pannels, at per foot long ———	5	0 10 0		0 7 6	0 5 0	
	4	0 7 6		0 6 0	0 4 0	
	3	0 6 0		0 4 6	0 3 6	
	2	0 4 6		0 3 6	0 2 6	
	1½	0 3 6		0 2 6	0 1 6	
Fillets for pannels, at per foot long ———	1	0 2 6		0 1 9	0 1 0	
	¾	0 1 9		0 1 0	0 0 9	
	½	0 1 0		0 0 9	0 0 6	
Striping, or ornamenting the pannels, per foot square ———		0 10 0		0 7 6	0 5 0	

SECT.

HEADS, WINGS, KNEEBOOTS, AND DASHING LEATHERS.

FROM PAGE 208, VOL. 1.

HEADS.	Without lining.			With a ferge lining.			With a fecond cloth lining.		
	£.	s.	d	£.	s.	d	£.	s.	d.
A fquare head fixed on the body, including the join⋅s —	7	0	0	8	10	0	10	0	0
A round or waggon ditto —	8	0	0	10	0	0	12	0	0

	Cloth.			Oilfkin.			Serge.		
A pair of curtains to flide —	0	18	0	0	16	0	0	12	0
Wrenches which turn the joints from the infide, to fet or unfet the head with —	—	—		—	—		1	10	0
A back glafs light —	—	—		—	—		0	6	0
The heads made on a frame for the convenience of taking off occafionally —	—	—		—	—		1	6	0

WINGS.	Large.			SIZES. Middling.			Small.		
A pair of iron framed wings trimmed with a 2-inch lace -	1	15	0	1	12	0	1	10	0
Ditto, with a 2½ ditto —	1	17	8	1	14	8	1	12	8
Ditto, with a 3 ditto —	2	0	4	1	17	4	1	15	4
Ditto with plated frames —	3	13	6	3	3	0	3	0	0

APRONS, or KNEEBOOTS.									
A kneeboot, fixed on the foot-board —	2	4	0	2	0	0	1	18	0
Ditto, to take off occafionally	2	8	0	2	6	0	2	2	0
An iron-jointed rod for ditto -	0	18	0	0	17	0	0	16	0

SECT.

DASHING OR SPLASHING LEATHERS.

	£.	s.	d.
A ſtrong daſhing-leather, with back ſtays, for a curricle — — ——	2	10	0
A light ditto for gig or whiſkey ——	1	15	0
A ſtrong ditto for a poſt chaiſe or coach carrage, to go round the boot — ——	3	0	0
A large ditto for the front of a poſt-chaiſe or coach, to fix upon the braces —— —	2	12	6
A leather pocket to either — —	0	5	0

SECT. 20.

BRACES AND POLE-PIECES.

FROM PAGE 213, VOL. I.

	Coach.			Chariot.		
	£.	s.	d.	£.	s.	d.
A pair of ſafe braces, with fixtures —	4	4	0	3	13	0
A pair of croſs check ditto, with plated buckles, for phaeton, &c. —	0	12	0	0	12	0
A ſet of point-ſtraps for the main braces -	0	6	0	0	6	0
French pole-pieces, in addition to the common ſort — ——	0	6	0	0	6	0

SECT.

SECT. 21.

TRAVELLING REQUISITES.

FROM PAGE 224, VOL. I.

TRUNKS, COVERS, STRAPS, AND BELTS.	Large for Coach, Chariot, or large Phaeton.	Middling, for middle or light Phaeton.	Small for Gig or Whiskey.
	£. s. d.	£. s. d.	£. s. d.
A best leather trunk, welted or nailed, lined with cloth, with inside straps and laths —	4 0 0	3 5 0	2 6 0
A trunk cover, made of neat's or ox-leather, welted —	2 5 0	1 15 0	1 1 0
A ditto of painted cloth —	0 10 6	0 7 6	0 5 0
Trunk-straps, per foot, per pair	0 1 9	0 1 0	0 0 9
A chain-belt, per foot, of either size —	0 2 9	0 2 9	0 2 9

IMPERIALS.		Coach.	Chariot.
A whole imperial for the roof	—	10 10 0	9 9 0
If divided in two for ditto	—	11 11 0	10 10 0
A three-quarter imperial for ditto	—	7 10 0	6 10 0

	Coach or Chariot.
	£. s. d.
A cap-box for ladies' head-dresses —	3 10 0
A hat-box for gentlemen's hats —	2 12 6
A well for the bottom of a body, which is hung on a crane-neck carriage —	2 12 6
Two narrow wells for ditto, hung on a perch carriage —	4 14 6
A set of splinter-bars complete, to hang on the pole end, when four horses are used, for them to draw by —	1 5 0

A drag-

	Coach or Chariot.
	£. s. d.
A drag-chain, with hook — —	0 8 0
A drag-chain, with shoe — —	0 15 0
The covering either with leather —	0 4 0
A drag-staff —— ——	0 10 6
For cording the set of springs, to prevent accident by being overloaded, &c. — —	1 1 0
A coachman's tool-budget — —	0 10 6

	Coach.			Chariot.		
	£.	s.	d.	£.	s.	d.
An oil-cover for the whole of the body, to preserve it while travelling —	5	5	0	4	10	0

ON

FINISHED CARRIAGES.

THE great variety of conveniencies and ornaments, with which carriages are finifhed, and the choice of them being optional to the proprietors only, no certain rule can be laid down for the value of finifhing any of them, further than what may be collected from the tables, where, by adding to the firft charge of each carriage, the feveral articles which are neceffary to complete them, the price of any pattern may be eafily obtained, which is the great advantage to be derived from the tables being here reftated; the following reprefentations will convey a proper idea of the kind of carriage moft fuitable for the various purpofes defigned : but the manner in which they are finifhed is not meant as a rule to abide by, as there are many things which may be excepted to, and others found neceffary to be added; it will, however, inftruct how to make the ftatements for any other pattern, or prove the value of thofe reprefented.

The fancy of the occupier is to regulate the mode of finifhing, as alfo the particular fhape of the carriage; but generally the prevalent pattern of the times influences his choice.

CHA"

CHAP. III.

C O A C H E S.

COACHES have the moſt uniform appearance
of any other carriage ; and, for families, are
the moſt convenient of any in uſe, as they can accommodate twice the number of paſſengers at one
time, but as the weight is ſomewhat increaſed by
the ſize, a proportion ſhould be obſerved according to the numbers it is meant to contain, whether
four or ſix paſſengers, the advantage of a light
coach is in the relief given to the horſes, and, of
courſe, being conveyed with greater expedition,
which are advantages too great not to be regarded;
the mode, therefore, of their conſtruction, as alſo
the method of finiſhing them according to the
intention of their uſe, is neceſſary to be attended
to.　Coaches, with perch carriages, in this com-
modious town, are to be preferred, being much
lighter than with crane-necks, and are leſs expenſive.

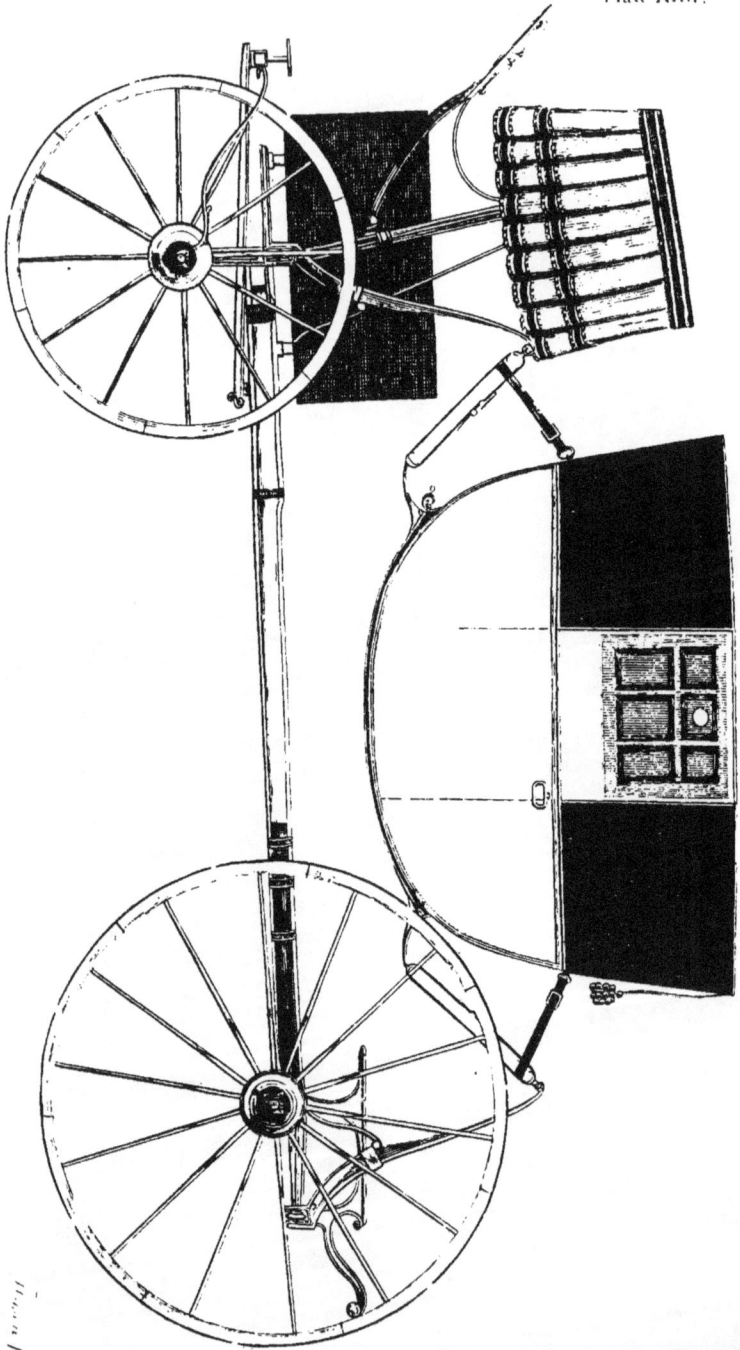

Plate XXII.

SECT. I.

A PLAIN · COACH.

PLATE XXII.

WHERE only one carriage is kept, and the ufe of it almoft conftantly required, a plain, fubftantial coach is to be recommended, in preference to a flight, ornamented one ; as, by being expofed to all weathers and rough roads, it is lefs liable to require expenfive repairs, and, if well formed, and neatly executed in the finifhing, will always preferve a genteel appearance ; in this pattern of a coach, there is nothing fuperfluous or wanting to make it compleat ; and, for convenience, may be confidered as one of the cheapeft of all four-wheeled carriages.

DESCRIPTION.

THE *Carriage* a perch, with a common coach-box, a fquare trunk boot, and raifed hind end, with plain plough handles, ftraked wheels of the neceffary height, common axletrees and fprings.

The *Body* part is alfo plain ; the lining with fecond cloth, and trimmed with two-inch binding lace, and holders two inches and a half wide, double folding fteps, feat-boxes, a Wilton carpet, plate glaffes, with cloth-covered frames, mahogany fhutters, and filk fpring curtains.

D   The

The *Hammercloth* is of livery, trimmed with three rows of lace two inches and a half wide, a pair of webb footman-holders two inches and a half wide, the *Plating* with *Silver*, an octagon frame for the back light, mouldings all round the middle, up the fides, and over the doors, and at the top of the back and fore parts, in all about thirty-four feet.

The *Braces* and *Pole-pieces* common, with half buckles, the painting of any colour, but plain and common varnifhed, the mouldings picked out one colour.

PRICE OF THE PLAIN PERCH COACH.

	£.	s.	d.
The firft charge for a perch coach —	105	9	0

EXTRAS.

	£.	s.	d.
A pair of plain plough, or guard handles —	2	0	0
A fquare trunk-boot — —	5	0	0
A common coach-box, with feat and cradle —	5	5	0
A puckered, or full-plaited hammercloth, with 3 rows, or 22 yards, of 2½ inch lace —	6	6	0
A pair of web footman-holders —	0	8	0
A fet of of filk fpring curtains — —	3	3	0
A plated octagon frame — —	0	10	0
Thirty-four feet of 4-8th moulding —	3	16	6
The painting picked out one colour —	1	11	6
	133	9	0

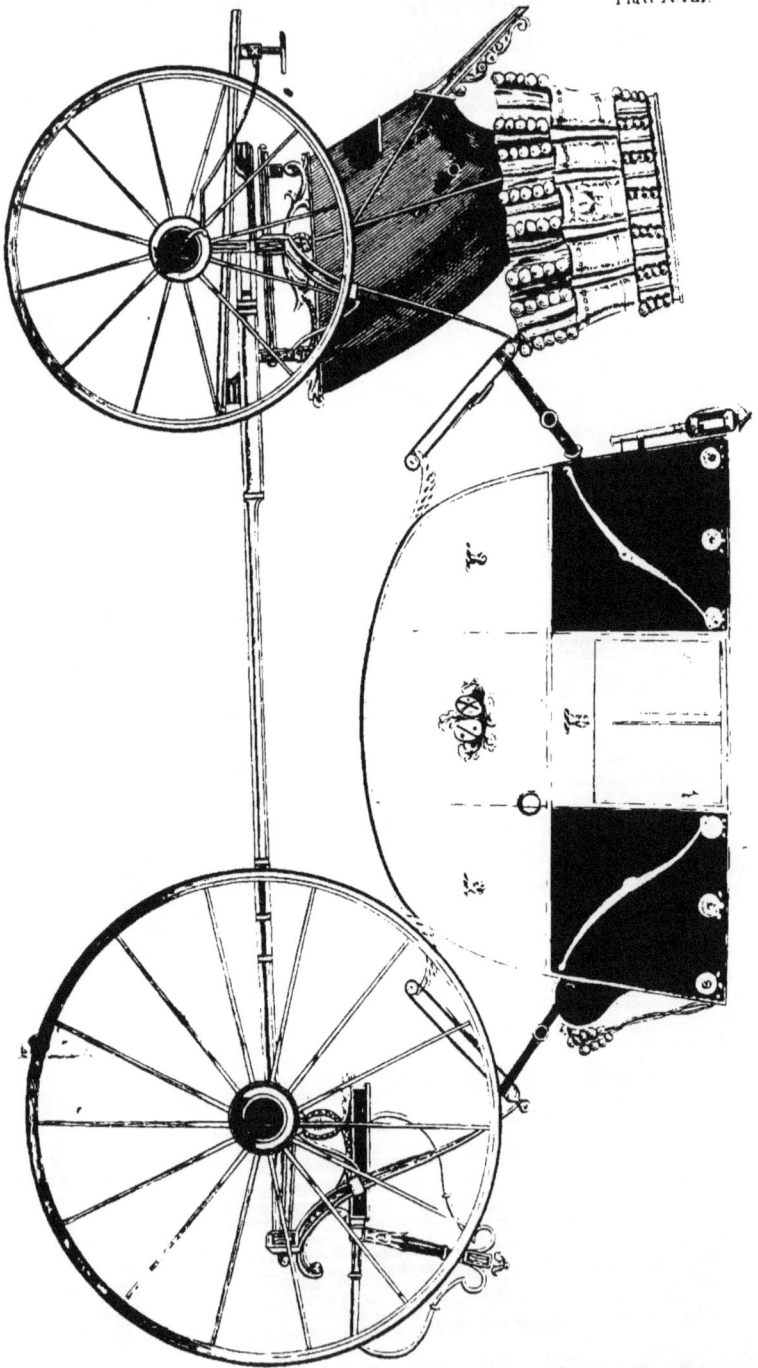

Plate XXIII.

SECT. 2.

A NEAT ORNAMENTED, OR TOWN COACH.

PLATE XXIII.

NOTHING contributes more to fafhion or grandeur, than a good difplay of ornaments about a carriage, of which there are a great variety of patterns; but, in this, neatnefs with elegance is to be regarded, as the expence which may be added above the former defcription increafes the price to almoft double that of a plain coach; but to finifh thofe carriages at a moderate expence, and preferve the elegance, it is neceffary to obtain a knowledge of thofe things which have the beft external appearance; the painting, and the plating for the outfide, and the trimmings for the infide, do moft readily attract obfervation, as it is impoffible to eftablifh a rule for the different modes of finifhing carriages, the feveral additions neceffary to form a middling handfome one, will be noticed in this defcription, thofe of a more expenfive, in a future.

DESCRIPTION.

THE *Carriage* a perch, plated on the fides with iron, a raifed hind end, on neat, fhort blocks, a footman's cufhion plated on the top frame, with carved hind ftandards, a raifed fore end with neat.

D 2.   fore

fore budget blocks, a half-wheel fore end, a Salifbury coach-box; hooped tyre wheels, with moulded fellies, common axletrees and boxes.

The *Body* with round fides; a fword cafe back;
lined with fecond cloth; trimmed with $2\frac{1}{2}$ inch lace,
and fwinging holders; quilted fides; double folding fteps; a Wilton carpet; with two fliding feat-
boxes; Venetian blinds, and a fet of filk fpring
curtains. The *plating* with *filver*, a half-inch moulding round the fide pannels, on the bottom fides, all
round the middle and roof, up the corner pillars,
and fides of the door lights; a 3-8th moulding all
round the door and front lights; four filver fcroll
ornaments; a fet of flat, pierced, creft head-plates;
a fet of light fham joints; and a pair of oval lamps
plated.

The *Hammercloth* of livery, trimmed with one
top, and two middle rows, or 22 yards, of $2\frac{1}{2}$,
and one bottom row, or 9 yards, of one-inch lace,
a top and bottom row, or 13 yards, of ornamented
fringe, 5 inches deep, two pair of lace footman's
holders, $2\frac{1}{2}$ inches wide.

The *Painting* of the carriage picked out two colours; the body polifhed; a pair of arms painted
on the doors in foliage mantles; four crefts on the
quarters, and two on the ftiles. The *Braces* common, and French pole-pieces.

PRICE

PRICE.

	£.	s.	d.
Firſt charge for a perch coach — —	105	9	0

EXTRAS.

	£.	s.	d.
The perch platèd on the ſides with iron —	3	3	0
A pair of neat carved ſhort hind blocks —	2	5	0
A footman's cuſhion, with a plated top frame, and carved hind ſtandard — —	6	18	0
A half-wheel fore end —— —	1	5	0
A pair of neat budget blocks — —	2	10	0
A Saliſbury coach-box, with ſeat, &c. —	10	5	0
Sixteen feet of plated moulding for ditto —	1	16	0
Hoop tyre wheels, with moulded fellies —	1	19	0
Round ſides to the body —— —	2	0	0
A ſword caſe to ditto — —	2	10	0
The lining, with ſwinging holders, and other lace, 2¼ inches wide — —	1	11	0
Quilted ſides to the lining — —	1	1	0
A ſet of Venetian blinds in lieu of ſhutters	2	15	0
A ſet of ſilk ſpring curtains —	3	3	0
A hammercloth, as deſcribed — —	10	10	0
The creſts embroidered in mantles on the ends	1	10	0
Four lace footman's holders — —	1	4	0
Eighty feet of half-inch plated moulding to the body — — — —	9	0	0
An octagon, and a pair of ſword-caſe frames	1	1	0
Four ſilver ſcroll ornaments — —	0	16	0
A ſet of plated joints — ——	6	0	0
A ſet of flat pierced creſt head-plates —	2	19	0
A pair of plated oval lamps — —	2	10	0
Picking out the painting of the carriage two colours — — — —	1	15	0
Varniſhing of ditto after painting ——	0	15	0
Arms in mantles, on the two doors —	1	9	0
Creſts on the four quarters, and two door ſtiles	1	4	0
French pole pieces —— ——	0	6	0
	188	19	0

D 3

SECT.

SECT. 3.

A LANDAU.

PLATE XXIV.

A LANDAU is a carriage in the form of a Coach, the upper part of which may be opened at pleasure, for the advantage of air and prospect in the summer time, principally intended for country use; they are the most convenient carriages of any, as so many persons may be accommodated with the pleasure of an open and a close carriage in one, without the care of driving, as in other open carriages, or the expence and incumbrance of keeping two, and the expence for duty saved thereby, are advantages worth the notice of those who wish to be thus accommodated.

The amusement many gentlemen may have in driving for themselves in light, open carriages has prevented the Landau being more generally used than what they otherwise would have been, and what, from their utility, might have been expected. The upper parts are covered with a black grain leather, which cannot be japanned, and of course, does not look so well as fixed roofs; they are also heavier, and more expensive than the common coaches, which are the principal objections to them, but are trifling when compared to the other advantages they possess.

DESCRIPTION.

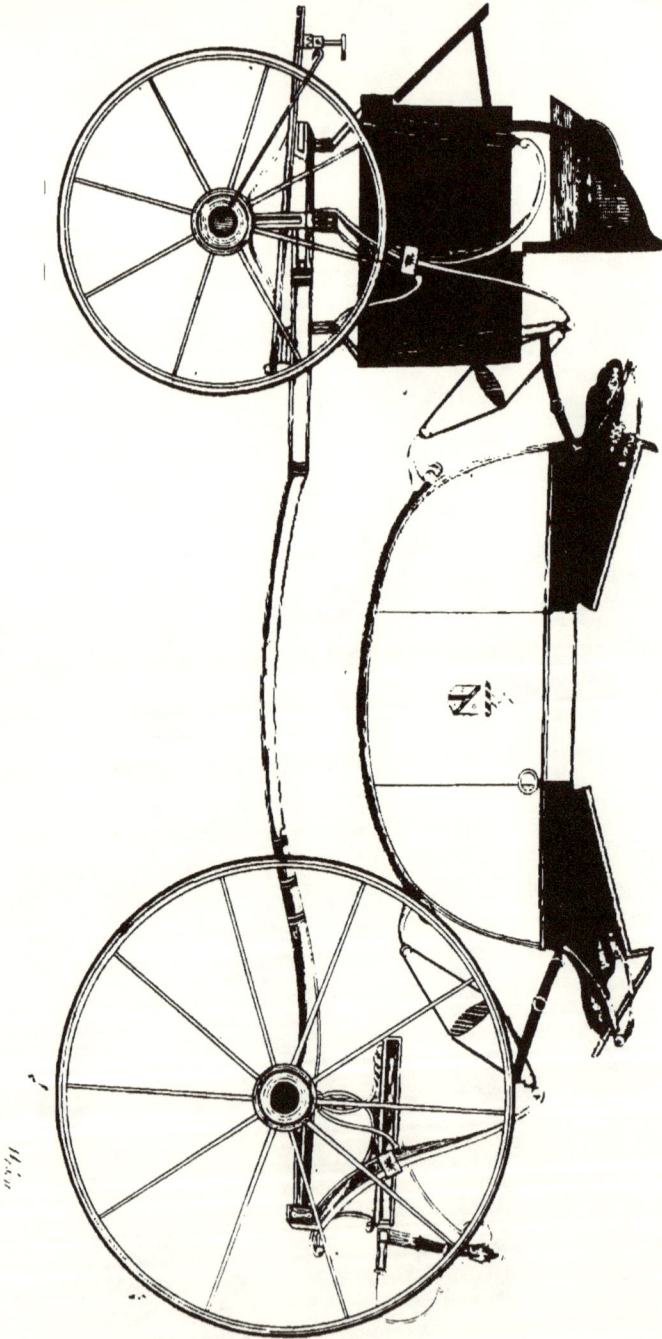

Plate XXIII.

DESCRIPTION.

THE *Carriage* a perch, of the compafs, or crooked form, *plated* on the fides with iron; a half-wheel fore end; a raifed hind end, with fhort, plain blocks; a footman's cufhion, with carved hind ftandards; a pair of double-returned fprings, for carrying a fquare trunk-boot, which makes into a coach-box occafionally; hooped tyre wheels, with common axletrees and boxes.

The *Body*, a Landau, with round fides; lined with fecond cloth; trimmed with a three-inch lace, and fwinging holders; the fides quilted; double folding fteps: a Wilton carpet; fliding feat-boxes; Venetian blinds; a fet of web footman's holders. The *mountings* of *Brafs*; a 4-8th moulding all round the middle, at the top of the back and front part, and round the doors; a fmall 2-8th moulding all round the door and front lights; a fet of fancy device head plates; the joints, the check-brace rings, the wheel-hoops, and body loops, on the whole furface plated; and a plated pole-hook.

The *Painting* of the body and carriage picked out two colours; the arms and crefts painted on the doors, the fore and back pannels. The *Main Braces* with worm fprings plated; French pole-pieces; a fet of braces to carry the boot, two inches wide; and four fhort check-braces underneath the boot.

PRICE

PRICE.

	£.	s.	d.
First charge for a Landau, with perch carriage	120	11	0

EXTRAS.

	£.	s.	d.
A compass perch, with iron-plated sides —	4	4	0
Half-wheel fore end — —	1	5	0
A raised hind end, with plain short blocks —	1	10	0
A footman's cushion, plated top edge of brass mouldings, with carved hind standards —	6	13	0
A pair of double-returned springs —	2	12	0
A trunk-boot, with a concealed coach-box —	10	0	0
Hooped tyre wheels — —	1	0	0
Round sides to the body — —	2	0	0
Trimmed with a three-inch lace, and swing-holders — — —	2	7	0
Quilted sides — — —	1	1	0
Venetian blinds, in lieu of shutters —	2	15	0
Forty feet of 4-8th brass moulding —	2	5	0
Thirty-two feet of 2-8th ditto —	1	1	6
A set of fancy pattern head-plates —	1	5	0
A set of joints, plated — —	6	6	0
A set of check-brace rings, ditto —	0	8	0
A set of wheel-hoops, ditto — —	1	15	0
A set of body-loops, ditto — —	1	12	0
A pole-hook, ditto — —	1	5	0
A set of worm-springs, ditto —	6	10	0
Picking out the moulding two colours —	2	5	0
Four arms and crests, middle size —	2	4	0
Twenty feet of two-inch braces for the boot	2	3	0
Four large buckles for ditto — —	0	8	0
A set of short check-braces for the boot —	0	5	0
French pole-pieces — —	0	6	0
	185	16	6

SECT.

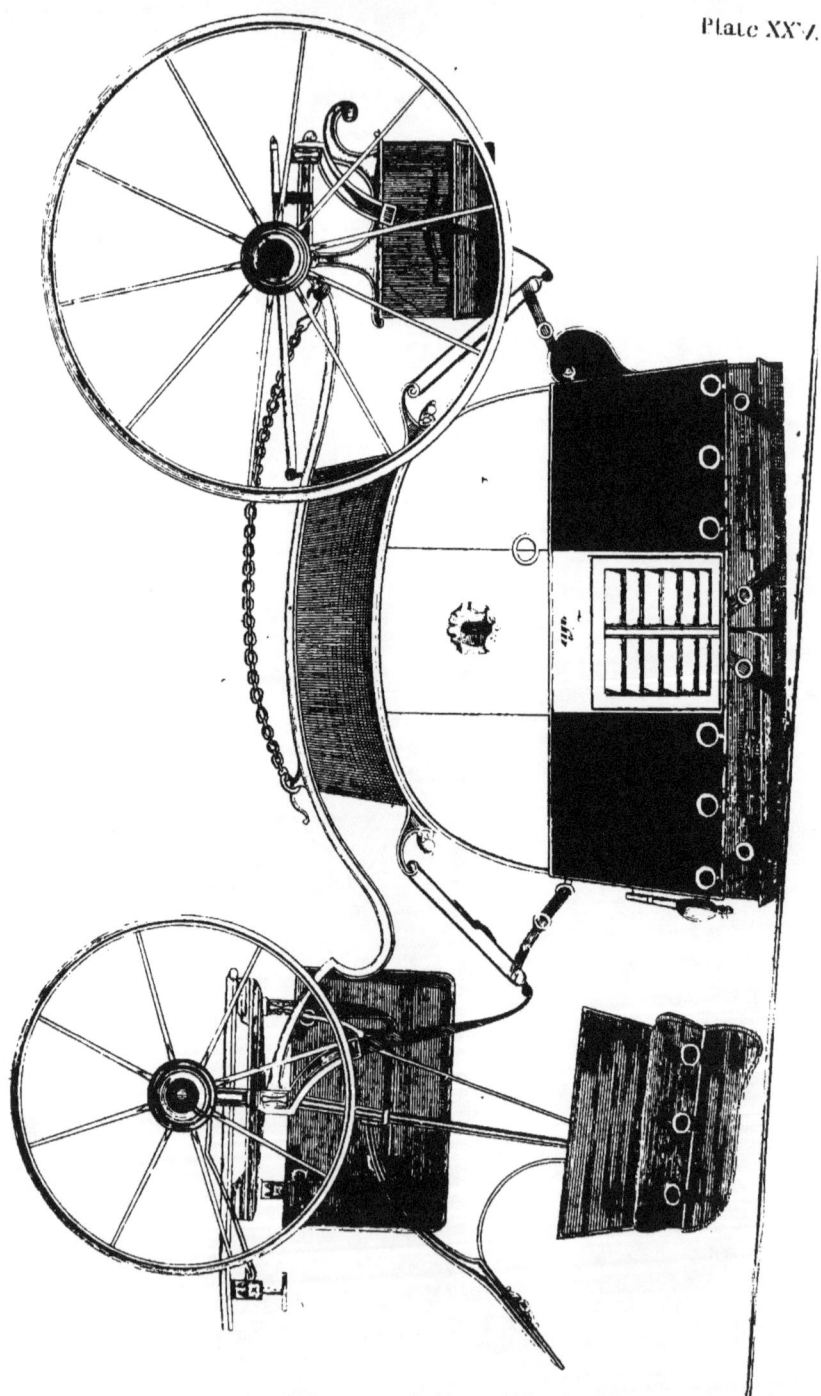

Plate XXV.

SECT. 4.

TRAVELLING COACH.

PLATE XXV.

STRENGTH and convenience are the moſt eſ-
ſential properties of this carriage, it being principally intended for continental journies, nothing
ſhould be omitted that can contribute to either;
plain, ſtrong-built, crane-neck carriages are to be
preferred on this occaſion, as the roads on the continent are very rough, and, in the towns, very narrow; and, as there is not much opportunity for
cleaning or mending on the way, the plainer and the
ſtronger they are built, the better for the purpoſe.
The great expence of theſe carriages is principally
on account of the many conveniences for luggage
neceſſary for the paſſengers' accommodation, it depends on the knowledge of the intended route, to
proportion the carriage and conveniences thereto,
ſo that all unneceſſary incumbrance may be avoided,
to ſave both toil and expence.

DESCRIPTION.

THE *Carriage* a crane neck; ſtrong ſtraked
wheels; patent anti-attrition axletrees and boxes; a
raiſed hind end, with ſhort, plain blocks; a common

mon coach box, with a travelling feat; a platform
budget before, with a large trunk within it, and infide ftraps and laths to ditto; a trunk behind with
ditto, and two leather-belts; a chain-belt for fecurity, and an oil-cover for the trunk; the fprings
corded; a drag-ftaff; a chain; and a tool-budget,
for the coachman's conveniences.

The *Body* plain, with a fword-cafe; lined with
fecond cloth, and trimmed with a two-inch lace;
and two and a half ditto for the holders; fquabs, or
fleeping cufhions, faced with filk; Venetian blinds;
feat-boxes; Wilton carpet; double folding fteps;
the *plating* with compofition metal a 5-8th of an
inch moulding all round the middle and roof, up
the corner pillars, and fide of the doors; a fet of
circles for head-plates; a pair of fword-cafe
frames; a well at the bottom; two imperials for
the roof; the *painting*, varnifhing, &c. plain;
mantles, with cyphers, on the door pannels: crefts
on the ftiles; the main and check *Braces*, with
whole buckles; French pole-pieces.

PRICE.

	£.	s.	d.
Firft charge for a crane-neck coach	121	14	0
Patent anti-attrition axletrees and boxes	15	14	0

EXTRAS.

A raifed hind end, with fhort, plain blocks	1	10	0
A common coach-box, with a travelling feat	9	3	6
Carry over	148	1	6

A large

	£.	s.	d.
Brought over	148	1	6
A large platform budget	8	0	0
A large trunk for ditto, with infide ftraps and laths	3	19	6
Leather belts for fixing the trunk	0	7	6
A large trunk for the hind end, with infide ftraps and laths	3	19	6
An oil-cloth cover for the trunk	0	10	6
A pair of leather belts, 9 feet long	0	11	0
A chain-belt for fecurity, 9 feet long	1	4	11
The fprings corded	1	1	0
A drag-ftaff, with a chain	0	18	0
A tool-budget	0	10	6
A fword-cafe, or boodge	2	10	0
A fet of infide filk fquabs	4	0	0
Sixty feet of 5.8th moulding	5	10	1
A fet of circles for the head-plates	1	4	0
A pair of fword-cafe frames, and an octagon do.	0	16	0
Venetian blinds in lieu of fhutters	2	15	0
A pair of beft imperials for the roof	11	0	0
A large well for the bottom	2	12	6
Two mantles, with cyphers, on the doors	1	2	0
Two crefts on the door-ftiles	0	8	0
	201	1	6

SECT.

SECT. 5.

AN ELEGANT CRANE-NECK COACH.

PLATE XXVI.

IN any grand proceffion, an elegant carriage forms the principal part; and, where fplendour is neceffary, a rich difplay of fanciful defigns in the carving and painting, chiefly contributes towards it: but, as it is difficult to form a regular judgment of the value of a carriage fo highly ornamented in the painting and carving, fuch only will be defcribed, as the value thereof may be afcertained from the former ftatements.

A profufion of carved ornaments and figures much gilt, with beautiful paintings, decorate the outfide—rich velvet linings, and filk trimmings, the infide; the value of fuch a carriage can only be gueffed at, as it depends on the artift who executes it to charge according to its merit in the execution. The carriage here reprefented, though not fo much ornamented, is built on the fame principle as the ftate equipage, but more exactly anfwers the defcription of a neat, light carriage for the Eaft or Weft Indies, it being made very airy, with fide and end lights, or windows; the kind of carriages ufed chiefly in thofe places, are crane-necked, but are

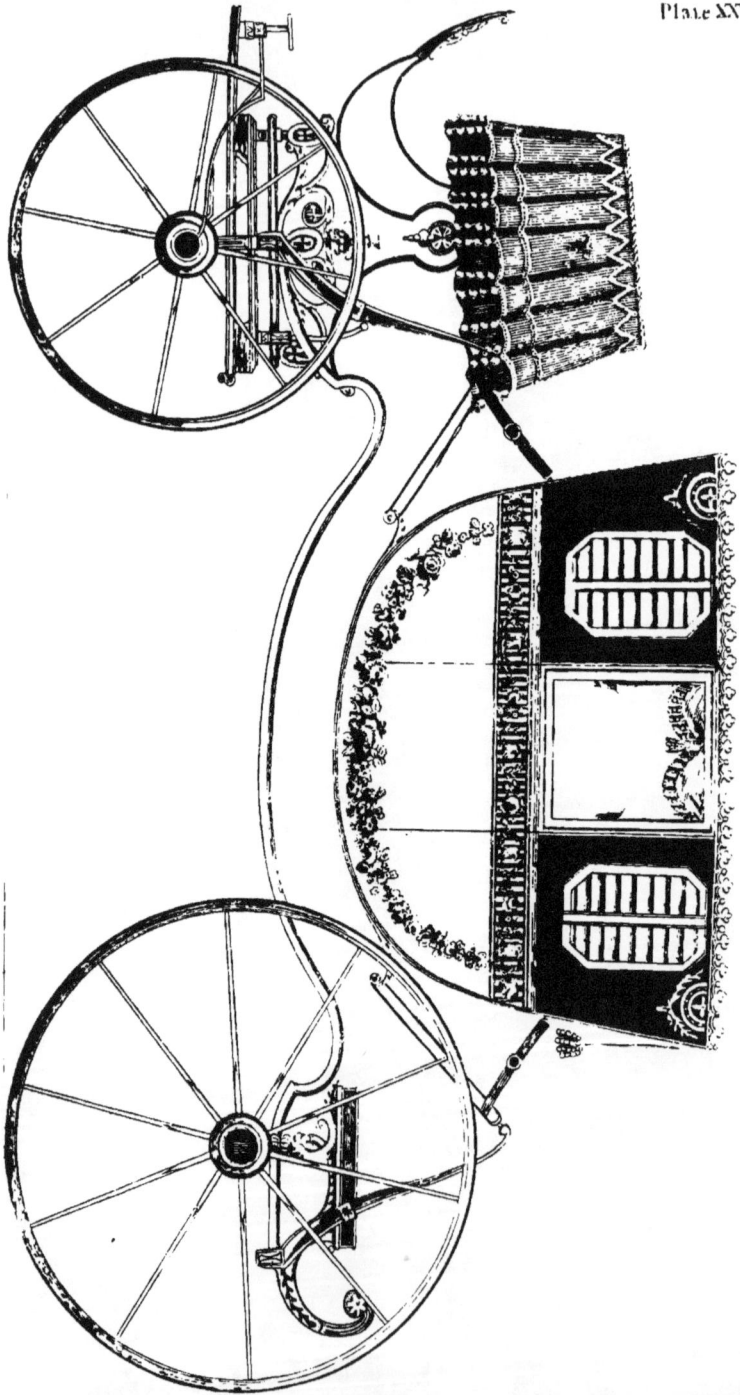

Plate XXVI.

are built much lighter than what is neceffary for
this country, as the horfes not being fo ftrong, and
the roads of foft, fandy foil, a heavy carriage would
fink therein, and be obftructed by its weight.

DESCRIPTION.

The *Carriage*, a crane neck; double bow
cranes; raifed hind end, with handfome, carved,
pump-handles, and a footman-cufhion, with a plated top and bottom edge; an iron coach-box, raifed
on handfome carved blocks; patent wheels, with
moulded fellies, new-pattern cylinder axletrees and
boxes.

The *Body* with carved ends to the bottom; fides
to cafe the body-loops; round fides; octagon fide-
lights, and one large back-light for glaffes and
fhutters to flide in; lined with Morocco leather, and
trimmed with handfome worfted and cotton lace,
four inches wide, with the arms worked therein;
treble folding-fteps; Wilton carpet; fliding feat-
boxes; one fet and a pair of feftoon curtains, with
fide drapery for the door, front, and back lights;
one fet of ditto, with top drapery only, for fide
lights; two fet and one large Venetian blind; laced
glafs-frames; one fet of glaffes for the fide lights,
and a large one for the back light extra, with the
frames covered with lace. The *plating* with *Silver*;
the mouldings 6-8ths of an inch wide, which goes
round

round the pannels, fides, back, and front, all round the middle and roof, up the corner pillars and fides of the doors, in quantity about 110 feet; a 3-8th of an inch moulding round all the lights, in quantity about 60 feet; four filver fcroll ornaments; four handfome, large head-plates, of about the value of a fet for a coach of the ufual pattern; four filver-plated nave-hoops; a plated pole-hook, a handfome cornice for the roof, of about the fame value per foot as the wide-plated mouldings, in quantity about 22 feet.

The *Hammercloth* fuperfine, trimmed with 13 yards of 2½-inch lace, 9 yards of eight inch ornamented fringe, 13 yards of four inch velvet, at 4s. per yard, and 36 yards of one-inch narrow binding-lace; filk crefts within filk mantles, embroidered on the ends; a double pair of arms-lace footman-holders. The *Painting* high varnifhed; a rich border, 5 inches wide, round the middle, meafuring about 21 feet; with handfome fwags of flowers on each fide, of about the fame value with the border; the mouldings of the carriage are gilt, and picked out in an ornamented manner; and amounts to about double the price of picking out with three colours. The main and check *Braces* with whole buckles; French pole-pieces, with plated buckles.

PRICE.

PRICE.

	£.	s.	d.
First charge for a crane-neck coach ——	121	14	0

EXTRAS.

	£.	s.	d.
Double bows to the cranes — ——	3	3	0
Raised hind end, with handsome carved pump handles — — —	4	4	0
A footman-cushion, plated at the top and bottom edge — — —	7	18	0
An iron coach-box, and carved blocks —	18	8	0
Patent wheels with moulded fellies ——	3	19	0
New-pattern cylinder axletrees and boxes —	17	14	0
Round sides to the body — ——	2	0	0
Side lights, and one large back ditto, for glasses and shutters — — —	9	0	0
Lining of Morocco leather in lieu of cloth —	8	0	0
The trimmings, worsted and cotton lace, 4 inches broad, with the arms worked in them —	9	6	8
Treble folding steps —— ——	2	10	0
A set of festoon curtains, with side drapery for the doors and front, and one ditto for the back light —— — ——	4	10	0
One set of ditto, with festoon tops only —	2	12	6
One set of Venetian blinds in lieu of shutters	2	15	0
One ditto ditto for the side lights	4	10	0
One large ditto for back light ——	1	10	0
Two-inch wide arms-lace for glass frames	1	17	0
One set of small glasses and frames, and the frames covered with lace — —	6	13	0
One large glass, with lace-covered frame —	2	7	0
Five extra glass strings, or holders, to match the rest — —— ——	2	10	0
Carry over ——_	237	1	2

	£.	s.	d.
Brought over — —	237	1	2
110 feet of 6-8ths of an inch size moulding	17	17	6
60 feet of 3-8ths of ditto — —	5	2	6
Four silver scroll ornaments — —	8	0	0
Four large handsome ornaments for the top in lieu of head-plates — —	2	10	0
Four silver-plated nave-hoops — —	6	6	0
A standing or raised cornice — —	3	11	6
A pole-hook, plated — —	2	10	0
The hammer-cloth, as described —	18	10	0
Two pair of arms-lace footman's holders, with ornamented tassels — —	2	16	0
The pannels high varnished — —	5	15	6
The mouldings gilt, and picked out three colours	5	0	0
Twenty-one feet of rich five-inch border —	11	0	0
A pair of handsome swags of flowers, painted on the pannels — — —	11	0	0
	337	0	2

SECT. 6.

VIS - À - VIS.

A NARROW, contracted coach on the seats, and where only two persons can sit facing each other, and is so called from the French: the advantage of it, independent of fashion, is its being so confined as to prevent the passengers being tossed about by the jolting of the carriage; and, by its being so narrow, they sit warmer than in other carriages; they

they are feldom ufed by any other than perfons of high character or fafhion, and are ufually finifhed in a fuperior manner to what the generality of carriages are; they are fomewhat lighter in the bodies than a common Coach, and, the carriage part being made proportionable thereto, does not, in general, exceed the weight of a Chariot;. the expence may be proportioned between the price of a Coach and a Chariot.

The quantity of materials being lefs for a Vis-à-Vis than what is ufed for a Coach, the price is proportionably lefs, and to reduce them to a regular ftatement, is to deduct 1-12th from the value of a Coach, and either of the reprefentations will ferve to afcertain the price of a Vis-à-Vis by, if of the fame defcription.

E   CHAP.

CHAP. IV.

POST-CHAISE AND CHARIOT.

A POST-CHAISE is a carriage intended only for expeditious travelling, and, for a clofe carriage, is the moft pleafant; the view in front not being obftructed by a coach-box, nor the draught impeded by any cumberfome weight: lightnefs and fimplicity are the principles on which this carriage ought to be built, if intended for poft work only.

The cuftom of the driver's riding the near horfe, in pofting, has long prevailed, and the abfurdity, it is feared, will not eafily be got rid of, although it has been the deftruction of fo many good horfes; for, it is evident, that if a man is a fufficient burden for a horfe to travel with, to impofe alfo an equal fhare of the draught of the carriage, with his yoked companion, muft foon fatigue him, and impede the travelling thereby, unlefs the poor animal is fcourged to exertion beyond his natural ftrength; to keep pace with the other horfe; any fimple con-trivance on the carriage, for the driver to fit in,

would

would leffen the fatigue, both to man and horfe, and be more likely to promote fpeed.

Chariots are built exactly the fame way as Poft-Chaifes, but are only fo called from having an uniform coach-box, intended for town-ufe, and are ufually built ftronger than what would be neceffary for a Poft-Chaife, though frequently ufed for both purpofes, and are then built between the two proportions: for fmall families, where only one carriage is kept, a Chariot, with a moveable coach-box, is to be preferred, being lighter, and more pleafant to ride in than a Coach.

SECT. 1.

A PLAIN POST-CHAISE.

PLATE XXVII.

FAMILIES who often journey from place to place with poft-horfes, do well to furnifh themfelves with a Poft-Chaife, although it faves nothing of the expences in travelling, whether with their own or poft-mafter's carriage; yet a convenience, more than adequate to the expence of the carriage, is, in the end, to be met with, as the neceffity of removing from one carriage to another, and fhifting the luggage, is thereby avoided; an inconvenience

E 2   too

too great to be fubmitted to by any gentleman who can afford the additional expence of keeping their own Poft-Chaife. A plain, light carriage is to be preferred, if only to be ufed for pofting work, but if the journies are occafional, a chariot, with fuch a coach-box as can be removed, will anfwer the purpofe beft.

DESCRIPTION.

The *Carriage* is a perch; with raifed hind end, on fhort blocks; a fquare trunk-boot; a dafhing leather over it; common ftraked wheels; common axletrees and boxes; a trunk and cover on the hind platform.

The *Body* is plain, lined with fecond cloth, and common trimmings; plate glaffes, cloth-covered frames; fliding feat-boxes; mahogany fhutters; an occafional feat on the infide for a third perfon; a Wilton carpet; double folding fteps. The *Plating* with *filver*; a 3-8th moulding on the eibow and back rails, up the ftanding pillars, over the doors and front lights, and on the top of the back behind, meafuring about 30 feet. The *Painting* plain. The *Braces* common, and Englifh polepices.

PRICE

Plate XXVII.

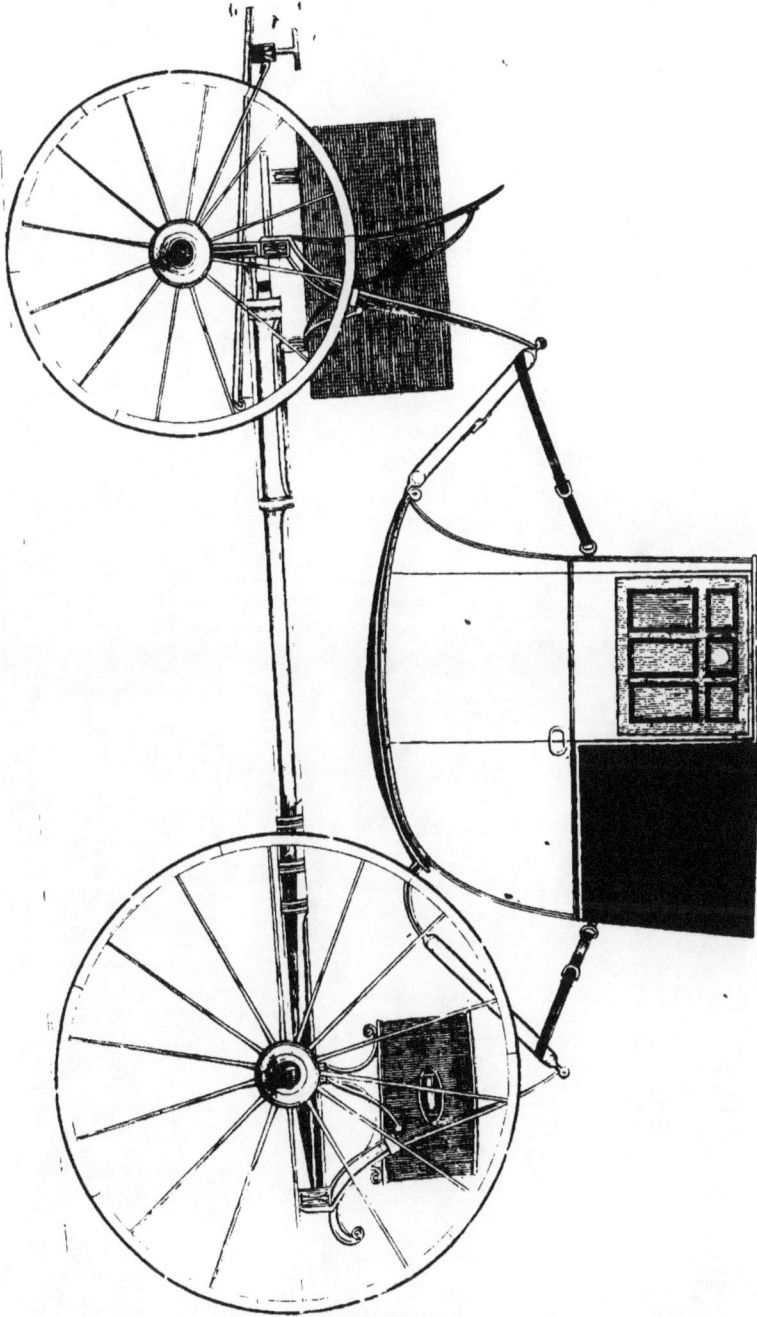

PRICE.

	£.	s.	d.
The firſt charge for a perch poſt-chaiſe	93	1	6

EXTRAS.

	£.	s.	d.
Short hind blocks, plain — —	1	10	0
A ſquare trunk-boot — —	5	0	0
A daſhing or ſplaſhing leather for ditto —	3	0	0
A large trunk behind, with inſide ſtraps and laths	3	19	6
Leather belts for ditto, 9 feet long . —	0	11	3
An oil, or painted, cloth cover for the trunk	0	10	6
A ſliding ſeat for a third perſon —	0	10	6
An octagon back-light frame — · —	0	10	0
Eleven feet of 3-8ths of an inch moulding —	2	12	6
	111	5	9

WITH A COACH-BOX.

For the value of a plain Chariot, deduct the price
of the daſhing-leather, the trunk and belts,
with cover, and ſliding-ſeat, and add the price
of a common coach-box, hammercloth, and
footman-holders, of the ſame deſcription as
that of the coach, and the amount is — | 115 | 3 | 6 |

SECT. 2.

A NEAT TOWN CHARIOT.

PLATE XXVIII.

THERE is no carriage looks better than a genteel Chariot; and, where much room for paſſengers is not neceſſary, none is more convenient, for,

E 3 being

being more light and airy than a coach, it is much
to be preferred on that account : on it, as few or as
many ornaments may be exhibited as on the Coach,
and wi h as good an effect; but, for a carriage in
frequent ufe, it is beft not to be too profufe with
them, as it adds to the weight, and trouble in cleaning, as well as to the expence. To form a genteel
Chariot, is to coliect fuch materials as are light in
their appearance, and of a fanciful device ; the more
novelty, if not to extremes, the more genteel the
carri ge; but as that is a matter of fancy, it muft
be left to the occupier of the carriage to make a
choice ; what is now moft fafhionable will only here
be noticed.

DESCRIPTION.

THE carriage is a perch, of the bent or crooked
form, with iron-plated fides; a whole wheel front;
an iron coach-box on a fquare trunk-boot, raifed
on neat, carved blocks; a raifed hind end, with
neat fhort blocks; a footman cufhion, with plated
mouldings to the frames, and carved hind ftandards; hooped tyre wheels, with moulded fellies,
and common axletrees and boxes.

The *Body* with round fides, a fword-cafe back,
contracted door-lights, lined with fecond cloth,
trimmed with a $5\frac{1}{2}$ inch lace, fwinging holders, a
pair of filk fquabs, plate glaffes, with laced glafs-
frames, and filk fpring curtains ; Venetian blinds ;
fliding

Plate XXVIII

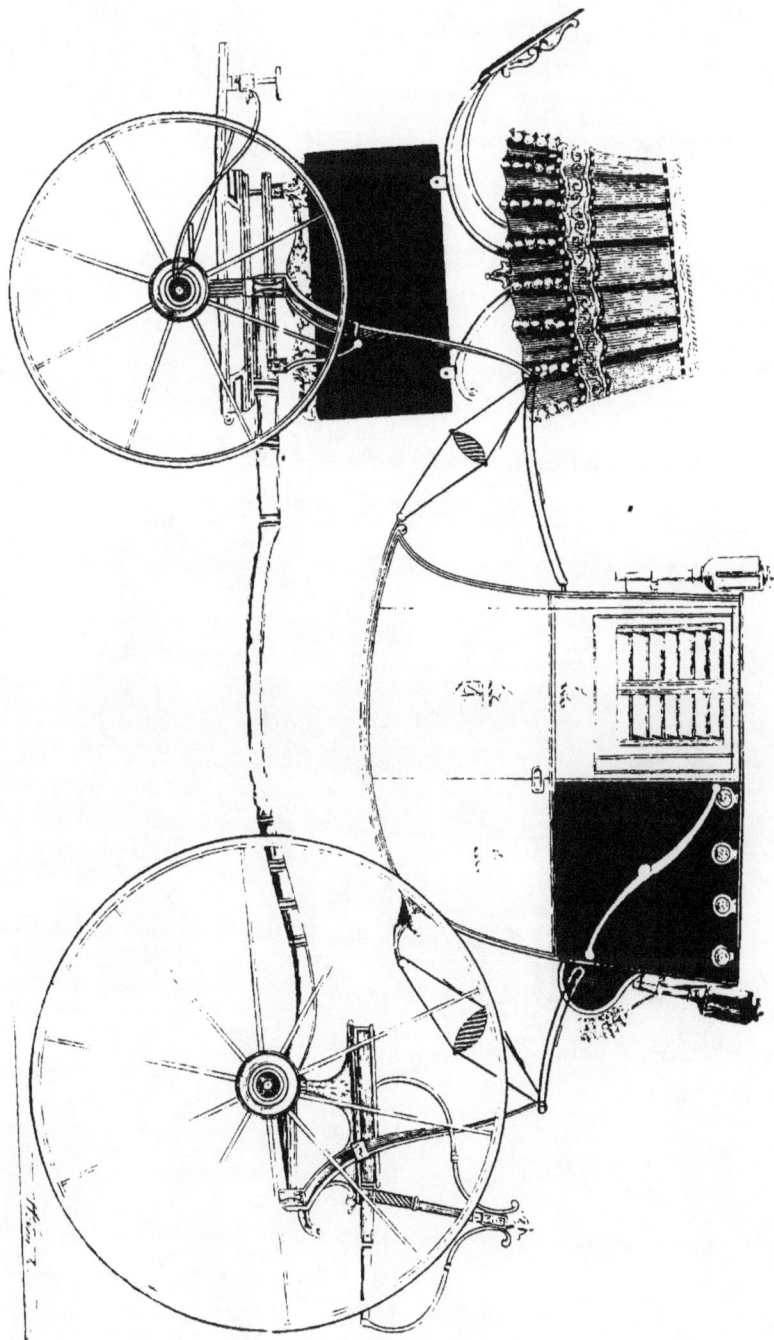

sliding seat-boxes; a Wilton carpet; double folding steps. The *Plating* with *silver*, a small 3-8th
moulding, or quill-bead, in double rows round the
side pannels, and in single rows round the front and
door-lights; a 4-8th moulding all round the middle and roof, up the corner pillars, and sides of the
doors, and along the bottom sides; 4 silver scroll
ornaments; an octagon; and a pair of sword-case
frames; a pair of plated thick joints, with barrel
props and caps for them; eight silver crest head-
plates, with silver circles; a set of cased plated
metal wheel-hoops; a plated pole-hook, and check-
brace rings; five Italian full-plated *Lamps*. The
Hammercloth of livery, trimmed with a top row of
$2\frac{1}{2}$ inch, a bottom row of one inch, and a middle
row of four-inch lace, one bottom row of seven-
inch ornamented fringe; four $3\frac{1}{2}$ inch double lace
footman-holders; the *Painting* picked out two colours; the pannels polished; the arms on the
doors and crests, on the quarters and stiles; the
main and check *Braces* with whole buckles; a set
of worm springs, with French pole-pieces.

PRICE.

	£.	s.	d.
First charge for a town chariot ———	93	1	6

EXTRAS.

	£.	s.	d.
A compass perch, iron plated on the sides —	3	16	0
A whole wheel front ——— —	2	5	0
A raised fore end, with neat carved blocks —	2	10	0
Carry over —	101	12	6

E 4   A square

	£.	s.	d.
Brought over — —	101	12	6
A square trunk-boot for an iron coach-box	6	0	0
An iron coach-box — —	10	0	0
Raied hind end, on neat carved short blocks	2	5	0
A footman-cushion plated at the top edge, with carved hin' standards — —	6	18	0
Hooped wheels, with moulded fellies —	1	19	0
The body with round sides — —	1	0	0
A sword-case back — —	2	10	0
Contracted door-lights — —	2	0	0
Swing holders, and other trimmings, 3½ inches wide — — —	1	18	0
A pair of silk squabs — —	2	12	6
A set of spring curtains — —	3	0	0
Ditto Venetian blinds — —	2	15	0
Laced glass-frame — —	1	10	0
Eighty feet of plated 2-8th moulding —	5	0	0
Forty feet of ditto 4-8th ditto — —	4	10	0
An octagon, and a pair of sword-case frames	1	1	0
A pair of thick joints, with four barrel props and caps — — —	4	14	0
A set of silver crest head plates, and silver circles	3	0	0
To a pair of ditto, extra — —	1	0	0
Four cased plated metal wheel-hoops —	3	0	0
A plated pole-hook — —	2	2	0
Six plated check-brace rings — —	1	4	0
Five Italian round-side lamps, with plated heads and barrels — — —	6	0	0
A hammercloth as described —	11	0	0
Four double lace footman-holders —	1	16	0
Main and check-braces, with whole buckles	0	10	0
Spiral or worm springs — —	1	10	0
French pole-pieces — —	0	6	0
	192	13	0

SECT.

SECT. 3.

A LANDAULET, OR DEMI-LANDAU.

PLATE XXIX.

THIS carriage has the fame advantage as the Landau, only that the number of paffengers are proportionably lefs; but, for convenience, where only one carriage is kept, none exceeds it for country ufe. When a Demi-Landau is ufed open, the common fort of coach-box is objectionable, being fo high as to take away the profpect in front, which is principally obfcured by the coachman fitting there. A boot with a concealed chair, or coach-box, when ufed as a Landau, anfwers beft. The common coach-box may be added occafionally for town ufe, the fame as to a Poft-Chariot: the mode of finifhing will anfwer for any other defcription, except only the difference in price between a Poft-Chaife and a Demi-Landau.

DESCRIPTION.

THE *Carriage* is a perch of the bent, or com-paffed form, plated with iron on the fides; a half-wheel fore end; a raifed hind end, with plain plough handles, and a footman-cufhion; a fquare trunk-boot; a light chair, or chaife body for the

coach-

coachman, fixed on the boot at the fore end, and hung on an iron bar which croffes the fore fprings by fhort braces; ftraked wheels, common axletrees, and boxes. The *Body* a landaulet, with round fides, lined with fecond cloth, and trimmed with a three-inch lace ; quilted fides; a fliding feat-box ; Wilton carpet; double folding fteps; plate glaffes, the frames covered with a two inch lace ; Venetian blinds. The *Plating* with brefs, a 4-8th moulding round the pannels, the middle, fides, and over the doors, along the back and front; two fcroll ornaments, and two tip ditto; the body-loops plated on the four bolt heads; fix fancy device headplates; the joints, check-rings, pole-hook, and wheel-hoops plated ; a pair of Italian lamps plated. The *Braces* common French pole-pieces; a fet of double web footman-holders. The *Painting* picked out one colour; a plain fillet round the pannels I inch wide ; the arms on the doors ; cyphers with crefts on the quarters, and crefts on the ftiles.

PRICE.

	£.	s.	d.
Firft charge for a demi-landau	107	2	6

EXTRAS.

	£.	s.	d.
A compafs perch, plated on the fides	3	16	0
A half-wheel front	1	3	0
A pair of plain plough handles	2	0	0
Carry over	114	1	6

A footman.

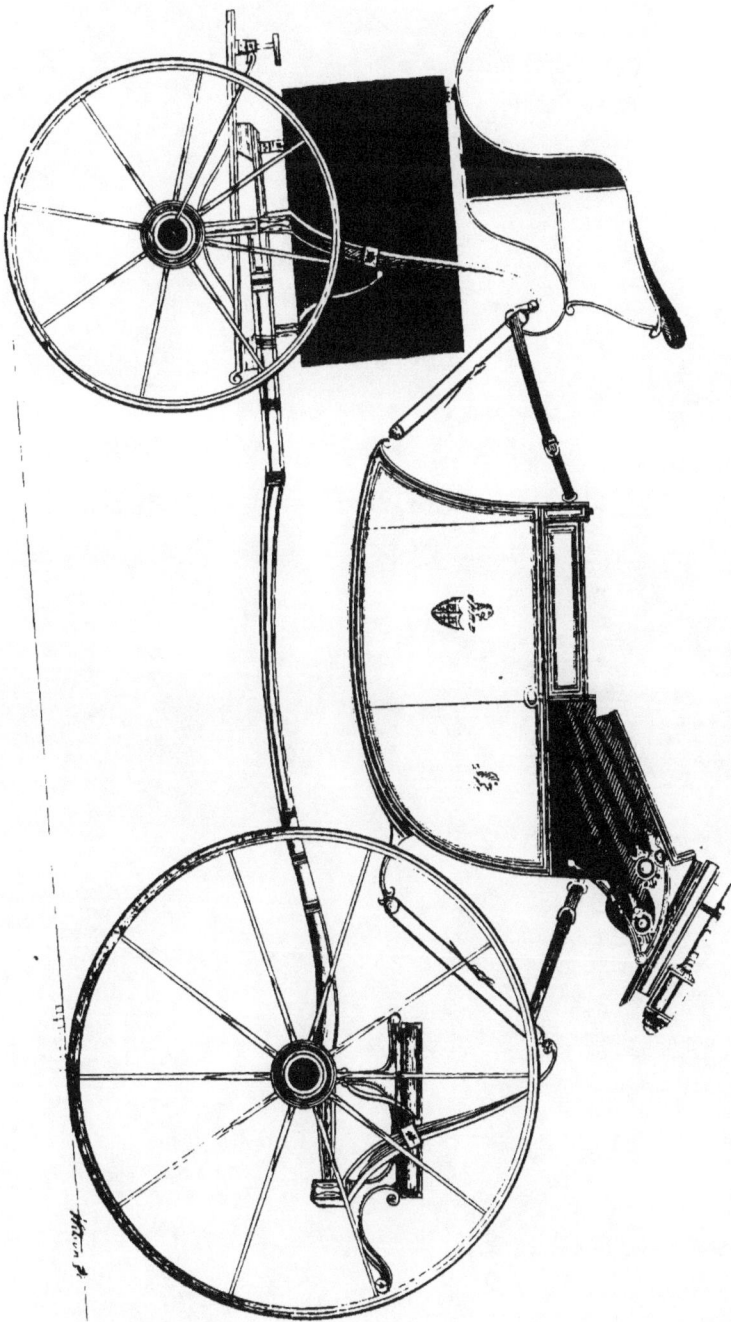

	£.	s.	d.
Brought over	114	1	6
A footman-cushion	2	2	0
A square trunk-boot	5	5	0
A chaise, or chair coach-box	10	0	0
Round sides to the body	1	0	0
The swing-holders, and other laces, three inches wide	1	2	0
Quilted sides	0	10	6
Lace-covered glass frames	1	10	0
Venetian blinds	2	15	0
Sixty-five feet of 4-8th moulding	3	13	1
Two scroll and two tip ornaments	0	5	0
Body-loop bolt heads, plated	0	5	0
Check-brace rings, ditto	0	5	8
Joints, ditto	3	3	0
Wheel-hoops, ditto	1	10	0
A pole-hook, ditto	1	1	0
A pair of Italian lamps	2	8	0
Painting of the body and carriage, picked out one colour	1	11	6
Forty-eight feet of one-inch plain fillets round the edge of the pannels	2	8	0
Arms on each door-pannel	0	14	0
Crests, with cyphers, on the two quarter ditto	0	11	0
Crests on the three stiles	0	9	0
	156	10	3

SECT.

SECT. 4.

TRAVELLING POST-CHAISE.

PLATE XXX.

A POST-CHAISE, for travelling with on the continent, requires, like the coach, to be built ftrong, and finifhed with conveniences fui:able for the journey ; to enumerate all that are ufed would be fuperfluous; fuch as the conveniences of beds, cupboards, table, &c. &c. which are but feldom required; and as the conftruction of them is fanciful, the price to be charged for them cannot here be ftated; therefore, only what is generally ufed will be valued. It is cuftomary with the foreign poft-mafters to drive three horfes abreaft, and they are always furnifhed with fhafts on purpofe for the near horfe to be placed in, for which it is neceffary to have hooks fixed in the fplinter-bar, for the fhafts to be hung by. The number of horfes ufed in travelling on the continent are proportioned to the luggage, for every trunk, or imperial to the carriage, another horfe is put, or charged for.

DESCRIPTION.

THE *Carriage* is a crane-neck, with raifed hind end, on plain, fhort blocks; a large platform budget,

Plate XXX.

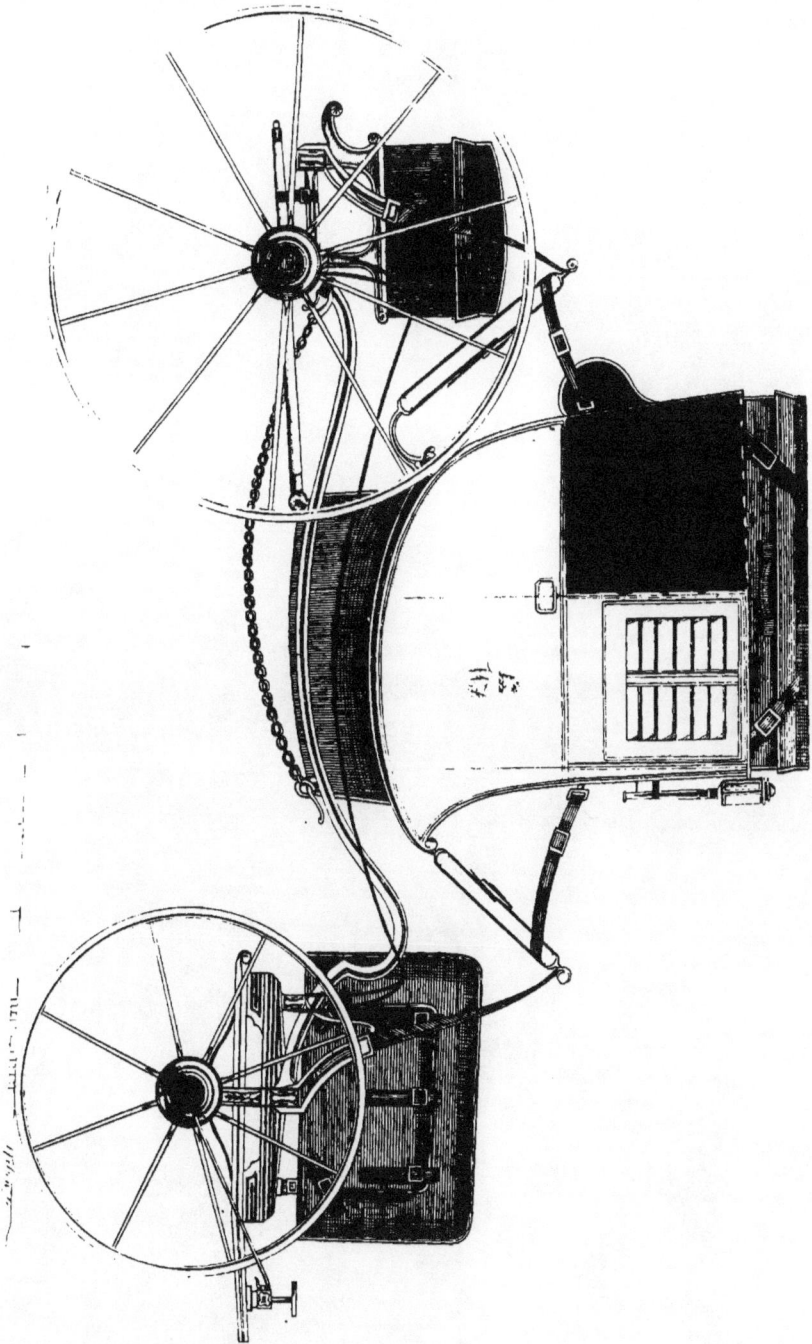

budget, with a trunk infide of it; a large trunk on the hind end; a drag-ftaff and chain; ftrong ftraked wheels; new-pattern axletrees, with double cafe boxes; the fprings corded. The *Body* has a fword-cafe back, and is lined with fecond cloth; trimmed with 2½-inch lace, and fwinging holders; quilted fides; double folding fteps; a fliding feat-box; Wilton carpet; Venetian blinds; and cloth-covered glafs-frames. The *Plating* with *filver*; an octagon, and a pair of fword-cafe frames; a 4-8th moulding all round the middle, up the corner, and ftanding pillars; Italian lamps, plain, and three in number. The *Painting* plain, with a cypher and creft on the doors only; the main and check *Braces* common, and Englifh pole-pieces; a pair of fafe braces and fixtures.

PRICE.

	£.	s.	d.
Firft charge for a crane-neck poft-chaife —	107	14	6

EXTRAS.

Axletrees, with double cafe boxes —	21	15	0
A raifed hind end, on plain fhort blocks —	1	10	0
A platform, or luggage boot —	3	0	0
A pair of trunks, with infide ftraps and laths	7	19	0
Sixteen feet of ftrap-belts for both trunks —	1	0	0
A drag-ftaff and chain — —	0	18	6
Cording the fprings — —	1	1	0
A fword-cafe back — —	2	10	0
Quilted fides to the lining — —	0	10	6
Carry over —	147	18	6

Swing-

	£.	s.	d.
Brought over ——	147	18	6
Swing-holders, and the lace 2½ inches wide —	1	11	6
Venetian blinds —— ——	2	15	0
An octagon and fword-cafe frames ——	1	1	0
Fourty four feet of 4-8th mouldings ——	4	19	0
Three Italian flat-fide lamps ——	2	12	0
A large broad well —— ——	2	12	6
A whole imperial —— ——	9	9	0
A large double cypher and creft on the doors	0	19	0
A pair of fafe braces and fixtures ——	3	13	0
	177	10	6

SECT. 5.

AN ELEGANT CHARIOT.

PLATE XXXI.

CHARIOTS are, generally, finifhed handfomer than Coaches, and form a material part in all grand proceffions; the elegance of them lies principally in the carved and gilt ornaments to the carriage part, with rich and fanciful paintings to the body, and the infides lined with velvet, and bordered with filk trimmings, taffels, &c. the value of fuch a carriage can only be afcertained by the builder, whofe fancy ought not to be reftricted, but when limited to a certain price; the reprefentation is rather out of the common ftyle, and is built on the principle of a ftate carriage, but more exactly

answers

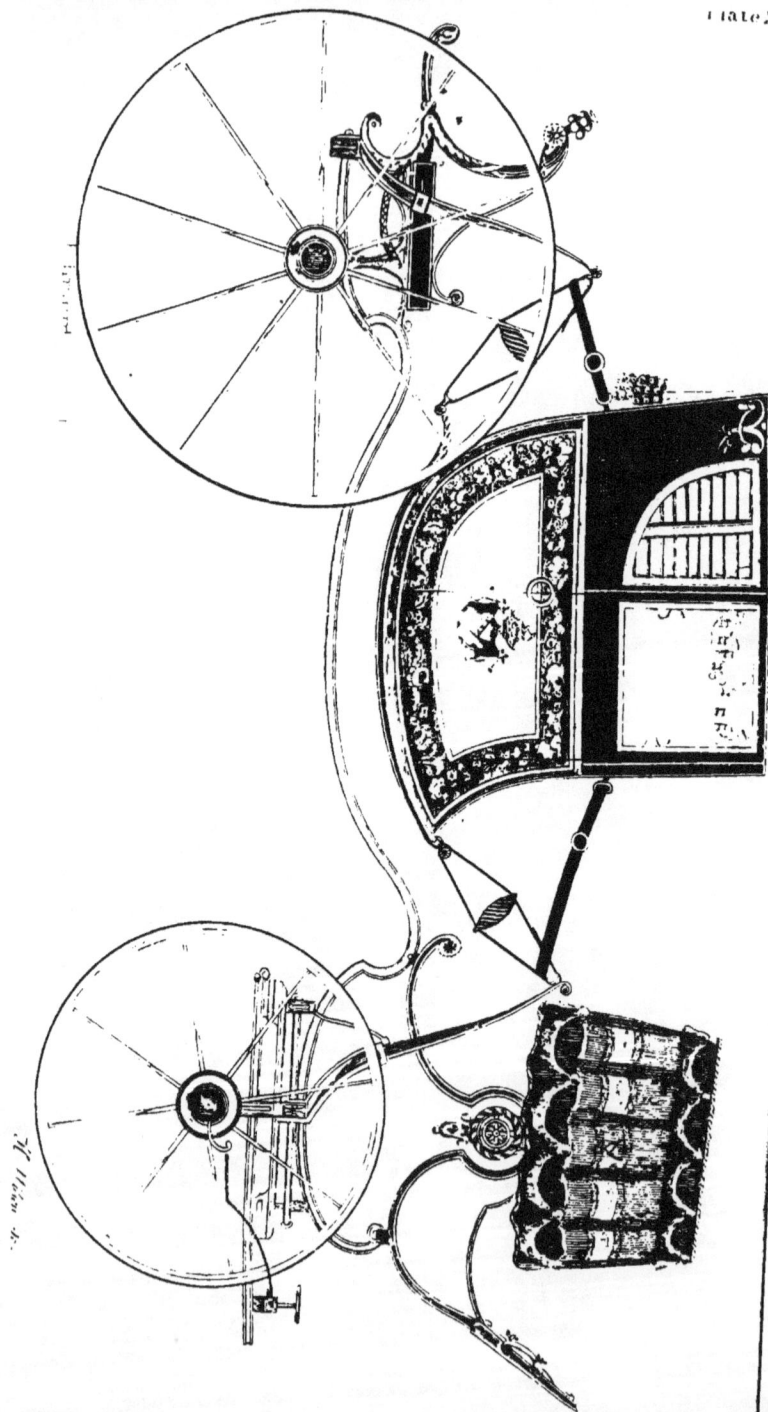

anfwers the defcription of a Chariot for the hot
countries, being light and airy for that pu-pofe ; it
being reprefented finifhed in a fuperior manner,
does not imply a neceffity for all to be fo, that
are built for the Indies, as they may be finifhed
with conveniencies fuitable to the place, but in as
plain a manner as any other carriage, excepting only the neceffity for fide and back lights for the advantage of air : from 100 to 200l. for carving and
gilding above what is here ftated, a very elegant
carriage may be built.

DESCRIPTION.

THE *Carriage* is a crane neck, with double-
bowed cranes, and long fweeped fore ends, on
which the iron coach-box is fixed ; a raifed hind
end, on handfome fhort blocks, with footman-
cufhion plated at the top and bottom edge, and
extra handfome carved hind ftandards ; patent
wheels, with moulded fellies, new pattern cylinder,
axletrees and boxes. The *Body* with fide lights,
and a divided back light, with plate glaffes, and
Venetian blinds ; lined with Morocco, trimmed
with filk creft lace; handfome feftoon curtains,
with fide drapery to all the lights; a fliding feat-
box ; a Wilton carpet ; and treble folding fteps.

The *Hammercloth* of a fecond cloth, trimmed
with a top and bottom row, or thirteen yards, of
narrow, and one row, or nine yards, of broad four-

inch

inch lace; with filk-embroidered arms in the middle: a top and bottom row, or thirteen yards,
of feven-inch fringe, over which filk drapery,
in feftoons, is placed; double footman-holders,
of lace, $3\frac{1}{2}$ inches wide, with handfome taffels.
The *Plating* with *filver*, a broad 5-8th moulding
round the pannels, the corners, pillars, and fides of
the doors; a 3-8th moulding all round the door,
the front and back lights; a pair of handfome ornamented head-plates; the body-loops plated on
the whole outfide furface; the check-brace rings,
the worm fprings, the out and infide wheel-hoops,
and pole-hook plated. The *Painting* has the
mouldings gilt or filvered, and picked out three
colours; the *Body* is ornamented with a border all
round the framing on the pannels, of the middling
kind, five inches wide, with a large rich mantle on
the fides and ends, having the arms and crefts within; a high-varnifhed body; an oil-varnifhed carriage.
The main and check *Braces* with whole buckles,
and a pair of worm fprings plated; a fet of point-
ftraps; French pole-pieces, with plated buckles.

PRICE.

	£.	s.	d.
Firft charge for a crane-neck poft-chaife —	107	2	6

EXTRAS.

	£.	s.	d.
Carriage. Double-bow cranes —	· 2	15	6
Additional fweeped-up fore end to the cranes	3	3	0
Carry over —	113	1	0

An

	£.	s.	d.
Brought over —— ——	113	1	0
An iron coach-box fixed on the cranes ——	10	0	0
A raised hind end, with handsome short blocks	3	0	0
A footman-cushion, with plated top and bottom frames, and hind standards ——	7	18	0
Extra carved ornaments to ditto ——	5	0	0
Patent wheels, with moulded fellies ——	3	19	0
The body with round sides — ——	1	0	0
Two side and one back divided light ——	9	15	0
Lining of Morocco leather — ——	6	0	0
Silk crest-lace for the trimmings ——	5	0	0
Extra for the small seaming laces, being of silk	2	12	6
Two sets of festoon curtains, with side drapery	7	7	0
Venetian blinds in lieu of shutters ——	2	15	0
An extra set of Venetian blinds for the side and back lights — —— ——	4	10	0
A set of glasses and frames for ditto ——	5	5	0
Four extra holders for glasses ——	2	8	0
Treble folding steps —— ——	2	10	0
A hammercloth, as described ——	17	17	0
Double-laced footman-holders, 3½ inches wide	2	4	0
Seventy feet of 5-8th plated moulding —	9	12	6
Fifty-six feet of 3-8th ditto — —	4	18	0
Two scroll, and two tip ornaments, of silver	0	14	0
Two handsome head-plates of silver embossed	2	8	0
The hind body-loops on the whole outside surface plated —— —— ——	3	13	6
The fore ditto, ditto —— ——	2	2	0
Four check-brace rings plated ——	0	16	0
A set of worm springs ditto — —	6	10	0
The inside and outside wheel-hoops ditto —	10	6	0
A pole-hook ditto —— ——	2	2	0
Carry over ——	255	3	6

F   The

	£.	s.	d.
Brought over —— ——	255	3	6
The wood mouldings gilt, and picked out three colours, and otherways ornamented —	5	0	0
Fifteen feet of a middling ornamented border, four inches wide, all round the pannel framings	13	10	0
The arms and crefts on the fide-pannels, in large rich mantles, with coronets — —	6	0	0
High varnifhed pannels — ——	4	4	0
The carriage varnifhed after painting —	0	15	0
Whole buckles to the main and check braces A fet of point-ftraps, with plated buckles —	0	8	0
French pole-pieces, with ditto ——	0	12	0

$$£. 285 \quad 12 \quad 6$$

SECT. 6.

A SULKEY.

A SULKEY is a light carriage, built exactly in the form of a Poft-chaife, Chariot, or Demi-Landau, but, like the Vis-à-vis, is contracted on the feat, fo that only one perfon can fit thereon, and is called a Sulkey, from the proprietor's defire of riding alone. The advantage peculiar to this is the lightnefs in draught ; and, by being fo fmall within the body, the paffenger fits more warm, and lefs incommoded by the jolting of the carriage. In the value of thefe carriages there is nothing reduced from that of the chariot, &c. but in the

proportion

proportion of the materials, which are lefs in quantity, and make a difference of ab ur one-twelfth lefs in the price than what is ftated for the other carriages; therefore, the value of a Sulkey, finifhed to any of the patterns defcribed, may be afcertained from either.

F 2 CHAP.

CHAP. V.

ON PHAETONS.

PHAETONS, for some years, have deservedly
been regarded as the most pleasant sort of
carriage in use, as they contribute, more than any
other, to health, amusement, and fashion, with the
superior advantage of lightness, over every other
sort of four-wheeled carriages, and are much safer,
and more easy to ride in, than those of two wheels.

The sizes and constructions of Phaetons are
more various than any other description of carriages, which gives fancy a greater scope; but
the sizes are mostly proportioned to the sizes of
the horses for draught, whether by ponies, or one
or two horses; so that a separate description of the
three sizes of phaetons, built with perch and crane-
neck carriages, of the best designs which are at
present in use, will make it necessary to represent
two of each size, viz. a perch and crane-neck,
with the different ornaments and conveniences,
making, in all, six descriptions, variously finished,
sufficient to direct a choice, and ascertain the value
of almost every sort of them. The form of the
bodies,

bodies, for either phaetons, curricles, or gigs, makes no difference in the price; the iron-work, or loops to the ſtep-piece, and gig bodies, the ſword-caſes, and doors, are the only things which make the prices vary any thing material. The ſhape for either body may be reverſed from the one repreſented, regarding only the ſize according to the intention of draught, whether with large horſes, galloways, or a ſingle horſe, adding or reducing the ornaments at pleaſure.

LARGE, OR HIGH PHAETONS.

AS by the ſize of the horſes for the draught, the ſize of the phaeton is moſtly regulated; a large phaeton is peculiarly convenient to thoſe who keep either a coach or chariot; as the ſame horſes which draw the one are of a ſize adapted to the other, and the greater variety of carriages may be kept without increaſing the number of horſes; the patterns, ſizes, and heights of thoſe phaetons are uſually followed by the public from ſuch as are introduced by perſons of high rank, and whoſe ſkill in driving, and judgment in carriages, are moſt diſtinguiſhed; the height of thoſe phaetons makes it neceſſary to add ſtrength to ſupport the weight, and are uſually, on that account, built as heavy as a common perch

F 3   chariot;

chariot; but, according to the prefent mode, they are not built of that extravagant height which they hitherto have been; it is ufual in thofe high phaetons to have the bodies placed directly over the fore wheels, the principal advantage of which is in the command the driver has over the horfes, but are more difficult to mount and difmount, and, on a fhort lock, are more likely to be overturned than if the weight was fufpended between the four bearings or axletrees.

SECT. I.

A PERCH HIGH PHAETON.

PLATE XXXII.

A PHAETON with a perch carriage may be built on a larger fcale than if with a crane-neck, and not be fo heavy; the advantage of turning is not fo great, yet the fafety is greater, as the perch prevents the fore carriage from locking fo far under as in crane-necks, whereby the danger of overturning is avoided, by having a large bafe for the fore-wheels to ftand on. As the danger arifes from the fituation of the body being directly over the bearings of the fore axletrees, and when thofe bearings are removed to a parallel with the centre of the carriage, as in crane-neck carriages they are, the

fafety

Plate XXXII

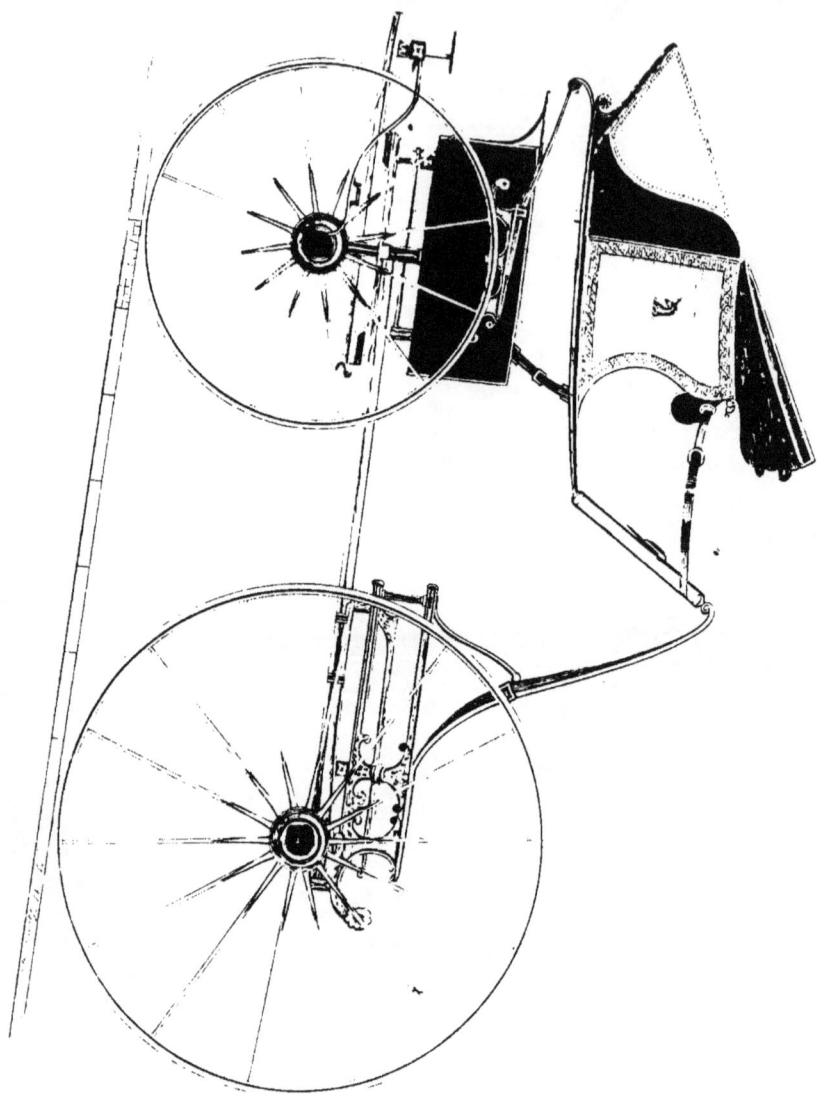

fafety then depends only on the chance of even ground, or that the weight of the body and paffengers does not preponderate over the weight of the hind part of the carriage; the longer the carriage, the greater is the fafety, by the fpace being wider between the bearings.

DESCRIPTION.

THE *Carriage* is a perch, with the fides plated with iron; a whole-wheel front; a fquare trunk-boot; hind and fore fpring-blocks; a hind platform, raifed with blocks; ftraked wheels; common axletrees and boxes.

The *Body*, a long-tail chair back, with fham doors and fword cafe; *lined* with fecond cloth, and *trimmed* with two-inch lace; a fquare, fixed *head*, lined with fecond cloth; a large, fixed knee-boot; a fliding feat-box; and a treble folding-ftep for occafional ufe. The *Plating* with *filver*, a half-inch moulding round the fham doors, the front and back of the head, and on the knee-boot at bottom, and round the fides of the trunk-boot; a pair of fword-cafe half frames; and fancy device head-plates. The *Painting* picked out two colours, with a rich fillet round the pannels; the arms on the back, and crefts on the fide pannels and foot-board, painted fmall; the main and check *Braces* common; a pair of crofs check braces; and Englifh pole-pieces.

F 4   PRICE

PRICE.

	£.	s.	d.
First charge for a large perch phaeton ——	47	19	6

EXTRAS.

	£.	s.	d.
The sides of the perch plated with iron ——	2	10	0
A whole-wheel front —— ——	2	5	0
A square trunk-boot —— ——	5	5	0
A hind platform raised with blocks ——	1	10	0
A pair of hind spring-blocks —— ——	4	4	0
A pair of fore ditto —— ——	1	0	0
Sham doors —— —— ——	0	15	0
A sword-case —— ——	1	10	0
A square, fixed head, lined with cloth ——	10	0	0
A knee-boot fixed on the footboard ——	2	4	0
A treble folding, or hanging step ——	3	3	0
Thirty feet of plated moulding ——	3	7	6
A pair of half sword-case frames ——	0	6	0
A set of fancy device head-plates ——	1	5	0
The painting of the body and carriage picked out one colour —— ——	1	5	6
Japanning the doors and sword-case ——	0	10	6
Twenty-six feet of rich fillet painted round the pannels —— —— ——	3	5	•
The arms on the back, and crests on the side pannels and footboard, painted small —	0	14	0
	£.92	19	0

SECT. 2.

A LARGE CRANE-NECK PHAETON.

PLATE XXXIII.

THIS being more weighty than a perch phaeton, is more folid on its bearings, but as the body
is hung over the fore bearings, or axletree, great
care fhould be obferved in turning fhort, left by
the height of the body, and weight of the paffengers, it fhould overfet, which is the only danger
to be apprehended from them ; on every other account they are to be preferred, as being a pleafant
and eafy vehicle to ride in, and, for appearance,
has much the fuperiority over every other kind of
open carriages in ufe.   They are peculiarly convenient for gentlemen to travel with, who are fond
of driving; and as many conveniences for carrying
luggage may be added, as would be neceffary for
a long journey, almoft as many as to a travelling
poft-chaife.   The expence for building fuch a carriage, in the fuperior manner, and furnifhing with
conveniencies, is very great, and nearly on a par
with the chariot.

DESCRIPTION.

THE *Carriage* is a crane neck, with a fquare
trunk-boot, raifed on neat carved blocks; a large
platform

platform budget behind, raifed with blocks; large hind and fore fpring-blocks, neatly carved; patent wheels with moulded fellies; patent cylinder axletrees and boxes.

The *Body*, a ftep-piece with fprings at the fore end; real doors; and a fword cafe; a round head, made on a frame to take off, with a pair of wings to put on occafionally; a knee-boot to take off, lined with fuperfine cloth, and trimmed with a $2\frac{1}{2}$ inch lace; a Wilton carpet; a double ftep to hang on occafionally. The *Plating* with *filver*, with fmall 2-8th moulding, in double rows, all round the pannels, the door, and fword-cafe ends. A large 5-8th moulding round the front of the head, the top and bottom behind, and round the fides of the boot; fix filver fcroll ornaments; the checkbrace rings; the collars, and ftar bolt-heads of the body-loops; the outfide wheel-hoops; polehook and worm-fprings, plated.

The *Painting* ornamented with rich ftriping; mantles, with fmall arms and creft, on the pannels, which are highly varnifhed; the mouldings of the carriage picked out three colours; the fwordcafe and doors japanned; the carriage varnifhed; the *Braces* common, with whole buckles; the pole-pieces French; a fet of fplinter-bars mounted with plated iron-work.

PRICE.

Plate XXXIII.

PRICE.

	£.	s.	d.
First charge for a large crane-neck phaeton —	61	9	6

EXTRAS.

	£.	s.	d.
A square trunk-boot — —	5	0	0
Neat fore budget-blocks — —	2	10	0
A raised hind platform — —	1	10	0
A platform or luggage-boot — —	8	0	0
Large hind spring-blocks — —	4	4	0
Large fore ditto — —	1	0	0
Patent wheels with moulded fellies —	3	19	0
Patent cylinder axletrees and boxes —	22	4	6
A set of splinter-bars — —	1	5	0
Real doors — — —	2	0	0
A sword-case back — —	1	10	0
A pair of single elbow springs —	1	0	0
A round head, lined with cloth, made on an iron frame — — —	13	10	0
A pair of wings with plated frames —	3	15	0
A knee-boot to take off occasionally —	2	4	0
A hanging-step with double treads —	2	2	0
The lining with superfine cloth —	2	0	0
Trimmed with a 3½ inch lace — —	0	10	6
Fifty feet of 2-8th plated moulding —	3	6	6
Twenty-six feet of 5-8th ditto —	3	9	6
Six silver scroll ornaments — —	1	4	0
Six check-brace rings plated —	1	4	0
Four star-heads to the body-loops, ditto —	0	10	0
Four collars for ditto — —	1	12	0
A pair of worm-springs, ditto —	3	0	0
A set of wheel-hoops, ditto, with cased metal	3	0	0
A pole-hook, plated — —	1	18	0
Carry over —	158	17	6

The

	£.	s.	d.
Brought over — —	158	17	5
The ferrels and loeps for the fplinters-bar, plated	1	15	0
The pannels painted with 9 feet of rich ornament-			
ed ftriping — — —	4	10	0
Four fmall mantles, with the arms and crefts in			
each — — —	2	12	0
The pannels high varnifhed — —	2	10	0
The mouldings of the carriage picked out three			
colours — —	2	5	0
The carriage varnifhed — —	0	15	0
A pair of point-ftraps — —	0	3	0
A pair of crofs check-braces —	0	10	6
French pole-pieces, with plated buckles —	0	12	0
	£. 174	10	0

MIDDLE-SIZED PHAETONS.

ALTHOUGH there are no eftablifhed rules for the fize of phaetons, yet a proportion fhould be obferved according to the fize of the horfes, whether fifteen, fourteen, or thirteen hands high; as the appearance of both ought to be conformable to each other, therefore a middling-fized phaeton, to the middling, or galloway, fized horfes, fuits beft; many perfons are very partial to this fize of equipage, being lefs formidable in the appearance than the high, and more elegant than the low, phaeton; from the moderate fize of them, they are, in general, called ladies' phaetons, and are beft adapted

for

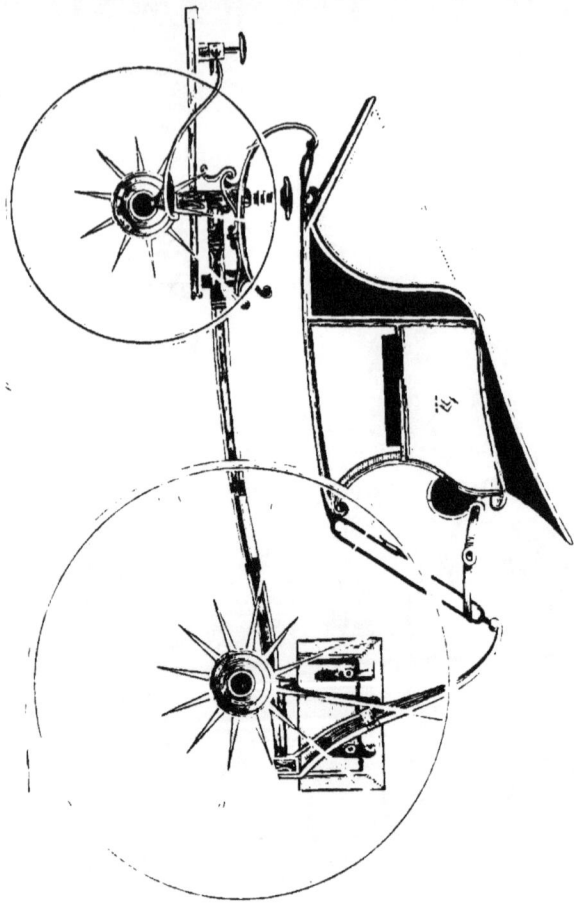

for their amufement. Although there is no rule for hanging the bodies, yet, as they are called ladies' phaetons, in regard to their perfonal fafety and eafe, it is neceffary to defcribe fuch a mode of hanging as fhall effectually fecure both.

SECT. 3.

A MIDDLE-SIZED PERCH PHAETON.

PLATE XXXIV.

SMALL horfes in a light carriage are more expeditious on their journies than heavy horfes with a heavy carriage, therefore a plain, light perch phaeton, with fuitable horfes, is more likely to be expeditious, and lefs expence, if not incumbered with too many fuperfluities.

DESCRIPTION.

THE *Carriage* a perch, with fore fpring-blocks; a middle-fized platform budget; ftraked wheels; common axletrees and boxes. The *Body* a chair back, half panneled, with fham doors and fwordcafe; lined with fecond cloth, and a two-inch lace; a Wilton carpet; a drop feat-box; a pair of wings; and a fixed knee-boot. The *Plating* with *filver*,

a half

a half-inch moulding round the doors, and on the footboard for the knee-boot; a pair of half fword-cafe frames. The *Painting* plain, with a fmall creft and cypher on the pannels ; the mouldings of the carriage picked out one colour ; common *Braces*, and Englifh pole-pieces.

PRICE.

	£.	s.	d.
Firft charge for a middle-fized perch phaeton	42	8	0

EXTRAS.

	£.	s.	d.
A pair of large fore fpring-blocks ——	1	0	0
A middle-fized platform budget ——	6	0	0
Sham doors —— — ——	0	15	0
A fword-cafe back —— ——	1	10	0
A drop feat-box —— ——	0	7	6
A pair of wings, middle-fize — ——	1	12	0
A fixed knee-boot, ditto —— ——	2	0	0
Sixteen feet of plated moulding for the doors and knee-boot —— — ——	1	16	0
A pair of half fword-cafe frames ——	0	6	0
The painting of the carriage picked out one colour —— —— ——	0	15	0
A fmall creft and cypher on the two fide pannels	0	10	0
	£. 58	19	6

S E C T.

SECT. 4.

A CRANE-NECK MIDDLE-SIZED PHAETON.

PLATE XXXV.

TO unite fafety with the other properties of a crane-neck carriage, is to fufpend the body behind the bow of the cranes, fo that the weight may be between the bearings; this can only be effected by a longer carriage, whereby the command over the horfes is not fo great, as if the body was more forward; yet it is otherwife preferable on account of its eafe and fafety, and thofe who are partial to phaetons, and cannot drive, may have a fixed, or temporary, feat for the coachman, concealed in a budget, or as defcribed in the plate; a long carriage is objected to by many perfons, on a fuppo-fition of a vaft increafe in the draught, which is er-roneous: the only material increafe is, the addi-tional weight of the materials of the carriage, be-ing fomewhat longer, and of courfe made ftronger than if otherways, to fupport the weight: the in-creafe of draught therefore is principally owing to the increafe of weight, but the carriage has much the advantage in its appearance.

DESCRIPTION.

DESCRIPTION.

THE *Carriage* a crane-neck, with double-bow cranes; a raifed hind end, on neat fhort blocks, and a footman's cufhion with a plated top edge; a trunk-boot, and large fore fpring-blocks; light chaife coach-box; double fteps; hooped tyre wheels; common axletrees and boxes. The *Body* a tub-bottom fhape, with fham doors; lined with fecond cloth, trimmed with a three-inch lace; a round, or waggon, fixed head and knee-boot; a Wilton carpet; a fliding feat-box; a driving-box; and a deep cufhion, with a plaited, or puckered fall, trimmed with lace. The *Plating* with *filver*, a 3-8th moulding all round the fham doors, the head, and footboard for the knee-boot; the check-rings, pole-hook, and wheel-hoops, plated. The *Braces* common, with an additional pair of crofs check ditto.

PRICE.

	£.	s.	d.
Firft charge for a crane-neck middle-fized phaeton — — —	54	6	0

EXTRAS.

	£.	s.	d.
Carriage with double-bowed cranes —	2	2	0
A raifed hind end with neat fhort blocks —	2	5	0
A middle-fized trunk-boot — —	3	10	0
Carry over —	62	3	0
	* A light		

	£.	s.	d.
Brought over	62	3	0
* A light chair coach-box	9	0	0
A pair of large fore spring-blocks	1	0	0
A footman's cushion plated at the top	2	18	0
Double steps	0	14	0
Hooped tyre wheels	1	5	0
Sham doors	0	15	0
A driving seat-box	0	10	6
Trimmings of a three-inch lace	0	7	0
A round, or waggon, head, lined with second cloth	0	12	0
A knee-boot	2	0	0
The cushion made of an extraordinary depth, with a fall trimmed with lace	0	12	0
Thirty feet of 3-8th plated moulding	4	12	6
Six check-brace rings, plated	1	4	0
A pole-hook, ditto	1	18	0
A set of wheel-hoops, ditto with cased metal	2	10	0
Eighteen square feet of middling ornamented striping of the zig-zag pattern on the pannels	6	5	0
The arms and crests painted in mantles on the back pannels	0	18	6
The moulding of the carriage picked out two colours	1	11	6
French pole-pieces	0	6	0
A pair of cross check-braces	0	10	6
	101	12	6

* This being much smaller than what is used to post-chaises, 1l. should
be reduced from the original price, which is 10l.

G   SECT.

SECT. 5.

PONEY, OR ONE-HORSE PHAETON.

PLATE XXXVI.

A PAIR of ponies from twelve to thirteen hands
high are about equal for draught with a horfe of
fifteen, and a phaeton of the fame weight is equally
adapted for either; excepting only, that each
fhould be built of a proportioned height, for the
advantage of both horfe and driver. A low phaeton and a high horfe, are equally as abfurd as a
high phaeton and a low horfe, yet timid and infirm
people prefer low phaetons ; the infirm, becaufe they
are eafy of accefs ; and the timid, becaufe they are
more eafy to efcape from in time of danger, without confidering that the danger often arifes from not
having a proper command of the horfe, when any
accident occurs to ftartle him. Thofe phaetons
are frequently defigned for one horfe, or a pair of
ponies, and fometimes for one or two horfes alternately, a medium fhould then be obferved in the
building, that it be neither too high for the ponies,
nor too heavy for the one horfe ; a pole and fhafts
are then neceffary, the pole for the pair, as ufual,
and the fhafts for the fingle horfe ; but the fingle
horfe fhould never be ufed without a breeching.

Poney

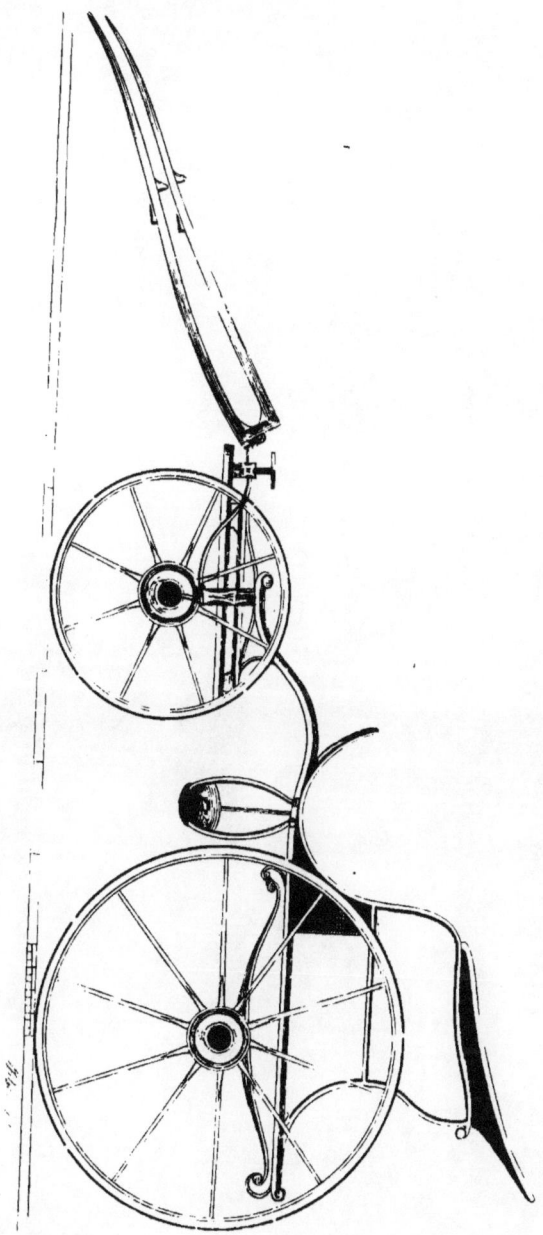

Poney phaetons are pretty equipages, and are beſt adapted for parks only; for, by being ſo low, the paſſengers are much annoyed by the duſt, if uſed on the turnpike roads; and one-horſe phaetons, where one horſe only is kept, are much to be preferred to any two-wheeled carriage for ſafety and eaſe, but are heavier in draught; to allow for that, it ought to be built as light as poſſible to be ſafe with.

SECT. 6.

A LIGHT ONE-HORSE, OR PONEY BERLIN PHAETON.

PLATE XXXVII.

FOR a ſafe, light, ſimple, and cheap, four-wheeled phaeton, the Berlin is to be recommended in preference to any: it is a crane-neck carriage, with the body fixed thereon, at ſuch a diſtance between the bearings as to be perfectly ſafe. The crane necks are made of wood, and are called ſhafts, on which a half-panneled chaiſe is fixed, and the carriage is united to the hind axletree by a pair of graſshopper ſprings, on which depends the eaſe in riding; the only objection to it is, on account of the diſtance the paſſengers are from the horſe, which, though it gives but an indifferent

G 2   command

command of his head, fecures them from the danger of his heels. The fhafts, or cranes, are alfo very liable to break at the bend, as it is nearly impoffible to find timber that is grown to the fhape; the chance of breaking arifes from the grain being croffed, by cutting it away to form the bow neceffary for the wheels to pafs under, and are obliged to be fecured by iron plates, which even feldom prove fufficient: the value in its firft charge may be confidered equal to that of a fmall perch phaeton, and by being more fimple in it's principle, there is lefs occafion for additions to be made in the expence.

DESCRIPTION.

THE *Carriage* a Berlin, with wooden cranes fupported on grafshopper fprings; two bars framed at the hind end; a whole wheel front; a pair of fingle fteps, and one-horfe fhafts; ftraked wheels; common axletrees and boxes. The *Body* a half-pannelled whifkey, or chaife; lined with fecond cloth: trimmed with two-inch lace; an oil-cloth at the bottom; and a pair of wings. The *Painting* picked out one colour.

PRICE

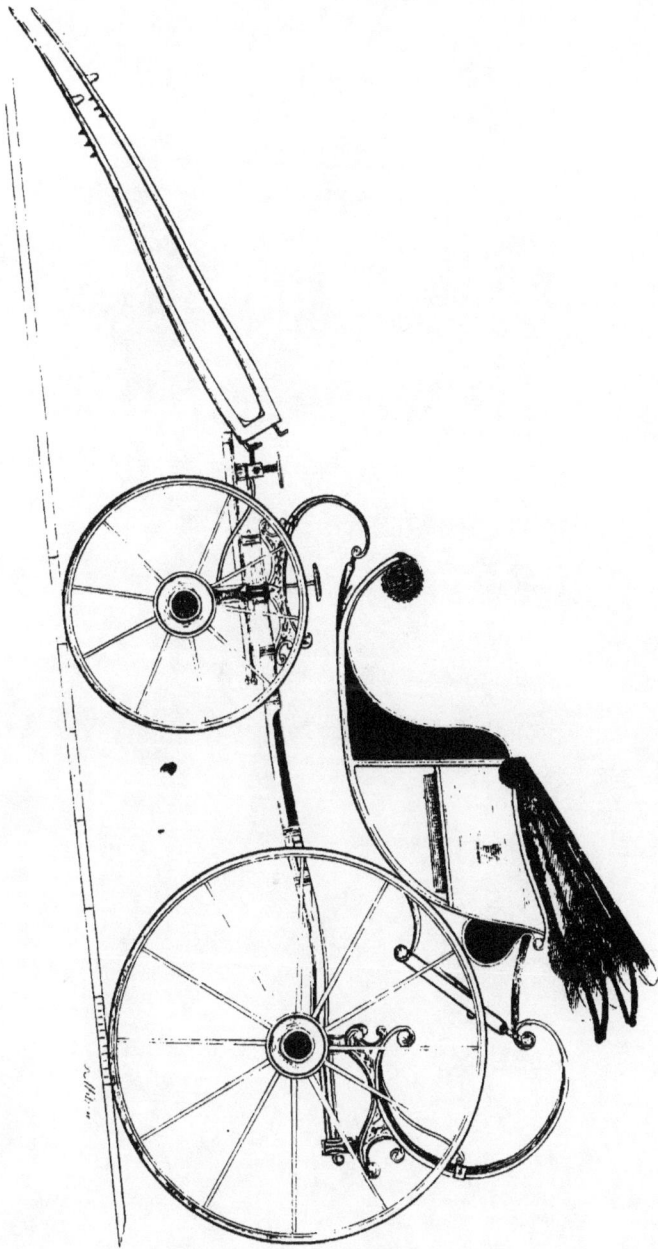

PRICE.

	£.	s.	d.
The firſt charge the ſame as a ſmall perch phaeton	37	8	0

EXTRAS.

	£.	s.	d.
A pair of wings	1	10	0
The mouldings of the body and carriage picked out one colour	1	2	6
	40	0	6

SECT. 7.

A ONE-HORSE, or PONEY PERCH PHAETON.

PLATE XXXVIII.

CARRIAGES built with iron cranes are moſtly too heavy for one horſe, or ponies, and perch carriages, on that account, are preferable; iron cranes being alſo more expenſive, become likewiſe an objection; a ſhort carriage for the purpoſe looks beſt, but affords little room for the hanging, unleſs the body is placed over the fore wheels, which is neither ſafe nor eaſy; the body between the bearings is much to be preferred, having both thoſe advantages, which is owing to the form and ſituation of the ſprings.

G 3   DESCRIPTION.

DESCRIPTION.

THE *Carriage* a perch, with fhafts for one horfe, and pole, with pole-pieces, for a pair of ponies; the fore and hind fprings of the fcroll form, raifed on neat blocks; a whole-wheel fore-end; ftraked wheels, ten and twelves; common axletrees and boxes.

The *Body* a half pannel, tub-bottom fhape; with fham doors; a fword-cafe; and a drop feat-box; lined with fecond cloth, and trimmed with a $2\frac{1}{2}$ inch lace; a Wilton carpet; a round, or waggon, fixed head, and knee-boot. The *Plating* with *fil-ver*, a 3-8th moulding all round the fham doors, the front and back of the head; and a pair of fword-cafe frames. The *Painting* of the body picked out two colours; crefts painted on the fide pannels.

PRICE.

	£.	s.	d.
The firft charge for a fmall-fized perch phaeton	37	8	0

EXTRAS.

		£.	s.	d.
Pole and pole-pieces (befides fhafts)	——	1	5	0
A whole wheel front	——	1	10	0
Small hind fpring-blocks	——	2	2	0
Large fore ditto	——	1	1	0
Scroll fprings behind and before	——	2	2	0
The body with fham doors	——	0	15	0
Ditto, with fword-cafe back	——	1	10	0
Carry over	——	47	13	0

The

	£.	s.	d.
Brought over ——— ———	47	13	0
The lining trimmed with a 2½ inch lace —	0	2	6
The lining quilted ——— ———	0	10	6
Round or waggon head ——— ———	12	0	0
A knee boot ——— ———	1	18	0
Thirty feet of 3-8th moulding ———	2	17	0
A pair of sword-case frames ———	0	9	0
The painting picked out two colours ———	1	4	0
Two crests on the side pannels ———	0	6	0
	£.67	0	0

SECT. 8.

A SOCIABLE.

PLATE XXXIX.

A SOCIABLE is a phaeton with a double or treble body, and is so called from the number of persons it is meant to carry at one time. They are intended for the pleasure of gentlemen to use in parks, or on little excursions with their families: they are also peculiarly convenient for the conveying of servants from one residence to another.

The bodies may be constructed so as to hang on the carriage of a coach or chariot, after removing its own body, and no other expence is then incurred but that of the Sociable body itself, which may be made on a very simple plan, if it is only required for an occasional convenience; but if the car-

G 4   riage

.s

riage is built with, and only for, the body, it may
alſo be built very light and ſimple, although they
carry many paſſengers; but as they are intended for
country uſe only, and in fine weather, they need
not be more heavy than a common phaeton, and a
great convenience for large families may be formed
at a little expence, except the duty.

DESCRIPTION.

THE *Carriage* is built the ſame as a large crane-
neck phaeton, with a raiſed hind end, on ſhort
plain blocks; large fore ſpring blocks; ſtraked
wheels, ten and twelve ſpokes; common axletrees
and boxes.

The *Bodies* are three in number, with drop ſeat-
boxes to each, and a ſword-caſe to one; they are
all built on one large bottom formed to the ſhape of
the crane, and are in value the ſame as three ſingle
tub-bottom chaiſe bodies. The ſides are cane inſtead of pannel; they are lined on the rails; with
cuſhions on the ſeats, and ſeat-fails; trimmings
plain; two oil-cloths for the bottom; a draw folding ſtep on each ſide; a ſquare fixed head to the
hind end, a large jointed umbrella for the centre of
the two fore ones; a common knee-flap for the
front body; a large knee flap, which buttons acroſs
the four elbows, which covers the vacant ſpace
between the two bodies. The *Painting* picked out
one colour to body and carriage.

PRICE.

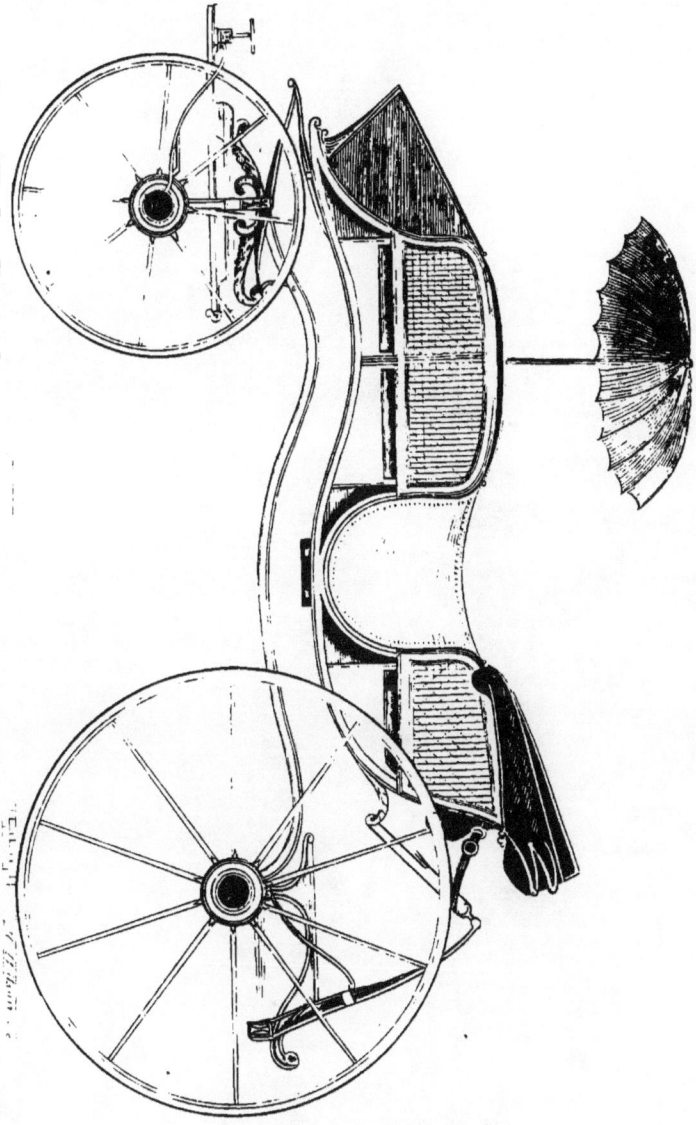

PRICE.

This differing from the common fort of carriages, a firft charge
cannot be collected from the tables in this volume, but a reference to the feparate parts, which are ftated in the other,
will prove the value to be as here ftated.

		£.	s.	d.
Body. Three tub-bottom fhape chaife bodies		19	10	0
A fword-cafe back ——— ———		1	10	0
Three drop-feats ——— ———		1	2	0
The lining for the three cane bodies of fecond cloth, and plain trimmings ———		10	0	0
A fquare fixed head ——— ———		10	0	0
A jointed umbrella ——— ———		2	2	0
Two middle-fized knee-boots ———		4	0	0
Double fliding fteps to fold — ——		3	0	0
Two oil-cloths for the bottom ———		0	15	0
Painting and picking out three cane bodies —		3	16	0
Japanning a fword-cafe ——— ———		0	7	6
Carriage. A crane-neck large phaeton carriage		33	10	0
A fet of ftraked wheels, tens and twelves		6	5	0
A pair of plain blocks ——— ———		1	10	0
A pair of large fpring-blocks ———		1	1	0
A pair of main braces, four feet long, each $2\frac{1}{2}$ inches wide, with plated half buckles —		1	0	6
A pair of check braces ——— ———		0	6	0
The painting of the carriage plain ———		1	15	0

$$£. \ 101 \ \ 10 \ \ 0$$

Caned bodies are ufually lined on the top rails only, and then
but one-third of the price ftated for linings can be charged.

SECT.

SECT. 9.

SHOOTING PHAETON.

PLATE XL.

THIS, like the Sociable, is an uncommon carriage, but alfo peculiarly convenient for the purpofe
defigned, which is that of fhooting from. Gigs
have been commonly ufed for the occafion, but
this being more fteady, and carrying more conveniencies than a Shooting Gig, is much to be preferred. There has not been many of them built,
but as there is every reafon to fuppofe that they may
be found ufeful, the different views of them are here
reprefented for the purpofe of fhewing their various
conveniencies, and giving proper information con-
cerning the manner of building them. The manner of hanging the body makes it not only eafy
but fteady ; and although defcribed only for this,
yet may be adapted to any other carriage.

The conftruction of the carriage part is exactly
like that of a phaeton. The body is a half-panneled chaife, fixed on a platform, and of a fufficient
width for two perfons to fit in ; at a diftance behind
it is an encircled chair body, fixed on the fame
platform, which can only contain one perfon to fit
in. The bodies are placed at a convenient diftance

from

from each other, in order to give room between them for a funk bottom, or well, for carrying fowling-pieces or game. When ufed for fhooting, the gentleman occupies the back feat, and the fervant drives; at other times, the gentleman drives and the fervant fits behind. The ends of the well and boots are bevelled to each others form, for the advantage of room; in the boot the dogs may be carried, but their fituation is more comfortable and eafy under the feat of the fore body, which may be railed on purpofe. They are ufeful carriages, at other times, to travel with, and the fervant may (without riding on horfeback) be alfo carried in a fituation that is proper, comfortable, and convenient at call.

THE DIFFERENT VIEWS OF THE SHOOTING PHAETON.

SEE PLATE XXXIX.

A. The Carriage. B. The Body, fhewing its platform by a dotted line at Fig. 2, on which the bodies are framed. C. The driving body made of a width for two perfons. D. The fhooting Body made of a width for one perfon only. E. The fprings, which are of the double elbow, placed acrofs the bottom. F. The iron work to which the

the fprings hang by fhort iron loops. G. The bevelled boots. H. The well for the guns and game. I. The kennel for the dogs.

Fig. 1. The Side.
Fig. 2. The Top.
Fig. 3. The Front.
Fig. 4. The Back Views.

—————

DESCRIPTION.

THE *Carriage* a middle-fized perch phaeton ; ftraked wheels, ten and twelve fpokes ; common axletrees and boxes ; a whole wheel front ; two middle-fized boots. The *fore Body* a half-panneled chair, with a fword-cafe and fham door. The *bind Body* a low chair feat, covered round with japanned leather ; each lined with cloth, and trimmed plain ; both fixed on a long platform, in which there is a large well ; an oil-cloth at the bottom of the fore body ; fmall wings to both ; two pair of check *Braces* ; four ftrong compafs-irons fixed to the fides of the boots for the fprings.

PRICE,

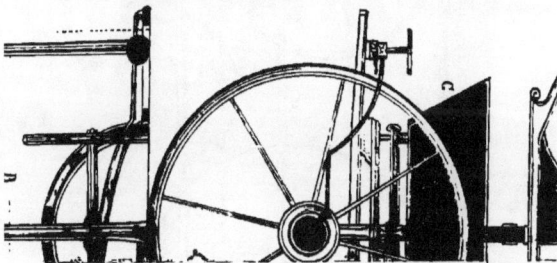

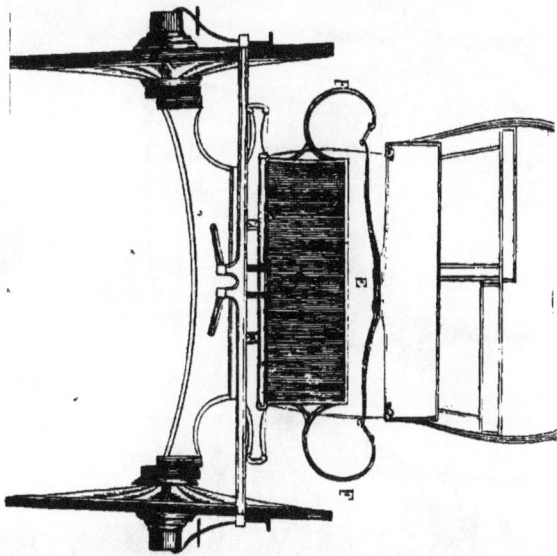

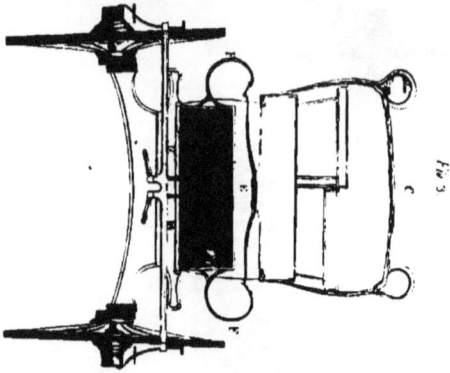

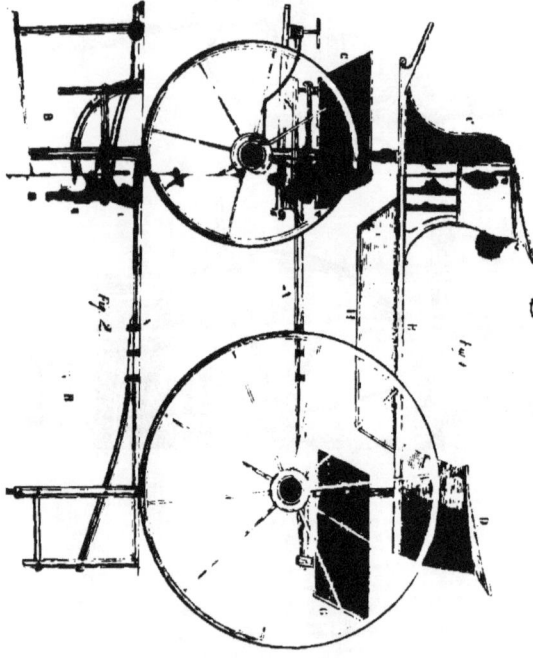

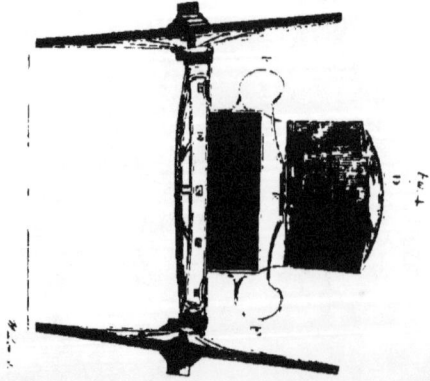

PRICE.

FROM THE FIRST VOLUME.

	£.	s.	d.
The carriage a middle-fized perch phaeton —	18	0	0
A fet of wheels ftraked tyre, ten and twelve fpokes — — —	6	5	0
A whole wheel-front — —	1	15	0
Two middle-fized trunk-boots —	7	0	0
Four ftrong compafs-irons for the fprings to hang by — — —	2	2	0
A platform-bottom for the two bodies, and a well at the bottom for the fowling-pieces	5	5	0
The fore body, a whifkey — —	5	5	0
A fword-cafe and fham-doors to ditto —	2	5	0
The lining the body with fecond cloth, and plain trimmings — —	5	0	0
The hind body, a fmall fimple chair, with a plain lining — —	7	10	0
A pair of wings, fmall fize — —	1	10	0
An oil-cloth for the body — —	0	7	6
Painting the carriage — —	1	11	6
Painting the body the fame as two whifkeys —	3	0	0
	£. 66	16	0

CHAP.

CHAP. VI.

TWO-WHEELED CARRIAGES.

FOR lightnefs and fimplicity two-wheeled carriages are preferable, but are lefs to be depended on for fafety ; the fmallnefs of their price,
and the difference of expence in the impofed duty,
are the principal reafons for their being fo generally ufed. They are not fo pleafant to ride in as
phaetons, as the motion of the carriage frequently
gives uneafinefs to the paffengers. Not having the
advantage of the fore wheels, they are neither fo
fafe in their bearings, nor fo eafy to turn about
with, and are therefore inconvenient where the turnings are narrow. There are two defcriptions of
two-wheeled carriages ; the curricle which is ufed
with two horfes, and the chaife that is ufed with
one horfe only. The one-horfe chaifes are of different patterns, and are diftinguifhed by a variety
of names, but moftly by the gig and whifkey, in
which there is a material difference ; but both the
curricle and chaife, like other carriages, are finifhed in various fanciful ways, agreeably to the tafte
of the occupier, or the prevailing fafhion of the
times.

The

The bodies of two-wheeled carriages are exactly the fame as the bodies of phaetons, and either pattern of the bodies may be ufed to either carriage by the alteration only of the height or form of the fprings.

———

SECT. I.

CURRICLE.

CURRICLES were ancient carriages, but are lately revived with confiderable improvements; and none are fo much regarded for fafhion as thefe are by thofe who are partial to drive their own horfes; they are certainly a fuperior kind of two-wheeled carriage, and, fiom their novelty, and being generally ufed by perfons of eminence, are, on that account, preferred as a more genteel kind of carriage than phaetons; though not poffeffing any advantage to be compared with them, except in lightnefs, wherein they excel every other, having fo great a power to fo fmall a draught. They are built much ftronger and heavier than what is neceffary for one-horfe chaifes, and the larger they are the better they look, if not to an extreme. They are often made to be ufed with one or two horfes, and are convenient when made fo for travelling; for if, by accident, one horfe fails, the

other

other may proceed with the carriage, as with a one-
horfe chaife, having the harnefs alfo fuitably contrived.   It is only for occafional purpofes that it
can be recommended, as a proper proportioned
curricle for two horfes is much too heavy to be
frequently ufed with one.

SECT. 2.

A CHANGEABLE CURRICLE, OR CURRICLE GIG

PLATE XL.

THIS is a kind of carriage which may be ufed
alternately as curricle or gig, being lighter than a
common curricle, and fo may be ufed with only
one horfe, and being longer in the carriage than a
common gig, makes the appearance more uniform
with that of a curricle, when ufed as fuch. If this
carriage is properly conftructed, it need not be too
heavy for one horfe, and a convenience is thereby
obtained, to thofe who keep but two horfes, of
having one at reft while the other is at work, fo
that a frefh horfe is always ready for ufe. Heads,
trunks, and dafhing-leathers, look beft for curricles when drawn by two horfes, but as they add to
the

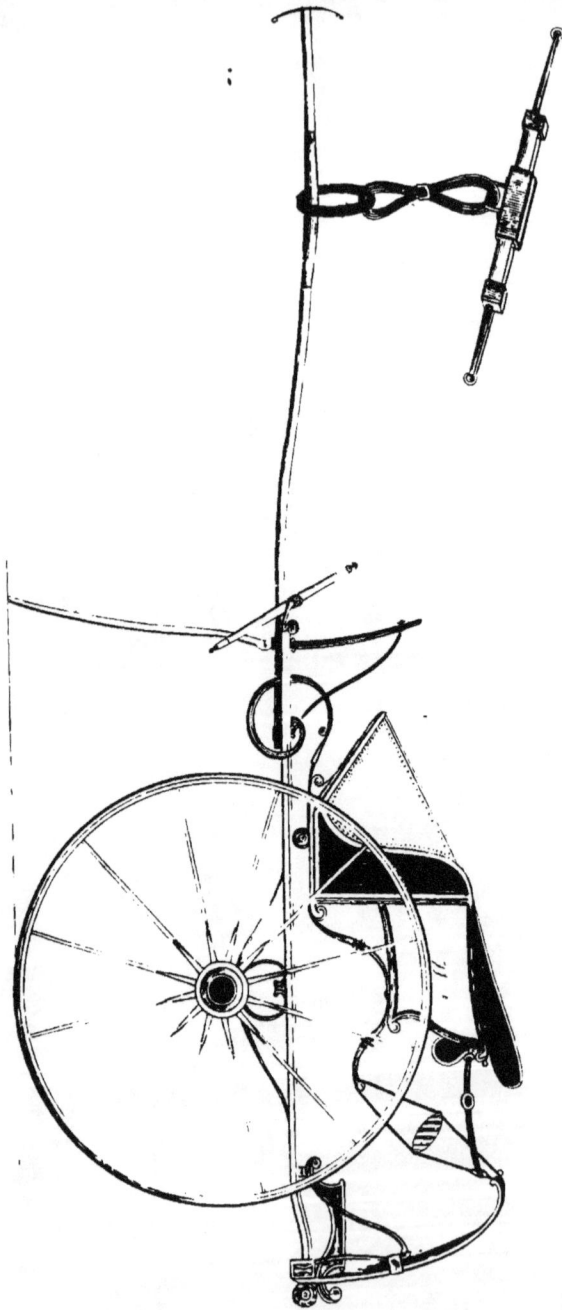

Plate 5

the weight, they may be fo made, as to be eafily removed when drawn by one.

DESCRIPTION.

THE *Carriage* made with fhafts and a pole, for alternate ufe; a light dafhing leather in front; a fmall platform-boot behind; ftraked wheels; common axletrees and boxes. The *Body,* a ftep-piece, with fham doors, and fword cafe; lined with fecond cloth; trimmed with two-inch lace; a pair of wings, with plated frames; and a middle-fized knee-boot. The *Plating* with *filver,* a 4-8th moulding round the fham doors, on the footboard, and at the top of the fword-cafe back. The *Painting* of the body and carriage picked out one colour, and crefts on the fide pannels. The *Braces* in front placed round the fore fprings, with jacks fixed on the bottom of the body; common pole-pieces.

PRICE.

	£.	s.	d.
Firft charge for a curricle made a gig ——	39	13	9

E X T R A S.

	£.	s.	d.
A dafhing-leather in front ————————	2	10	0
A fmall platform-boot behind with wood fides	3	0	0
Sham doors —— —— ——	0	15	0
A fword-cafe back —— ——	1	10	0
The trimming of a 2½ inch lace ——	0	3	6
A pair of middle-fized wings, with plated frames	3	2	0
Carry over ——	50	14	3

H　　　　　　　A middle-

			£.	s.	d.
Brought over	—		50	14	3
A middle-fized knee-boot	—	—	2	0	0
A pair of fword-cafe frames	——		0	9	0
Twenty feet of 4-8th moulding	—		2	5	0
The body and carriage picked out one colour			0	19	6
Japanning the doors and fword-cafe	—		0	10	6
Two fmall crefts on the fide pannels	—		0	6	0
Five feet of two-inch brace for the fore fprings			0	10	0
A pair of fmall fpring-jacks	—	—	0	15	0

£. 58 9 3

SECT. 3

A FIXED OR PROPER CURRICLE.

PLATE XLI.

THE proprietors of this fort of carriage are in
general perfons of high repute for fafhion, and
who are, continually, of themfelves, inventing
fome improvements, the variety of which would be
too tedious to relate; thofe only will be noticed
which are beft calculated for eafe and fafety; the
whole weight of the carriage refting on the pole,
it principally depends on it for both; and to it the
contrivances are moftly applied, either to relieve it
from the weight of the carriage, or give eafe to the
rider, which may be done by fprings, or a rope,
fixed to, or a joint in, the pole; as there is fomething

thing of novelty in the ufe of the rope to thefe car-.
riages, it is the moft prevalent contrivance in ufe.
To hanging the body of a curricle with eafe,
every attention fhould be paid, and it is moftly with
high, light fprings, and long braces, that this is effected, with the body low between the framings of
the carriage, which is built long and ftrong ; fuch
a curricle is the moft fafhionable in ufe.

DESCRIPTION.

THE *Carriage* a Curricle, for two horfes only ;
a dafhing-leather in front ; a fmall-fized platform-
budget behind ; the new-pattern cylinder axletree
and boxes, the axletree cranked or bent to admit
the body hanging low ; patent wheels, with moulded fellies ; a long rope, united with a double brace
and buckle at the fore end of the pole, and a fingle
brace at the other end, which is fixed to a jack on
the axletree, and, by means of the brace and jack,
the rope is drawn very tight ; near the bearing, a
piece is buckled clofe between the pole and the
rope, and keeps it at a proper diftance, by this
contrivance the pole is releafed from the weight ;
and, by the elafticity of the rope, the rider has
more eafe ; and, by the preffure of the weight on
the rope, which is fixed on the axletree, it is of
fome advantage to the draught.

The

The *Body* a chair back, with fham doors, and
a fword-cafe; long fprings fixed underneath, and
hung to the inner fore bar by a loop; lined with
a fecond cloth, and trimmed with a three-inch lace;
quilted fides; and an extra deep cufhion; a driving-box; a round or waggon head, with curtains;
and a knee-boot of a middle fize. The *Plating*
with *filver*, a fmall-fized quill, or 2-8th fize moulding, in double rows, round the fides of the pannels
and doors; a 4-8th moulding on the bottom edge
of the bottom fides, round the head, and on the
knee-boot; a pair of fword-cafe frames; four filver fcroll ornaments; a pair of plated check-brace
rings; a pair of plated worm-fprings, and a pole-
hook; the joints of the head plated. The *Painting*
of the carriage picked out three colours; the pannels high varnifhed; the doors and fword-cafe japanned; arms, crefts, and mantles, on the three
pannels; and a pair of crofs check braces.

PRICE.

		£.	s.	d.
Firft charge for a curricle — —		37	10	6

EXTRAS.

A platform budget — —		4	0	0
A dafhing leather — —		2	10	0
New pattern cylinder axletrees and boxes —		8	10	0
Patent wheels with moulded fellies —		2	0	0
Carry over —		54	10	6

A crank

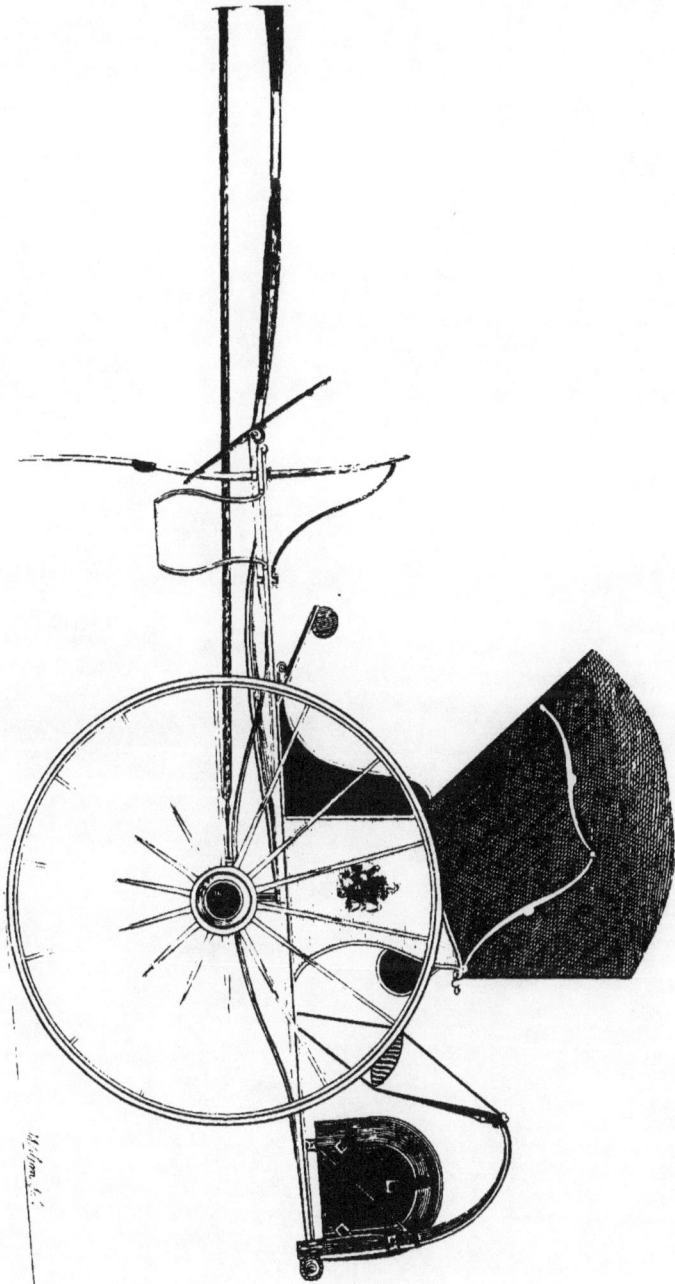

	£.	s.	d.
Brought over	54	10	6
A crank axletree	1	0	0
The rope and apparatus	3	3	0
Sham doors	0	15	0
Sword-cafe back	1	10	0
A pair of elbow fprings, three feet long	3	10	0
The trimmings of three-inch lace	0	5	0
Quilted lining	0	10	6
Extra for a deep cufhion and plaited fall, trimmed with lace	0	8	0
A driving-box	0	12	0
A round head, lined with cloth	12	0	0
Cloth curtains for ditto	0	18	0
A middle-fized knee-boot	2	0	0
Fifty feet of 2-8th moulding	3	2	6
Thirty feet of 4-8th ditto	3	7	6
A pair of fword-cafe frames	0	9	0
Four filver fcroll ornaments	0	16	0
A pair of check-brace rings, plated	0	8	0
A pair of worm-fprings, ditto	3	0	0
A pole-ring, ditto	2	12	0
The head-joints, ditto	8	8	0

£. 103   5   0

H 3   SECT.

SECT. 4.

THE NEW-PATTERN CURRICLE.

PLATE XLII.

FROM the novelty of curricles the number of them is daily increasing, and like every other thing, which is a prevailing fashion, excites the speculation of ingenious men to alter and improve.

Curricles, which are only drawn by two horses, cannot be materially injured in the draught by the additional weight of springs, and other conveniencies, which are intended either to give ease, or make the carriage more secure to travel with, those are the apparent properties of the patent Curricles, but as they have been so lately constructed, a positive proof of their real or superior advantages over the other sort cannot as yet be ascertained, with sufficient accuracy, so as to justify a full recommendation, further than that the mechanical ingenuity in the construction of them merits a trial from those whose circumstances can afford the increased difference of expence, which, with their being also more complicated, and thereby more subject to be out of order, are, at present, the only likely

likely objections to hinder their general use; but both these objections, by experience and practice, may be removed; yet, as they are not common, nor likely to be so from the great difference of price, they may, on that account, be preferred by a few persons who chuse to appear distinguished.

DESCRIPTION.

THE material difference of this Curricle from others, is in the carriage part only, and that chiefly at the fore end, where there are both shafts and pole for a double security, so that if the pole should break, the shafts may support the carriage. The shafts A. are united to the fore bar B. with strong joints at C. for the purpose of extending outwards. The fore bar and shafts are formed to the shape of the horse, and strengthened in the bend with strong iron plates at top and bottom, and also with broad flat plates at the sides, fixed on the outside of the fore bar, and main side of the carriage, to strengthen the framings; each main side has a piece of about five inches cut out at D. and are supported together by flat spring-plates E. at the top and bottom, fixed with a bolt through each division F. and G. the purpose of which is to lessen or ease the motion of the carriage by the trotting of the horses; the fore springs H. are not fixed to the fore part of

the carriage as ufual, but to the axletree, and has
a long tail, I. extending backward, which is united
with a ftay, K. which clips the eye at the loop, and
is fixed to the bottom of the axletree ; a bottom
ftay, L. the fame as common, fixes the carriage
to the axletree, which is fupported by a raifer, or
block, between each. At the bottom of the body
a double ftay body-loop is fixed, and hangs to a
brace which goes along the back of the fpring, and
is fixed in a jack, P. at the hoop, a fmall fpring
plate, Q. is fixed to the fore bar for the check
braces, which is fixed to the bottom, or body-
loop ftay ; a compafs fpring plate, S. is fixed to
the hind fpring ftay head, with a loop at the top
for the hind check braces to pafs through, which is
fixed to a loop at the ftay head : the hind part is
moftly hung, as common, from whip fprings by
long braces, which are fixed by fpring jacks, having alfo worm, or fpiral, fprings between them.

The draught fometimes is taken from roller-
bolts fixed on the fore bar, the fame as the coach
or chariot fplinter-bars, but are moftly from fhort
fplinters, which are curved to the fhape of the
fore bar, and are each fixed to the axletree by a
long trace, V. which makes the draught more
fteady and eafy, than if taken from the fore bar, as
ufual.

There is alfo another pattern Curricle, made on
a principle fomething fimilar to this, but with fome
                                        pretended

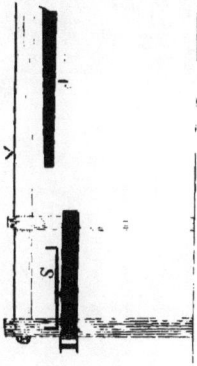

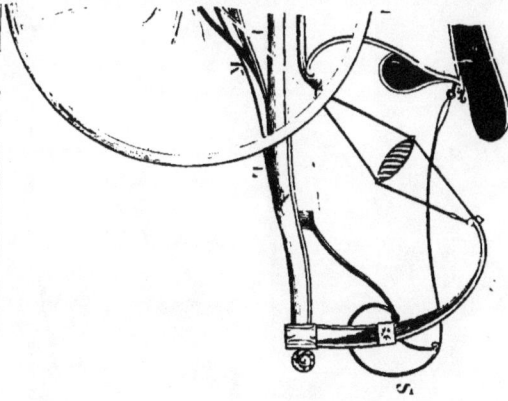

Plate XLII

pretended improvement, the principal object of which is to do away the neceſſity of the pole, the ſliding-bar, and the props, by having two pair of ſhafts, in which the horſes are ſeparately placed, and are ſupported by the harneſs in the ſame manner as one-horſe chaiſes uſually are; thoſe ſhafts act on a ſemi-circle, at the fore part of the carriage, inſtead of rule joints, and at about the middle are jointed with ſpring joints, for the points to be turned down in the manner of a claſp knife, to form a reſt for the carriage inſtead of the prop; and alſo, that if one of the horſes ſhould fall, the points of the ſhaft fall with him without injury, or incommoding the other horſe, further than ſtopping him, in conſequence of the accident.

By what is repreſented of the former new-pattern Curricle, the principle of this may be eaſily explained. The dotted line deſcribes in what manner the ſhafts turn down, and how they become a ſubſtitute for the pole.

The price for either of the two may be reckoned, as an advance for the invention, of from 40 to 50l.

From the complexity and expence of both patterns, it is much to be doubted if either ever becomes general; yet as a few of them are in uſe, it is neceſſary to ſatisfy the public with a deſcription, without injuring the proprietors or public, by detracting

tracting from, or recommending either, in preference to the common fort.

The proprietors of each invention make alterations upon every one they build, fo that thefe
defcriptions cannot be expected to be fo correct in
every particular, yet the principle of both is
nearly defcribed.

CHAP.

CHAP. VII.

ON GIGS.

G IGS are one-horſe chaiſes, of various patterns, deviſed according to the fancy of the occupier; but, more generally, meâns thoſe that hang by braces from the ſprings; the mode of hanging is what principally conſtitutes the name of Gig, which is only a one-horſe chaiſe of the moſt faſhionable make; Curricles being now the moſt faſhionable ſort of two-wheeled carriages, it is uſual, in building a Gig, to imitate them, particularly in the mode of hanging. The Gig moſtly hangs from the middle of the hind pillars, and is built as light and eaſy as poſſible; all one-horſe chaiſes, that are neat and fancifully conſtructed, are named Gigs, and called by the name that the body is diſtinguiſhed by; ſuch as a ſtep-piece, a tub-bottom, or a chair-back Gig, &c.

A CHAIR-BACK GIG.

PLATE XLIII.

INDEPENDENT of fashion, this is the neateft fort of a one-horfe chaife in ufe, and affords much room for luggage, both in the body and on the carriage. To burthen a one-horfe chaife with fuperfluous weight is very improper; but as it is only on neceffary occafions that luggage may be wanted, the conveniencies for carrying them may always remain, without being of much incumbrance, and the carriage has a more genteel appearance thereby. Fixing the body to the fore fprings prevents its being fo eafy to ride in, as if it were hung by braces, or by fprings fixed under the body; but that the difference may be underftood is the reafon of its being thus reprefented, as they are frequently fo built.

DESCRIPTION.

THE *Carriage* with a pair of hind fpringblocks; a fmall platform-budget behind; ftraked wheels; common axletrees and boxes.

The *Body* a chair back, with fham doors, and fword cafe; lined with fecond cloth; trimmed

with

Plate XLIII

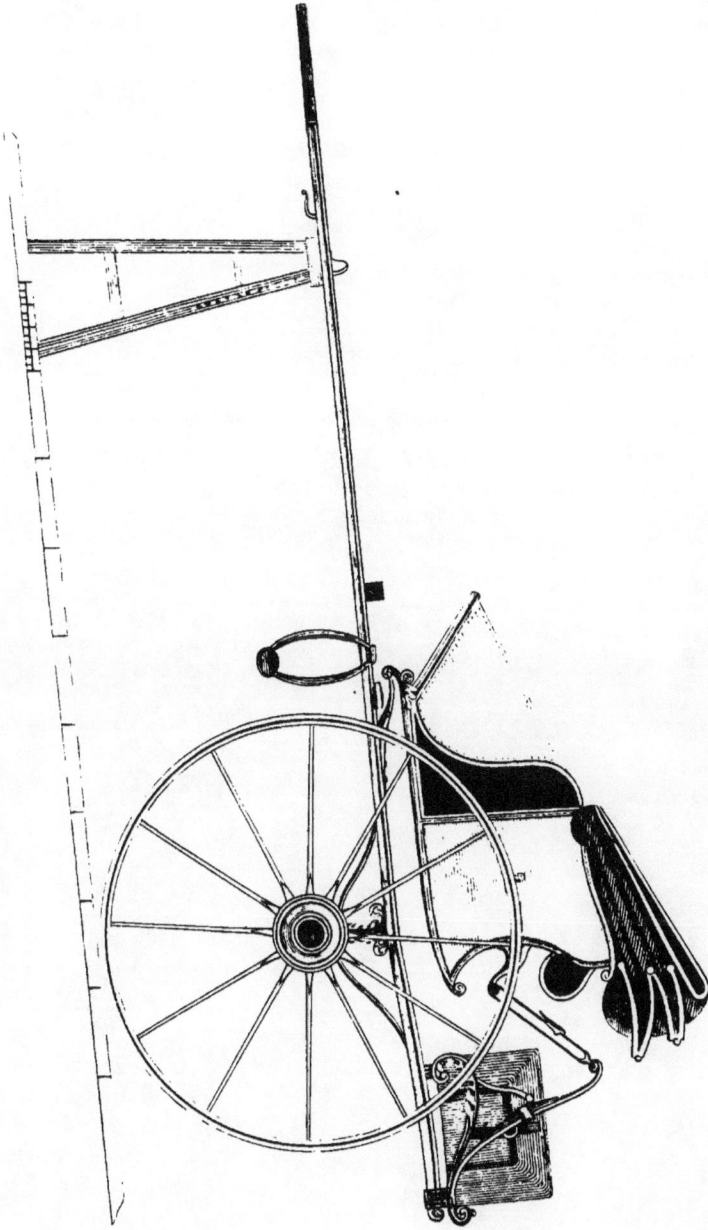

with 2½ inch lace ; a sliding seat-box, and a carpet ; a round fixed head, and a knee-boot of a small size ; a small platform-budget. The *Plating* with *silver*, a 4-8th moulding round the sham doors, the head and knee-boot; a pair of sword-case frames. The *Painting* of the body and carriage picked out one colour; the arms on the back, and the crests on the two side pannels. The *Braces* common.

PRICE.

	£.	s.	d.
First charge for a Gig	31	14	6

EXTRAS.

	£	s	d
A pair of small hind spring-blocks	2	2	0
A small platform-budget, with wood sides	3	0	0
A sword-case back	1	10	0
Sham doors	0	15	0
Trimmings, 2½ inches wide	0	2	6
A round head lined with serge	10	0	0
A small knee-boot	1	18	0
Thirty feet of 4-8th plated moulding	4	2	6
The mouldings of the body and carriage picked out one colour	0	19	6
Japanning the doors and sword-case	0	10	6
The arms and the two crests	0	11	0
£. 57	5	5	

SECT.

SECT. 2.

THE GIG CURRICLE.

PLATE XLIV.

THE two-wheeled carriage, which is intended
to be principally ufed with one horfe, and only as
by chance with two, fhould not be built more
heavy than the common Gig, and the fhafts fo contrived, as when placed together, they may form a
pole, which will fave incumbrance, and be always
ready, on any emergency, for the carriage to be
converted to either purpofe. As the pole requires
to be of a much greater length than the fhafts, it
has been common to have an additional focket-end,
to fix on the fhafts ; but as that is an incumbrance
to travel with, it is beft to have the fhafts of a length
fufficient to anfwer the purpofe of a pole, which is
done by having three fockets on the carriage,
A. B. C. inftead of two, for the fhafts to be fixed
in to a greater length, and the two middle fockets
for the pole fhould be made to receive the fhafts at
thofe parts which fit to the two hind fockets, B. and
C. ; and the pole-ring to fix on the points of the
fhafts, when united as a pole, which makes all
fnug, and eafy to change about for either purpofe.

Thefe Curricles are very convenient where the .
roads

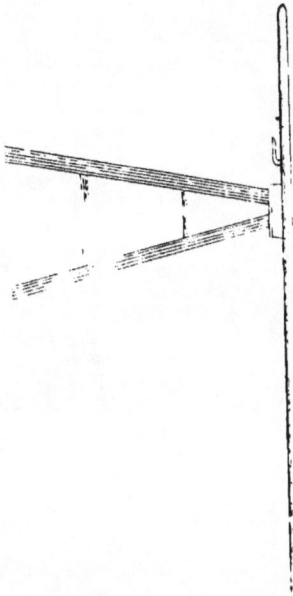

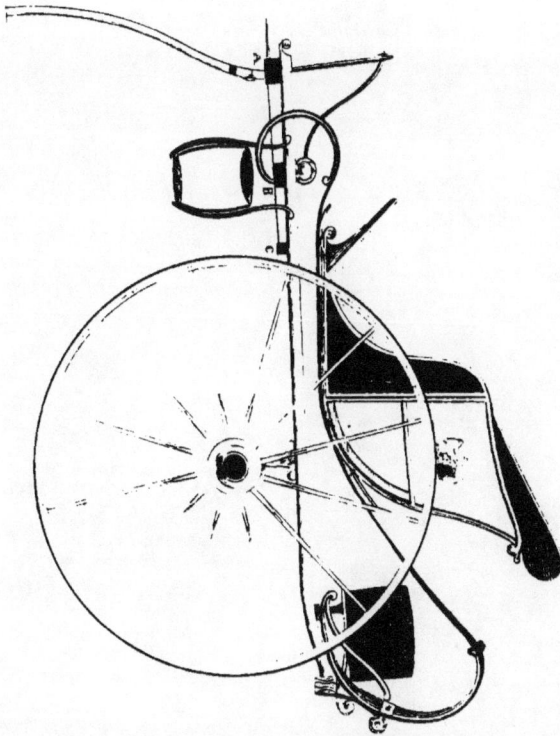

roads will not admit horfes abreaft, as all the appa-
ratus may be eafily reverfed, for the horfes to draw
in team.

DESCRIPTION.

The *Carriage* a gig curricle, with a fmall trunk-
boot behind, raifed on fmall plain blocks; a light
dafhing-leather in front, with a pocket; C-formed
plain fprings behind, French-horn fprings before,
with jacks to both; and a long fingle main brace,
which goes round each fpring, along the bottom of
the body, and fixed only to the jacks, by which the
body is raifed or lowered, and removed either
backward or forward at pleafure, which makes the
riding very eafy; double fteps; common axletrees
and boxes.

The *Body* a long-tail, tub-bottom, half-panneled Gig, lined with leather, and plain trimmings;
a drop feat-box; a Wilton carpet; fmall wings;
and knee-boot. The *Plating* with *brafs*, a 3-8th
moulding all round the framing, and for the knee-
boot; a pair of wing-frames; four check-rings:
and a pair of nave wheel-hoops plated. The
Painting ornamented with $1\frac{1}{2}$ inch plain border;
a fmall mantle on the three pannels, with the crefts
in each; the painting picked out one colour. The
Braces twelve feet additional length.

PRICE.

PRICE.

		£.	s.	d.
Firſt charge for a Gig Curricle	—	36	3	0

EXTRAS.

		£.	s.	d.
A ſmall trunk-boot	—	2	10	0
A pair of ſmall plain blocks	—	1	0	0
A light daſhing-leather, with a pocket	—	2	0	0
Two pair of ſmall ſpring jacks	—	1	10	0
A pair of double chaiſe-ſteps	—	0	14	0
Leather lining	—	2	0	0
A ſmall knee-boot	—	0	18	0
A pair of ſmall wings	—	1	10	0
Forty-four feet of 3-8th moulding	—	0	18	0
Four check rings	—	0	8	0
A pair of nave wheel-hoops	—	0	12	6
Twenty feet of 1½ inch plain border	—	1	10	0
Three ſmall mantles, with creſts in each	—	1	4	0
Twelve feet of two-inch main-braces extra	—	1	4	0

£. 54   1   6

CHAP.

CHAP. VIII.

WHISKIES OR CHAIRS.

WHISKIES are one-horſe chaiſes of the lighteſt conſtruction, with which the horſes may
travel with eaſe and expedition, and quickly paſs
other carriages on the road, for which they are called
Whiſkies. The principles on which they are built
are the moſt ſimple and light; any thing which adds
to the weight or complexity ſhould, in this carriage, be particularly avoided; to give eaſe in riding, and lightneſs in draught, are the main objects
which ought to be attended to; they, being principally intended for lightneſs, need not be furniſhed
with that extraordinary number of ſprings which are
uſed for other carriages, and from which the bodies
are ſuſpended; the ſprings of this carriage are fixed
on the axletree, and on the ſprings the carriage is
placed, and with the carriage the body is united,
ſo that all the dependence for eaſe is on the ſprings
from the axletree, which, if properly manufactured,
and of ſufficient length, gives as much eaſe to the
rider as thoſe which are differently formed, and,
in ſome inſtances, more, as they are not ſubject to

I ſuch

fuch frequent vibrations as are in others fo frequently experienced. They are now the moſt prevailing faſhion of two-wheeled carriages, and are lighter and cheaper than any other.

———

SECT. I.

A CANE WHISKEY,

PLATE XLV.

CANE Whiſkies are the lighteſt and cheapeſt of all others, and have, for ſummer uſe, a light, airy appearance; they are not ſo ſtrong as pannel bodies, but are leſs in the expence for painting and lining, and are principally intended for country uſe in fair weather; ſo that heads and knee-boots, which add to the weight and expence, are judiciouſly avoided; but if found neceſſary to have them, the whiſkey ſhould be built ſtronger than otherwiſe.

DESCRIPTION.

THE *Carriage* plain; common axletrees and boxes; ſtraked wheels. The *Body* cane, with a drop ſeat-box; lined with ſecond cloth; the top rails only trimmed; a pair of ſmall wings. The
Painting

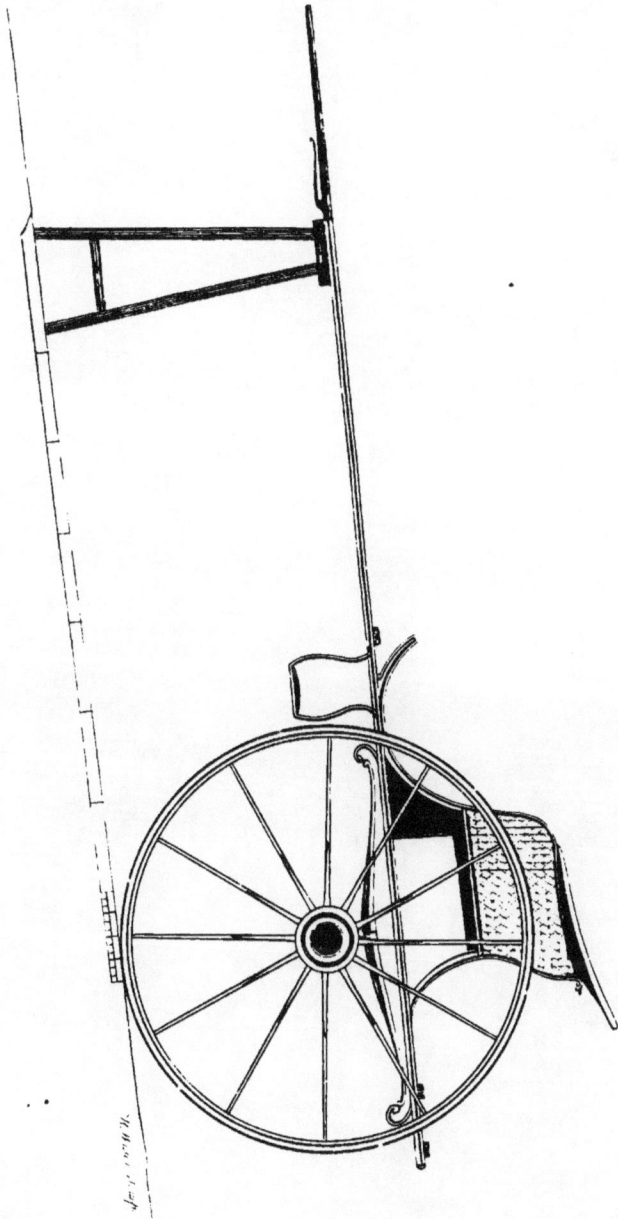

Painting of the body and carriage picked out one colour.

PRICE.

	£.	s.	d.
Firſt charge for a cane whiſkey — —	22	12	6

EXTRAS.

	£.	s.	d.
A drop feat-box — — —	0	7	6
A pair of ſmall wings — —	1	10	0
	£. 24	10	0

SECT. 2.

A HALF-PANNEL WHISKEY.

PLATE XLVI.

THIS carriage is built exactly like the laſt, ex-cepting with pannels inſtead of cane-work, and is lined throughout with cloth; the pannels are a great addition to the ſtrength, and it is therefore better to beſtow on it the expence of a head, a knee-boot, or whatever other conveniencies may be found neceſſary, than on the other chaiſe; it being a light, ſmall carriage, to load it with much lug-gage would not only ſpoil the appearance, but in-jure the carriage for uſe; yet it may be urged that, as they are of ſo light a draught, more convenien-

I 2   cies

cies than in other chaifes may be carried with it, without being more heavy in draught, but they fhould be judicioufly placed, according to the ftrength, and on fuch parts of the carriage as are beft fuited to bear them.

DESCRIPTION.

THE *Carriage* a Whifkey, with a fmall platform budget, made with wooden fides; a light dafhing-leather in front; double fteps; hooped wheels; common axletrees and boxes.

The *Body* with a drop feat-box, fham doors, and a fword-cafe; a fquare head lined with ferge; a fmall knee-boot; the lining with fecond cloth, trimmed with $2\frac{1}{2}$ inch lace; quilted fides; and a Wilton carpet.

The *Plating* with *filver*, a 3-8th moulding round the fham doors and pannels, round the head, and for the knee-boot; a pair of fword-cafe frames. The *Painting* of the body and carriage picked out one colour; the fham doors and fword-cafe japanned; a cypher and fmall creft on the two fide pannels.

PRICE.

	£.	s.	d.
Firft charge for a half-pannel whifkey —	24	9	0

EXTRAS.

	£.	s.	d.
A fmall platform budget with wooden fides	3	0	0
A light dafhing-leather in front — —	1	15	0
Carry over —	29	4	0

Double

		£.	s.	d.
Brought over	——	29	4	0
Double steps —— ——	——	0	14	0
Hooped tyre wheels ——	——	0	10	0
A drop seat-box — ——	——	0	7	6
Sham doors —— —	——	0	15	0
A sword-case back ——	——	1	10	0
A square head lined with serge	——	8	10	0
A small knee-boot ——	——	1	18	0
The trimming 2½ inches wide	——	0	2	6
The lining quilted ——	——	0	10	6
Forty feet of 3-8th moulding — —		3	10	0
The painting of the carriage and body picked out one colour —— ——		0	17	6
Two small crests and cyphers ——		0	10	0
		£. 48	19	0

SECT. 3.

THE GRASSHOPPER, OR THREE-QUARTER PANNEL CHAISE, OR WHISKEY.

PLATE XLVII.

THIS is a very ancient pattern of a chaise, but an exceeding good one, as all the framings form an agreeably-connected line; it is exactly on the same principle as the whiskey, which was built from them, having the springs, in the same way, fixed to the axletree, and the body united with the carriage,

I 3   but

but only different in its shape; the framings of the body, being much wider, shews more pannel, which extends to the shafts at the corners, and are arched up, in an agreeable form, between the bearings: they have a more solid appearance than the whiskey, and are, on that account, preferred by some persons, and, in particular, by those called Quakers, and for that reason are by some called Quakers' Chaises, and, by others, Serpentine, or sweeped-bottom Chaises; as they are built on so near a principle with the last-described carriage, there is nothing more to recommend them than the design, and the superior strength on account of the pannels filling most of the framings.

DESCRIPTION.

THE *Carriage* a whiskey pattern, with double steps; straked wheels; common axletrees and boxes.

The *Body* a three-quartered pannel, lined with second cloth, and trimmed with a two-inch lace; a Wilton carpet; an inside seat-box; and a pair of small wings. The *Plating* of *silver*, a pair of wing-frames, and wheel-hoops. The *Painting* of the body and carriage picked out one colour; three middle-sized crests on the pannels.

PRICE.

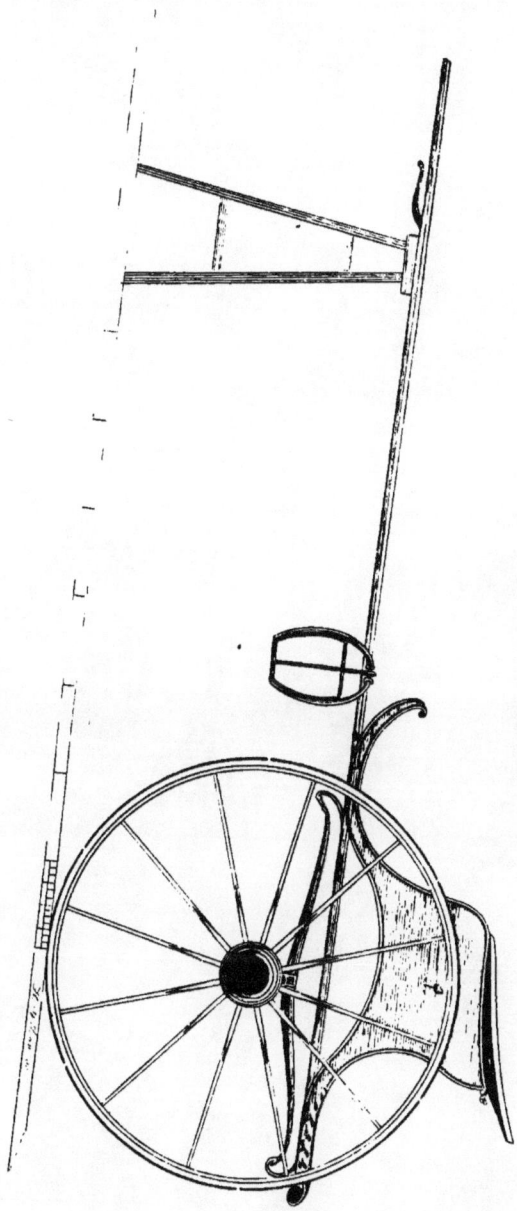

Plate XLVII.

PRICE.

		£.	s.	d.
Firſt charge for a half-pannel whiſkey	—	24	9	0

EXTRAS.

				£.	s.	d.
Double ſteps — — —				0	14	0
The body extra above the whiſkey —				2	2	0
A pair of ſmall wings with plated frames —				2	15	0
A pair of wheel-hoops, plated with caſed metal				1	5	0
The painting of the body and carriage picked out one colour — — —				0	17	6
Three middle-ſized creſts — —				0	10	6

£. 32 13 0

SECT. 4.

THE WHISKEY CURRICLE.

THE Whiſkey Curricle is made exactly in the ſame way as the Gig Curricle, and a further repreſentation would be uſeleſs; it is in the carriage part only where the alteration lies; the Whiſkey Curricle is only intended to be uſed with a pair of ſmall, light horſes, or one occaſionally. It is principally intended for expeditious travelling. The price to be charged in addition to thoſe already ſtated, for either cane or pannel whiskey is 4l.

I 4

SECT.

SECT. 5.

A TANDUM.

MANY people imagine a Tandum to be a one-horse chaise of a peculiar form, whereas it is only two horses in a team, or one before the other, to draw a two-wheeled chaise; where the roads are very bad and heavy, it is neceſſary to add one horse in this way to relieve the other and promote ſpeed; but, like many things which have been introduced by accident, it is now become a faſhion from its novelty; it can, however, only be uſed by thoſe who are expert in driving, unleſs the fore horse is rode by a poſtillion; as there is a convenience in having the chaiſe ſo contrived, it is to be recommended to all, being only a loop fixed to the point of each ſhaft, for the leading horse to be fixed to; and, if never wanted for that purpose, is neceſſary to preſerve the points of the ſhafts from wearing by rubbing on the ground, as may be frequently obſerved.

The expence to be charged in addition for a chaiſe with loops, for tandum uſe, is 5s.

SECT.

SECT. 6.

A BUGGY.

A BUGGY is a cant name given to phaetons or chaifes which can only contain one perfon on the feat ; they are principally intended for lightnefs in draught, for the rider to fit fnug in, and to preclude the poffibility of an affociate ; moftly ufed by out-riders.

They are built like other phaetons or chaifes, and to afcertain their value, is to fubtract onetwelfth from the ftatement of a common-fized car·· riage, finifhed to any pattern.

SECT. 7.

THE RIB CHAIR, OR YARMOUTH CART.

PLATE XLVIII.

FOR lawns or parks thefe fort of chaifes have been moftly ufed, and, for that reafon, do not require to have fprings, or to be lined, as they are frequently left out, expofed to the weather; they are fometimes made to go on four wheels, and are made very low and light, with the rim of the
wheels

wheels broad, and rimmed with a thin plate of
sheet iron, so as to prevent them making a track
on the ground which they roll over; they are of a
variety of shapes, but the most general is the one
described, which now seems to be a prevalent fashion among the gentry as a substitute for the
whiskey, and, for that use, are obliged to be built
stronger than what would be sufficient for a Garden
Chair; whatever may be the motive for using this
carriage in preference to the whiskey, certain it is,
that if a carriage in the shape of a wheelbarrow
was, by accident, introduced, it would become a
fashion, independent of either appearance or ease,
neither of which these new-fashioned garden-chairs
possess, when used on the roads, unless built upon
springs, and lined as other carriages are; but, as
they are likely to become general, one of the common sort will be described.

DESCRIPTION.

THE *Carriage* is built in the form of a whiskey,
but without springs, and is raised from the axletree by short blocks, or raisers, and strengthened
by short iron stays; the wheels are straked tyre,
with ten spokes; common axletrees and boxes.
The *Body* is made on a solid board, which is the
seat, round the back and sides of which the ribs
are fixed, and also in the top rail, which is of a se-
micircular form. This seat is fixed on with two
light

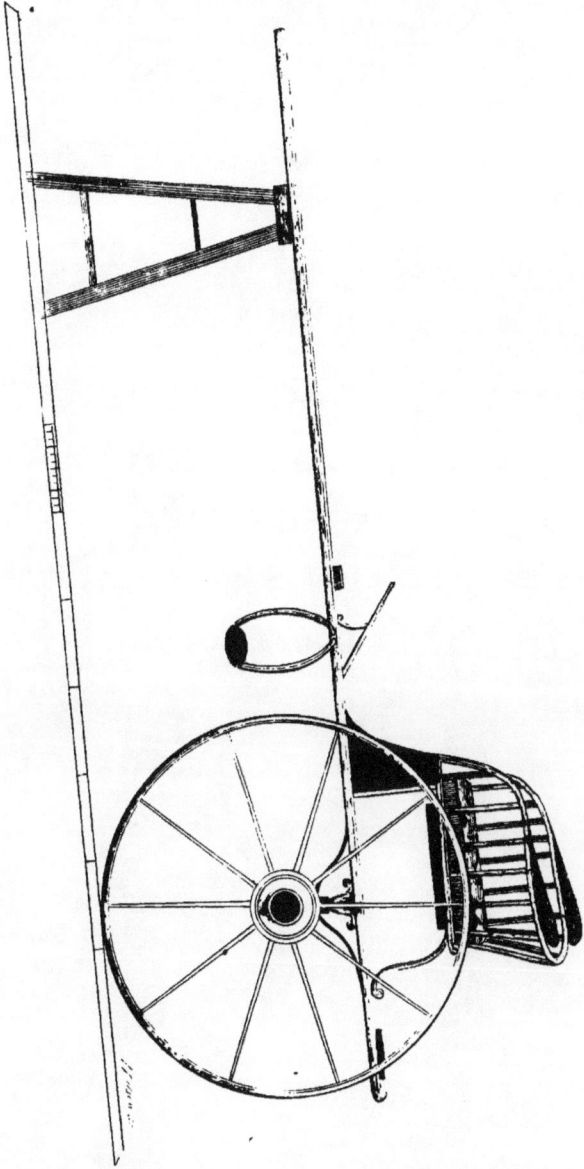

light iron props behind, and two broad wooden props before, made in the fhape of the bottom part of a fham door; a cloth cufhion for the feat, and a heel-leather to fhelter the legs behind.

PRICE.

	£.	s.	d.
The carriage a whifkey, dedufting the price of the grafshopper fprings ——— ——	6	10	0
A pair of ftraked wheels, tens — —	2	15	0
The body, including the cufhion and heel leather	4	10	0
The painting the fame as a cane chair ——	1	19	0
	£. 15	14	0

They are fometimes made on an inferior plan, fo as not to exceed the price of 10 or 12l. by having the words 'A Taxed Cart' painted on the back will fave the duty; fome are made equal to the value of a high-finifhed chair, with fprings, &c. But, as a caution to the public, for perfonal fafety, it is neceffary to obferve, that many of thefe chairs are made by country wheelwrights and carpenters, of very bad materials and workmanfhip, in order to fell them at a low price in London, and thereby injure the fair trader, who, for a reafonable profit, will not produce a bad article.

CHAP.

CHAP. IX.

THE COVERINGS.

AFTER a carriage has been finished, it appears like an imposition to add any thing further as extra charges ; yet there are some things which, though no way essential to the carriage, are materially so to the horses, the coachman, and passengers : therefore, as they are matters of convenience, though not of necessity, they ought to be charged for ; yet many scruple to pay for them, supposing them to be impositions ; and, though but trifling, separately, yet, when added together, amount to a sum which becomes an object. It is all leather-work, and principally for covering the splinter-bar rolls, the treads of chaise-steps, and the points of the shafts, or the vacant space behind the coachman's legs, called heel-leathers.

SECT. I.

SPLINTER-BAR ROLLS COVERING.

THE ufe of covering fplinter-bar rolls is to make them fafer for the coachman to ftep on, to prevent the horfe being hurt by rubbing againft them, and alfo to prevent any rattling by the trace-rings; they are fometimes covered on the cap or top only, or on the cap and roll, or cap, roll, and bottom on the fplinter-bar, according to the feveral conceits of the builder or coachman. The top or cap only is what is principally covered.

———

SECT. 2.

POLE COVERING AND STUFFING.

THE covering and ftuffing the pole is for the purpofe of preferving the horfe from injury by his rubbing againft the fides of the pole. They are frequently covered at two places, the hip and fhoulder parts, but moftly at the fhoulder only; the covering is a ftout, but foft, piece of leather, nailed on the top and bottom, and ftuffed, or padded, on each fide; it is, in general, about twenty-

twenty-feven inches long; and is of great fervice to the horfe, by preventing him from being galled.

SECT. 3.

TREADS OF CHAISE-STEPS COVERING:

THE covering the treads of chaife-fteps is to prevent the accident of flipping off, and thereby hurting the leg of the perfon while getting in or out of the carriage; and for the purpofe of looking neater than the plain iron tread would do. Sometimes they are covered round the back part of the ftep, and forms a cafe to prevent the leg from flipping through, which would probably be of dangerous confequence.

SECT. 4.

POINTS OF THE SHAFTS COVERING.

THE covering the point of the fhafts is to prevent them rubbing the fhoulders of the horfe; they are only covered, but without any ftuffing, and preferves them from any injury by frequent handling

ing and rubbing, when placing them in the tugs of
the harnefs.

———

SECT. 5.

HEEL LEATHERS.

HEEL Leathers are for the purpofe of fhelter-
ing the legs of the coachman from cold; they alfo
prevent the coachman from flipping through between the footboard and feat, without which he
moft likely would do.   They are broad pieces of
leather, which cover all the vacant fpace between
the footboards and the framed crofs-bars, to each
of which they are nailed. Thofe for Salifbury boots
have flaps, or checks, at the fides.

———

PRICE of COVERINGS and HEEL LEATHERS.

THOSE coverings and heel leathers, in particular for Salifbury boots, are included by fome in the
price of coach-box, or carriage; but as by many
they are made extra charges of, and are not included in the former ftatements, it will be neceffary to
ftate their value here, in particular, as they are not
always ufed.

SPLINTER.

SPLINTER-BAR ROLLS.

	£.	s.	d.
Covering the four caps	0	6	0
Covering the four rolls	0	4	0
Covering the top of the fplinter-bar on each end, and the middle where the fplinter-bar rollers are fixed	0	4	0

POLE COVERING.

	£.	s.	d.
Covering and ftuffing the fhoulder part	0	9	0
Ditto at the fhoulder and hips	0	18	0

CHAISE STEP.

	£.	s.	d.
Covering the treads of a pair of chaife fingle fteps	0	4	0
Covering the four treads of a pair of chaife double fteps	0	8	0
Covering round the back part of the fteps to prevent the feet from flipping through	0	8	0

SHAFTS POINTS COVERING.

	£.	s.	d.
Covering the points of a pair of chaife fhafts	0	4	0

HEEL LEATHERS.

	£.	s.	d.
A heel-leather for a common coach-box	0	10	6
A heel leather and cheeks for a Salifbury coach-box	0	15	0

CHAP.

CHAP. X.

ON HARNESS.

THE manufacturing of harnefs by coach-makers is equally as inconfiftent, as the building of coaches by harnefs-makers; and, though joined together, as mentioned in the Introduction, under the general title of coach-makers, yet, as there noticed, are very different profeffions; but one material circumftance, in favour of having the harnefs made at the coach-maker's is, that the furniture both to carriage and harnefs may be fuitable to each other, and now that they have become experienced, through practice, it is beft always to have the harnefs manufactured by them for the fake of propriety, in matching both together, and readinefs in the execution.

The principal properties of a harnefs are fimplicity and fufficiency, of which there is but little variation, except in the increafe of fize, th r-naments, or drefs; harnefs made for com.ɷn work fhould not be incumbered with any fu,er-fluities, as the lefs a horfe is burdened with trap-

K   pings,

pings, with the more eafe and freedom he per-
forms his work. The appearance of that noble
animal, fo handfome by nature, is not much, if
at all, improved by drefs, though it certainly is
a great ornament to the equipage, to have the
harnefs difplay a grandeur equal with it; and one
advantage is, that the extra ornaments, ftrappings, breechings, &c. may, at any time, be
taken off, or put on at pleafure, without any injury to the remaining neceffary parts, fo that fimplicity or grandeur may, at any time, be preferred, as the proprietors choofe.   Harnefs, within
thefe few years, has much increafed in the breadth
of the leather of which it is made, almoft double
to their former fize, and the great advance on the
price of that article, is the principal reafon for
the increafed price on harnefs, independent of
the expence of the ornaments, which now are
moftly plated with filver, when formerly they
were only brafs; fo that the increafed price, and
fize of leathers, and the odds of filver-plated furniture, makes almoft double the price, in general, on harnefs.

The prefent fafhion of harnefs is to beftow an
extravagant fuperfluity on the head of the horfe,
contracting and gagging it, to a feverity, with
fharp bits, bridoons, and chains, which, in time,
harden the mouth to almoft an infenfibility of
feeling;

feeling; befides ornamenting with car-bows, rings, rofes, &c. fo that, with the furniture, the head of the horfe imitates much the head-drefs of a French lady, while the pofteriors are left fans-culotted; breechings are of no ufe to them but in hilly places, falfe belly-bands being an exceed-ing good fubflitute, and are now moflly ufed in-flead thereof.

———

SECT. 1.

OF THE LEATHER, AND PROPORTIONS OF HARNESS IN GENERAL.

THE leather of harnefs is of one fort, but of different fizes, the traces of a thick and double, and the reins of a thin fize, the ftrapping and col-lars between both. Very good leather fhould be felected, in particular, for the reins, which to rifk would be madnefs. The belly part of a hide fhould not be ufed but for lining between two ftraps to give them a proper thicknefs, as it is of a foft, fpongy quality, and of fo little ftrength as not to be depended on.

Coach, chariot, or phaeton harnefs, are all made alike, and, if for the fame fize of horfes,

are

are cut the fame in breadth, the difference of
ftrength may be given in the fubftance, according
to the weight of draught; but as the fizes of
coach and chariot horfes, and the draughts are
generally different, the leather fhould alfo be
proportioned, both in width and thicknefs. For
a coach, with the horfes fixteen hands high, the
traces are $2\frac{1}{2}$ inches wide, the collars fix, the
breechings five, the ftrappings $1\frac{1}{2}$, the reins one
inch. For a chariot, the horfes fifteen hands
high, the traces $2\frac{1}{4}$, the collars five, the breechings $4\frac{1}{2}$, the ftrappings $1\frac{1}{2}$, the reins 7-8ths.
Large phaeton harnefs the fame as the chariot;
but fmall, or poney, phaetons, the horfes $13\frac{1}{2}$
hands high, the traces two inches wide, the col-
lars four, the breechings $3\frac{1}{2}$, the ftrappings $1\frac{1}{4}$,
and the reins 7-8ths; therefore, to prevent un-
neceffary repetitions of the variety, they will be
defcribed under three heads, viz. large, middle,
and fmall, each of the above proportion. Curricle and chaife harnefs is of the fame breadth as
the common-fized phaeton, though lighter in
proportion to the draught required.

———

THE HARNESS DESCRIBED.

A. the houfing or pad, a fmall faddle cut in
different fhapes, but moftly of a long fquare; it

is

is made of two thicknesses of leather, for the top, sewed together, with a thin plate of sheet iron between, which, when bent, keeps it to its form; at the bottom is a soft pad, or cushion, to lie easy on the horse's back, in the top of which the sockets are fixed, in which the territs are screwed, and by which the cushion is fixed to the top. The watering-hook is fixed in the centre at the front, and fastened between the top and the pad, the top is mostly ornamented with rims or plates; on each side, and at the middle behind, a short strap is fixed between the top and the pad, and is fastened by the hook and territ-screws; in each strap a bridge is sewed, to which is fastened the Newmarket and crupper straps.

B. the crupper, a long strap with a loop or dock at the back end, which fixes under the horse's tail, the fore end is looped through the housing bridge, and buckled about the middle; under the buckling part a broad piece of leather is sewed to prevent galling. The crupper-dock is mostly stuffed, or filled, with a tallow candle, to make it easy for the horse's tail. On the crupper-strap is fixed the different strappings which hold up the breeching or traces.

C. the breast-collar, a broad strap against which the horse opposes his breast for the pur-
K 3   pose

pofe of draught, all round the middle of which is
fewed an additional ftrap to ftrengthen the other,
near the middle whereof is fewed the dee, for the
pole-piece to be looped through; and at each end
of the collar a ftrong buckle is fixed for the
traces and breeching to be faftened by; two
fquare.pipes are fewed on near the buckles, and
receive the point of both.

D. the Breeching, a broad ftrap of leather
which goes round the horfes breech; on each
end are two ftrong, long ftraps, fewed about two-
thirds of the diftance round the breeching-ftrap,
and extend to the collar buckles, to which they
are faftened; its ufe is for the horfe to fet his
ftrength againft, and back the carriage by.

E. the Traces, the two ftrong leathers, of double or treble thicknefs, by which the carriage is
drawn; a fquare, bent ring is fewed in the end,
which, with the trace, forms a loop to hitch round
the fplinter-bar rolls: it is buckled to the collar
along with the breeching-ftrap.

F. the Back-Strap, a ftrap which croffes the
horfe's back, is looped to the crupper-ftrap; and
buckles to the tugs to hold up the traces.

G. the

G. the Hip-Strap, a ſtrap with a piece cut out of the middle, by which means it is ſewed together, to lie obliquely on the horſe's hips; it is fixed to the crupper, and buckles to the tugs of the breeching to hold it up.

H. the tugs are ſhort ſtraps, with buckles and loops ſewed upon a broader piece of leather to prevent galling the horſe, and are ſewed to bridges in the breeching or collar, and buckled to the back, hip, or neck-ſtrap. The trace-tugs are loops for the trace to run through and hang by, with a buckle at the top to receive the back-ſtrap.

I. the Newmarket ſtrap; a ſtrap with a buckle and loop, by which the collar is hung to the houſing, at a proper diſtance; it is placed round the collar-buckle and houſing-bridge.

K. the Belly-band, ſuppoſed to be one, but is two ſtraps of leather, by which the harneſs is faſtened on the horſe; each ſtrap is fixed in the houſing between the top and the pad by the ſcrews and terrets; the long ſide is broad, with a roller buckle and loops ſewed under a narrow ley; the ſhort ſide is broad at the top, but is reduced to a narrow ſtrap at the bottom, to ſuit the buckle, this is girded tight round the horſe's bel-

ly,

ly, and makes faſt the houſing, to which moſt of the harneſs is hung.

When breechings are not uſed, back-ſtraps are not neceſſary, except for the traces; when a harneſs is much ornamented, there are ſeveral back-ſtraps, but one is as much as is neceſſary, and even that is by ſome omitted.

This is the body part of the harneſs neceſſary for the purpoſe of drawing by; the other is the head part, or bridle, by which alone the horſe is managed.

L. the Winker, a broad leather on each ſide the bridle, which prevents the horſe from ſeeing any way but before him. They are almoſt of an equal ſize for length and breadth; made of two pieces of leather ſewed together, with tin or thin iron plates between them to preſerve their ſhapes; the outſides are moſtly ornamented with plates, pieces, or frames, the ſame as the houſing, and are cut in a form to match them. On each ſide of the winkers is ſewed a ſtrap, with a buckle at the top, a ſtrap and a buckle, with a billet, at the bottom, to hold the bit; this ſtrap is called the check of the bridle: at the top of the outer part of each winker is ſewed a ſtrap, which buckles to the head-ſtall, and is called a winker-ſtrap.

M. the

M. the Head-Stall, or Crown-Piece, is a broad
ftrap which lies on the top of the head, in which
the head-ring is fcrewed : about one-third of the
length at each end of this ftrap is cut up in the
middle, to make two ftraps at each end, one to
hold the winker, the other the throat-band, in the
middle of this ftrap is fewed a buckle which receives the winker-ftrap.

N. the Front, or Forehead-Piece, a broad
ftrap to go round the forehead, fewed in four
loops, two at each end, which receives the four
ftraps of the crown-piece; this ftrap is moftly
covered with taping.

O. the Reins, are the long ftraps with which
the horfe is guided, and are the moft material
parts of the harnefs to be regarded for quality,
which fhould be of the very beft leather, made
from 7-8ths to one inch wide. They are called
the long hand-reins, the coupling, and the bearing-reins. The long hand-reins are what the
horfes are guided by; they are made with a
buckle and billet at each end, by which they are
faftened to the outfide of each horfe's bit. At
about the middle, on the infide, two buckles are
fixed to receive the coupling reins, which are
what both horfes are checked by, fo as to turn
one way, being faftened from the rein of one
horfe to the bitt of the other; they are buckled

to

to the infide of the long rein, and croffing each
other, are buckled to the infide of each bit ; the
bearing-rein is what prevents the horfe from
holding his head down ; it is a fhort rein, with
buckles and billets to be faftened to the bit with,
and is hitched with a hook on the houfing, it being neceffary to have it lengthened or fhortened
at times ; it is made with a fhort fide-piece
which has a buckle to receive the end of the long
fide, and is thereby taken in, or let out, at pleafure.

P. the Throat-Band, a narrow, fhort ftrap,
with a buckle at each end : its ufe is to keep the
bridle faft ; it is placed under the throat of the
horfe, and is buckled to the ftraps of the crown-
piece.

What is thus defcribed is a fufficient quantity
of harnefs to be ufed with any four-wheeled carriage, but there are few made without fome fuperfluities, which are alfo neceffary to be defcribed, and likewife what are neceffary for two-
wheeled carriages.

Q. the falfe Belly-Band, a broad ftrap, with a
buckle and billet at each end, which is placed
under the horfe's belly, and buckles to the rim
of the collar-buckle, on each fide, to tighten and
keep

keep the collar down, fo that a breeching need
not be ufed, except in very hilly places, and
there are fome drivers who will not ufe the
breeching, but it is not fo fafe; the crupper-
ftrap, when a breeching is not ufed, ought to be
very ftrong, as a great ftrefs lies on it and the
Newmarket ftraps.

R. a Heam, a Round or Neck Collar, is a
thick, padded collar made to fit, and fit eafy
round the horfe's neck and fhoulders; it has two
wales, or rifings, on the outfide, called the fore
and back wales; the fore wale is made very hard
with ftraw, which preferves the form of the collar,
and the under one ftuffed foft with ftraw; between the wales the heams for drawing by are
fixed; they are made of different forts of leather,
but the beft are of Neat's leather only; thofe are
the beft collars for the horfe to draw by, as they
come more round the fhoulders, by which his
purchafe is greater and more eafy.

S. the Heam-Tugs, are two broad, fhort ftraps,
made exactly the fame as the ends of a breaft-
collar, with buckles and pipes for the traces, and
are riveted to the heam-loops.

T. a Falfe Collar, is a broader ftripe of leather
than the real collar, and placed under it, to prevent

vent the other from galling the breaft or fhoulders of the horfe, by its rubbing, which it does every ftep he takes.

V. the Shaft-Tugs, are two ftrong, leather loops, about two inches wide, with a buckle at the top of each.   Their ufe is to carry the fhafts of a one-horfe chaife, which are placed in them, and they are hung on each fide of the faddle to a ftrong ftrap called a back-band.

U. the Back-Band, is a long ftrip of leather, about 6½ feet long, with a buckle at one end, and the ftrap at the other; it is placed acrofs the faddle to flide in a trough under the feat; the tugs are buckled on it at each fide of the faddle, and fupports all the weight which is on the fhafts; for which about one-third of it is ftrengthened with an additional ftrap fewed to it, the other buckles round the fhafts, and under the horfe's belly, to keep the fhafts down and fteady.

W. the Martingale, a ftrap flit up the middle above the collar, which makes two ftraps at the top, with a buckle and billet fewed at the end of each; the broad end is looped through a buckle, by which it is fixed round the belly-band, and paffes through a loop, which is fewed on the collar, and buckles at the top in each fide of the bit;

bit; its ufe is to prevent the horfe from throwing his head back, but is fometimes ufed for ornament only.

X. the Bridoon-Head, or Rein, is an additional bridle with a bearing-rein; its ufe is to
make the horfe carry his head better; it is hung
to the head of the bridle in various methods, but
moftly with ornamented links, or chains. The
head of it is a narrow ftrap, which lies round the
top and fide of the head, with a front-piece fewed round the fide, to flide up or down; this fide-
piece and the crown-piece are fometimes fewed
to the bridoon bit-ring, or buckled on with billets, but fince chains and fwivels have been fo
much in ufe, the head-piece and bearing-reins
are all in one, and the bridoon is only held to
the rein by fmall ftraps and buckles, on which
fwivels or links are placed for the rein to run
through, and which is made round for the purpofe; a fwivel or link is hung by a fmall ftrap to
the crown-piece, for the bearing-rein alfo to run
through; the rein being fo contracted, keeps the
horfe's head in a proper pofition, and gives it a
little more freedom than if made without the
links; when the reins are fixed to the bridoon,
the bearing-rein is moftly hung on a dee to the
throat-band.

Y. the

Y. the Nofe-band, a ftrap made broad in the middle, and narrow at the extremities, placed round the lower part of the jaw, and is fixed through a loop at the check of the bridle, and buckles underneath ; it is of little ufe but to ornament the head, by having a plated piece fixed on the nofe part. It is fometimes only fixed on the front to the check of the bridle.

Z. the Forehead-Piece, a piece of leather, of different fhapes, made to carry an ornament, and is buckled to the head-ftall, or crown-piece, and hangs loofely on the horfe's forehead.

———

SECT. 2.

THE FURNITURE FOR HARNESS

PLATE XLIX.

THE furniture for harnefs confifts chiefly of the neceffary buckles for the ftrapping ; the territs and hooks for the reins; the rings and dees for the collars and traces ; the bits for the bridle ; and heams for the collar ; the other furniture is only for ornament, and confifts chiefly of pieces

or

or plates for the houfing or winkers, and ſtuds
for the ſtrapping.

The buckles for the ſtrapping and reins are always made of brafs, and are fometimes finiſhed of
that metal only, but are moſtly plated with filver.
Thofe buckles which exceed 1½ inch in fizeſhould
be made of iron, and, to match the other furniture, muſt be plated either with brafs or filver ;
for, whatever part of the leather requires to be
above 1½ inch wide, a brafs buckle is not of fufficient ſtrength for it. If the furniture is plated,
the territs ſhould be of iron ; but, if the furniture is brafs, the folid brafs, not being of value
equal to the trouble of plating, is moſtly ufed ;
but it is not fo good as if made of iron and
plated.

The bits, rings, dees, hcams, &c. which are
always made of iron, are, if required to match
the other furniture, obliged to be plated with the
fame fort of metal, but, in general, they are only poliſhed, and require much care from the
coachman to preferve them bright.

The ornaments, if the furniture is of brafs,
are folid, but if otherwife are plated with filver, except thofe ornaments which are raifed or
emboffed, fuch as crefts and cyphers, they are
then

then moftly made of thin filver, and filled on the
infide with lead.

THE FURNITURE DESCRIBED.

a. The Territs are what fcrews in the faddle,
or houfing, for the reins to run through, and they
are made to anfwer the form of the buckle, whether round, fquare, or octagon ; the number for
a faddle, or houfing, are two, but a centre one is
often added for ornament : a fhort territ is often
fixed at the top of a bridle, called a head-territ,
for the leading-reins to go through, or for ornament only.   The head territ is often called a
head-ring.

b. The Trace-Rings are iron fquare loops
fewed in the ends of the traces, a part of which
they receive, and loops round the fplinter bar.

c. The Watering, or Bearing-Hook, is a
hook, fixed on the top edge of the houfing, or
faddle, in the middle, and is faftened with one
or two nut-fcrews at the bottom ; its ufe is to receive the bearing-rein, which is eafily hung on
or off, when there is occafion to water the horfe.

d. The

Plate XLIX

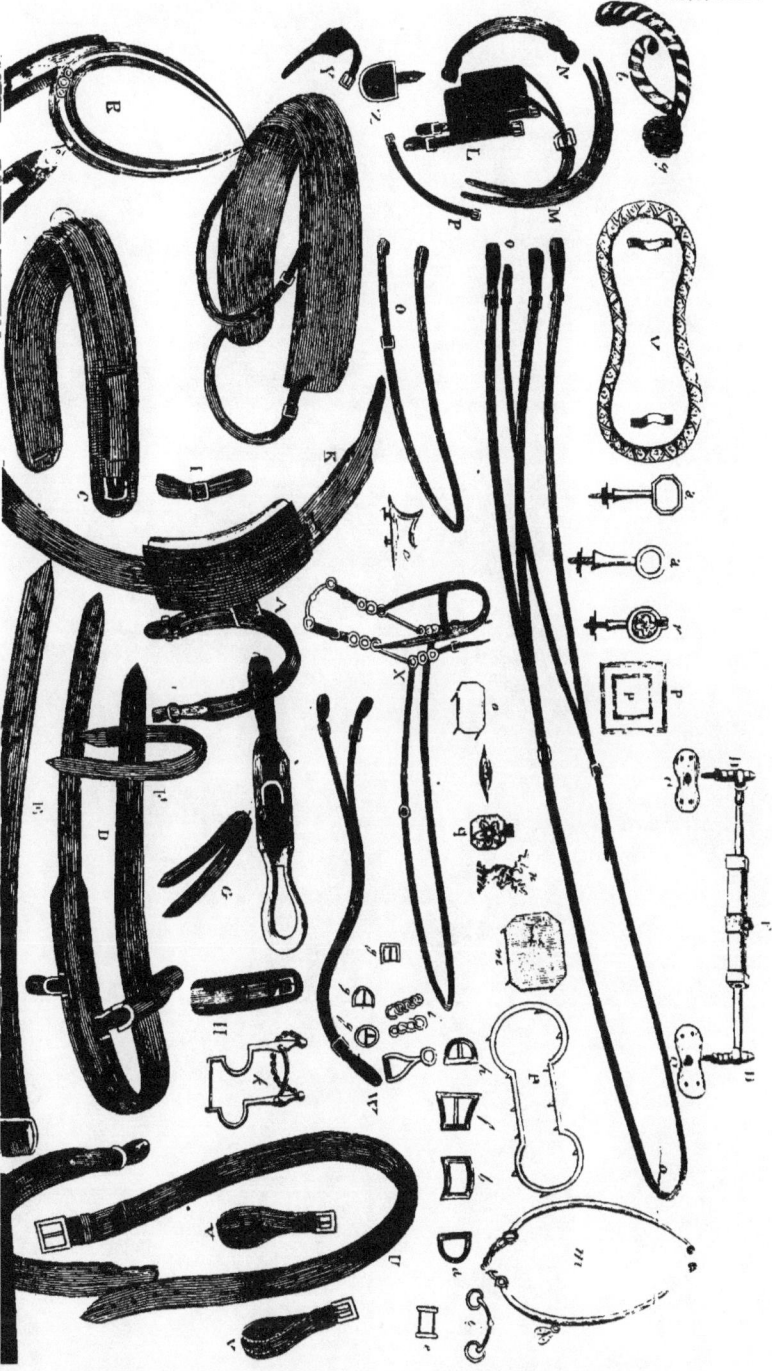

d. The Collar-Dee, an iron ring in the form of a D, fewed in the front of the collar, for the pole-piece to loop through; there are various other dees ufed about fome harnefs, but of a fmall fize, and moftly plated.

e. The Bridge, a thing made on the fides to refemble the buckle, but with two bars acrofs, on the under fide, called bridges; its ufe is to receive two feparate ftraps, one of which is fome-times fewed round one bridge, and looped round the other, fometimes fewed round both.

f. The Collar Buckles, are ftrong, iron buckles, fewed in the collar ends, by which the traces and breeching-ftrap are faftened.

g. The Buckles, which are of various patterns, but are all made to be fewed in the leather, hav-ing only a middle bridge and a tongue, but no chape.

h. The Throat-Band Dee, a thing made in the form of a D, with a roller-bridge acrofs the middle, fewed in the throat-band for the bridoon-rein to run in.

i. The Swivel, a convenience for the bridoon-rein to run in, made with an eye at the top, to

L hang

hang by, and a bar, with a roller at the bottom for the bridoon-rein to run on ; this is frequently ufed inftead of a chain-link.

j. The Chain-Links, the ornaments ufed to a bridoon to contraƈt the bearing-rein ; they are made of different numbers of links, but moftly three to each ; one link the ftrap is faftened to, while another receives the rein.

They are of different forms, fome with round, others with oval links, and fome are made like a double curb-chain, of a confiderable length.

k. The Bit, which is of iron, is placed in the horfe's mouth, and by it he is governed ; they are of different forms, fome are made to be fharper in the mouth, and for a ftronger purchafe than others, and are called the ftraight cheek, the duke, and Portfmouth bit. The bit is buckled in the top loop to the cheek of the bridle, the middle loop to the bearing rein, and the bottom loop to the hand rein.

l. The Bridoon Bit, an additional bit for the horfe's mouth, jointed in the middle, with a ring at each end for the reins to be faftened to.

m. The Heams, are the two irons made to fix round the neck collar, and of a length and
                                                                form

form to fit it; at each end, and in the middle of
each heam, are loops wrought out of the folid;
in the middle other loops are hung, to which the
tugs for the draught are fixed; at the bottom
loops are links, with a hook on one fide, for the
heams to be let out or taken up by; the top
loops are for a ftrap and buckle to faften them to
the collar. If, to the harnefs for a pair of horfes,
heams are ufed, a large iron ring muft be placed
in the middle links for the pole-pieces to be faftened to. The heams are either covered with
leather, polifhed, or plated.

*Thefe are the neceffary parts of the furniture: the
following are only for ornament:*

n. The Houfing and Winker-Plates, or Pieces,
are flat plates, of various forms and fizes, with
the creft, or cypher, chaced, or engraved, on
them, ufed to ornament the houfing and winkers.
The pieces are the fmaller-fized plates; when the
arms, crefts, or cyphers, are emboffed, they are
alfo called pieces, and are for the fame purpofe
as the plates; they are fixed by thin wire fhanks,
foldered to the bottom of the plate, or piece,
which goes through the leather, and are rivetted
on the infide. Circles, or rims, are what en-
circle the fmall plates, or pieces, and are faftened on the fame way.

L 2   o. Studs,

o. Studs, are small ornaments, sometimes used for the strapping, of a round, square, or octagon, form, about an inch diameter.

p. Frames, are the beads or mouldings fixed round the top edge of the housings and winkers, in double or single rows.

q. Forehead-Piece, Nose-Piece, Breast-Piece, or Side-Pieces, are ornaments usually made to match those on the housing, and fixed on those leathers called the nose-band, martingale, &c.

r. A Fly Head-Ring : this is a territ with an ornament piece, which plays to and fro with the motion of the horse's head.

s. Roses are the round ornaments fixed on the outside of the bridle, made of leather, worsted, silk, or tape, in various fanciful ways, and are fastened, by a loop at the back to the straps of the crown-piece.

t. Earbows, are of stiff leather, made flat, or sewed round; and covered with lace, or tape, to match the roses; one end is sewed on the front, the other is fastened on the crown-piece by the head-territ.

v. Pad-

v. Pad-Cloth, a cloth that lies on the horfe's back for the houfing to lie on, trimmed with lace round the edges, and faftened down by the belly-band.

Thefe are all ornaments, but fome of them being generally ufed, it will be proper firft to defcribe the neceffary harnefs, with the different prices thereof; and next to ftate the prices of the feveral appendages that are ufed for ornament only.

SECT. 3.

THE NECESSARY QUANTITY OF LEATHER-WORK
AND FURNITURE FOR A PAIR OF HARNESS.

THE LEATHER-WORK.

TWO pair of winkers, with ftraps and cheeks; two fronts; two crown-pieces; two throat-bands; a long hand-rein; a pair of coupling and bearing-reins; a pair of houfings and belly-bands; two cruppers; two breaft-collars; two pair of traces; two back-ftraps; two Newmarket ftraps; a pair of neck or wither ftraps; and two pair of collar tugs.

L 3   For

For a fingle or chaife harnefs, half the quantity, only with the addition of a back-band and tugs, and a faddle inftead of the houfing.

THE FURNITURE.

BUCKLES one inch or 7-8ths to the reins and bridle. To the winkers, eight; to the throatbands, four: to the crown-pieces, two; to the hand-reins, eight; to the coupling-reins, four; to the bearing-reins, fix.

Buckles 1½ inch, or 1¼. Four for the neckftrap; one for the belly-band; four for the Newmarket-ftraps; and two for the crupper.

Dees, or Bridges, 1½ inch. Three for the houfing; two for the collar-tugs; and two for the trace-bearers, or tugs.

Territs. Four for the houfings.

Watering or Bearing-hooks. Two for the houfings.

Screws. Eight for the houfings.

Scutcheons. Fourteen for the territs, hooks, and fcrews.

Collar-Buckles. Four, of polifhed iron.

Trace-Rings. Four, of ditto.

Collar-Dees. Two, of ditto.

Bits. Two, of ditto.

Only

Only half the quantity for a single horse harness, except two 2-inch buckles for the shaft-
tugs, and one $1\frac{1}{2}$ inch for the shaft or belly-band.

SECT. 4.

THE WHEEL HARNESS.

THE wheel harnefs is that worn by the horfes
neareft the carriage, and is faftened to it; this is
the moft general fort of harnefs, and is made
with long reins for the coachman to command the
horfes by from the coach box. It is faftened behind by the traces to the fplinter-bar rolls, and
before by two ftraps from the pole to the collars.
This is the only harnefs to which breechings are
at all neceffary; but, with falfe belly-bands to
the collars, they may be ufed without, except in
very hilly countries.

SECT. 5.

LEADING HARNESS.

A LEADING harnefs is exactly the fame as the wheel harnefs, only that the reins and traces are much longer, and that, with them, breechings are never ufed. The traces are fometimes faftened to the fplinter-bars, which hang on the pole, and then they are no longer than ufual; the draught is better when taken this way, but does not look fo neat as when faftened to the collars of the wheel harnefs; the make of all the reft is the fame as the wheel harnefs, except the reins, which are double the length for the leading horfes, and they go through two head-territs on the bridles of the wheel harnefs, which are fo much additional to the furniture. The coupling or bearing reins are the fame as thofe ufed to the wheel harnefs.

The extra expence for long traces is the fame as the extra expence for the fplinter-bars to the carriage; fo that there can be no advantage in price either way. If fix horfes are ufed, there can be no fplinter bars for the leaders to draw by, and, of courfe, the additional price of the traces muft be added to the price of a poftillion wheel-harnefs.

SECT. 6.

POSTILLION HARNESS.

WHEN the carriage goes poft, the near horfe is rode by a poftillion, which makes no other difference in the harnefs than the omiffion of the long hand and the coupling reins. A fhort hand rein is buckled to the infide of the off horfe's bit, by which he is led; a riding faddle, with deep, fingle fkirts, is fubftituted in the place of a houfing, and, including the ftirrups, is much on a par with the houfing furniture and reins; fo that a poftillion, wheel, or leading harnefs is the fame expence as either the poftillion or wheel harnefs of the other fort, if of plated furniture; but is rather more if of brafs, as the price of the faddle is more than equal to the price of the brafs furniture to the pads.

SECT. 7.

CURRICLE HARNESS.

A curricle harnefs is exactly the fame as that ufed to a coach or chariot, only that fmall faddles, inftead of pads, or houfings, are preferred, being eafier for the horfe, and ftronger

to

to fupport the weight of the carriage, which refts thereon by means of the iron-work which is ri-vetted on them, and which receives the bar for the pole to hang by.

———

THE CURRICLE BAR.

(SEE PLATE XLIX, FIG. I.)

THIS is an ingenious contrivance for the purpofe; it is made of iron, and is about twenty inches long and 2¼ fquare; in it are two fquare receffes, in which are placed two fliding bars, one on each fide the other; and, from each end, draws out to the fame length as the bar, making a length, when drawn out to its extent, of about four feet fix inches. The end of each flide is placed in the ftands D. D. and are faftened by round pins on which they act, and the pins are fecured by fpring keys. The ftands are faftened on the plates C. C. fo as to turn round with the bar; the advantage of this bar, with the fliders and joints, is to give room for the motion of the horfe in every fituation. On the middle of the cafe is a ftaple, F. to which the brace that fup-ports the pole is hung: the bar, with the brace and bearer, is an extra to the harnefs; the fad-dle would alfo make an increafe, but the ftrap-ping, being much lighter, makes them equal; therefore,

therefore, to know the price of curricle harnefs, add the price of a bar to a common wheel harnefs.

A coach or chariot harnefs, with the addition of two faddles and a bar, will make a complete curricle harnefs, having the trace-rings alfo made with a fcrew, whereby they may be changed, and woodcock eyes fubftituted in their place.

SECT. 8.

A CHAISE HARNESS.

A CHAISE harnefs is intended as well to fupport the carriage as to draw it by; it is made fimilar to the other; the only material difference is the faddle inftead of houfing, and through which flides a back-band, which has loops, or tugs, fixed by buckles thereon, in which the fhafts are hung. The harnefs for a four-wheeled chaife, or phaeton, is made exactly like this for a two-wheeled; but as the tugs do not carry any weight, but only hold up the fhafts, they need not be made fo ftrong.

To the harnefs for a four-wheeled carriage, drawn by one horfe, a breeching is abfolutely neceffary, but for a two-wheeled carriage it is not, provided there are ftops, or hooks, fixed on the fhafts, for the tugs to hold the chaife back by. This harnefs is half the value of the others.

SECT.

SECT. 9.

PRICE OF HARNESS.

THE value of harnefs is proportioned to the quantity of ftrapping and ornaments it is made up with; a fuperfluous quantity of one or the other is upon moft of the harnefs that is ufed. The value of the leather-work is eafily afcertained, as to what is neceffary; but the furniture being of many different patterns and qualities, varies the price of the whole. To afcertain, therefore, with any correctnefs, the prices of the different kinds of harnefs, it will be proper to ftate the value of the neceffary harnefs, made up with furniture of different forts, feparate, fo that the price for any additional ftrapping, and any different kind of furniture, may be added to the plain harnefs, and the price obtained with accuracy, in whatever manner they are finifhed.

Harnefs is frequently made without breeching or bridoon, and fometimes with one, at other times with both; it will therefore be proper to ftate the prices of them feparate, as alfo the back-ftraps and falfe belly-bands, which are but occafionally ufed.

Round or neck-coilars, and faddles inftead of breaft-collars and houfings, are fometimes ufed;

therefore

therefore it will be neceffary to ftate the value of each, that either way may be preferred, with a knowledge of the different expences.

___

THE FIRST CHARGE FOR A PAIR OF WHEEL HARNESS.

	Plated.			Compofition Metal.			Brafs.		
	£.	s.	d	£.	s.	d	£.	s.	d.
For a coach — —	11	14	0	10	7	6	9	11	6
For a chariot, or large-fized phaeton —	10	14	6	9	8	0	8	15	0
For a middle, or fmall-fized phaeton —	10	4	3	8	19	0	8	7	0
For a fmall poney phaeton —	9	14	0	8	9	0	7	19	0
* A pair of breechings for the coach, chario:, or large phaeton harnefs —	1	6	0	1	4	0	1	2	0
* A pair of falfe belly-bands for ditto —— —	0	12	0	0	11	0	0	10	0
* A pair of breechings for the middle and fmall-fized phaetons, or curricle harnefs —	1	1	0	0	19	6	0	18	0
* A pair of falfe belly-bands for ditto — — —	0	10	0	0	9	0	0	8	0

* One or other of thefe things are neceffary, but only with a wheel harnefs.

A PAIR

A PAIR OF LEADING HARNESS, WITH LONG REINS.

	Plated.			Composition Metal.			Brafs.		
	£.	s.	d	£.	s.	d.	£.	s.	d.
* For a coach — —	12	14	0	11	4	3	10	6	6
* For a chariot or large phaeton	11	14	6	10	4	9	9	9	6
For a phaeton of the middle or small fize — —	11	4	3	9	15	9	9	11	6
EXTRA.									
If either of the leading harneffes are made with long traces, it will make to each the addition of — —	1	15	0	1	15	0	1	15	0

THE POSTILLION, OR RIDING HARNESS.

	Plated.			Compofition Metal.			Brafs.		
	£.	s.	d.	£.	s.	d.	£.	s.	d.
The wheel harnefs for a coach	11	14	0	10	12	6	9	16	6
The leading ditto, with long traces — —	13	9	0	12	7	6	11	7	6
The wheel, or riding harnefs for a phaeton or chariot —	10	14	6	9	13	0	9	0	0
The leading ditto, with long traces — —	12	9	6	11	8	0	10	15	0

The extra or metal furniture for the poftillion harnefs, being of lefs value than the filver plating, makes the price of the faddle more than equal with the houfing and reins, as above ftated.

* The long reins and head-rings are the only articles in addition to the former price of wheel harnefs, which makes, for the coach and phaeton harnefs, 1l. more.

A CURRICLE

A CURRICLE HARNESS.

	Plated.			Compofition Metal.			Brafs.		
	£.	s.	d.	£.	s.	d.	£.	s.	d.
A curricle harnefs —	10	14	6	9	8	0	8	15	0
Bar-ftands and pole-bearers —	3	16	0	3	16	0	3	16	0
For plating the ftands and bar	3	3	0	2	2	0	1	11	6
An extra faddle, with its furniture, a back-band, a pair of tugs, and long hand-reins, by which one of the harnefs may be made to anfwer for a one-horfe chaife harnefs —	3	0	0	2	10	0	2	5	0

———

A CHAISE HARNESS.

	Plated.			Compofition Metal.			Brafs.		
	£.	s.	d	£.	s.	d.	£.	s.	d.
A fingle harnefs for a one-horfe chaife or phaeton —	5	7	0	4	15	0	4	7	0
A breeching to either —	0	10	6	0	9	6	0	8	6

SECT. 10.

EXTRA PARTS OF HARNESS AND FURNITURE,
WHICH, IF USED, ARE TO BE ADDED TO THE
PRICE OF HARNESS BEFORE STATED.

ROUND OR NECK-COLLARS, WITH POLISHED HEAMS AND TUGGS, INSTEAD OF BREAST-COLLARS.

	Plated			Compofition Metal.			Brafs.		
	£.	s.	d.	£.	s.	d.	£.	s.	d.
A pair for a coach, chariot, or large phaeton — —	1	5	0	1	3	0	1	2	0
A pair for a middle-fized phaeton or curricle — —	1	3	0	1	2	0	1	1	0
One for a chaife — —	0	12	0	0	11	0	0	10	0
A collar houfing for either harnefs — —	0	4	0						

FALSE COLLARS.

	£.	s.	d.
A falfe round collar — — —	0	9	0
A falfe breaft collar — —	0	13	0

SADDLES INSTEAD OF HOUSINGS.

	£.	s.	d.
A pair for a coach — — —	1	4	0
Ditto for a chariot, or large phaeton —	1	1	0

BRIDOONS,

BRIDOONS, per pair.	Plated.			Composition Metal.			Brass.		
	£.	s.	d.	£.	s.	d.	£.	s.	d.
A pair with throat-latch dees —	1	8	0	1	4	0	1	2	0
Each {A pair with single-link chain} chains or swivels —	1	18	c	1	15	0	1	12	0
3 inch. long {A pair with curb or double-link chains}	2	10	0	2	2	0	1	18	0
Conveniencies not generally used.									
A swivel — —	0	3	0	0	2	3	0	1	6
A throat-latch dee —	0	2	6	0	1	9	0	1	3
A hook for the bridoon-chain to hang on instead of a strap —	0	2	0	0	1	6	0	1	0
A rein-hook — —	0	3	6	0	2	3	0	1	9
A coupling-ring — —	0	1	6	0	1	0	0	0	9
If the bridoon-chains are more than three inches long each, add for each inch of single chain	0	0	6	0	0	4	0	0	3
For the curb-chain —	0	1	0	0	0	9	0	0	6

For a single harness only half the above prices is to be charged.

EXTRA STRAPPINGS.	Plated with Silver.			Composition Metal.			Brass.		
	£.	s.	d.	£.	s.	d.	£.	s.	d.
Hip or back straps, with tugs for a pair of coach or chariot harness —	0	18	0	0	16	0	0	14	0
Ditto, for a small phaeton or curricle —	0	16	0	0	14	0	0	12	0
MARTINGALES, per pair.									
Whole martingales —	1	0	0	0	18	0	0	14	0
A half ditto —	0	14	0	0	10	0	0	8	0
FOREHEAD PIECES, and NOSE BANDS, per pair.									
Forehead pieces, plain —	0	3	0	0	3	0	0	3	0
Nose-bands to buckle round —	0	6	0	0	5	0	0	5	0
Ditto for front only —	0	4	0	0	4	0	0	4	0

M   ROSES,

ROSES, per pair.		Worsted or Tape.			Silk.		
		£.	s.	d.	£.	s.	d.
A pair of rofes, and lapping the fronts of a pair of harnefs —	—	0	8	0	0	16	0
Ditto, with ear-bows for ditto —	—	0	11	0	1	0	0
A pair of rofes, and lapping the front of a chaife harnefs — —	—	0	7	0	0	14	0
Ditto, with a fingle ear-bow	—	0	8	6	0	17	0

PAD and SADDLE-CLOTHS, per pair.		Plain bound.			Bound with 2½ inch lace.		
A pair of pad-cloths —	—	0	7	9	0	12	0
A pair of faddle-cloths —	—	0	9	0	0	16	0

EXTRA FURNITURE.

FRAMES FOR THE OUT EDGES OF HOUS-INGS OR WINKERS, each.

	WINKERS.					HOUSINGS.			
Width of the mould-ing.	Silver.	Plated with Silver.	Com-pofition Metal.	Brafs.		Silver.	Plated with Silver.	Com-pofition Metal.	Brafs.
	s. d.	s. d.	s. d.	s. d.		s. d.	s. d.	s. d.	s. d.
Of an Inch.									
4-8ths	18 0	6 0	4 0	3 0		12 0	8 6	6 6	4 3
3-8	14 0	5 0	3 9	2 6		10 0	7 0	5 3	3 6
2-8	11 0	4 0	3 0	2 0		8 0	5 6	3 2	2 9
A faddle cantle of 2-8th or 3-8th moulding —			—	8 0		4 0	3 0	2 0	

TERRITS, per pair.

		Plated with Silver.			Compofi-tion Metal.			Brafs.		
		£.	s.	d.	£.	s.	d.	£.	s.	d.
For the houfings —	—	0	12	0	0	9	0	0	6	0
For the head-ftal's —	—	0	13	0	0	10	0	0	6	6
For ditto with flies	—	0	14	0	0	10	0	0	7	0

EXTRA

EXTRAS TO THE FURNITURE.

ROUND, OVAL, OCTAGON, or SQUARE PLATES, or PIECES, RIMS, EMBOSSED CRESTS or CYPHERS.

Different Sizes.	Emboffed CRESTS or CYPHERS.*								PLATES or PIECES†.								CIRCLES or RIMS.							
	Silver.		Plated with Silver.		Compofition Metal.		Brafs.		Silver.		Plated with Silver.		Compofition Metal.		Brafs.		Silver.		Plated with Silver.		Compofition Metal.		Brafs.	
Inch. Inch. Inch	s.	d.	s.	d.	s.	d.	s.	d.	s.	d.	s.	d.	s.	d.	s.	d.	s.	d.	s.	d.	s.	d.	s.	d.
4 by 3 or 3½	12	0	10	0	6	8	5	0	6	0	3	6	2	4	1	9	4	0	2	4	1	8	1	2
3½ by 3 or 3¼	11	0	9	6	6	4	4	9	5	6	3	3	2	2	1	7½	3	6	2	2	1	6	1	1
3 by 3 or 3	10	0	9	0	6	0	4	6	5	0	3	0	2	0	1	6	3	3	2	0	1	4	1	0
3 by 2½ or 2¾	9	0	8	0	5	8	4	0	4	6	2	9	1	10	1	4½	3	0	1	10	1	3	0	11
2½ by 2½ or 2½	8	0	7	6	5	4	4	0	4	0	2	6	1	8	1	3	2	9	1	8	1	2	0	10
2½ by 2 or 2¼	7	6	6	6	5	0	3	6	3	9	2	3	1	6	1	1½	2	6	1	6	1	0	0	9
2 by 2 or 2	7	0	6	6	4	8	3	0	3	4	2	0	1	4	1	0	2	3	1	4	0	10½	0	8
2 by 1½ or 1¾	6	6	5	6	4	0	3	0	3	0	1	9	1	2	0	10½	2	0	1	2	0	9½	0	7
1½ by 1½ or 1½	6	0	5	0	3	8	2	9	2	6	1	6	1	0	0	9	1	9	1	0	0	8	0	6
1½ by 1 or 1¼	5	6	4	6	3	4	2	6	2	0	1	3	0	10½	0	7½	1	6	0	10½	0	7	0	5
1 by 1 or 1	4	6	4	0	3	0	2	3	1	9	1	0	0	9	0	6	1	3	0	9	0	6	0	4½
7/8	4	0	3	6	2	8	2	0	1	6	0	10½	0	7½	0	5	1	0	0	7	0	5	0	3½
6/8	3	6	3	0					1	3	0	9	0	6	0	4½	0	10	0	6	0	4	0	3
5/8	3	0	2	6					1	0	0	7½	0	5	0	3½	0	8	0	5	0	3	0	2½
4/8	2	6	2	0					0	9	0	6	0	4	0	3	0	6	0	4	0	2½	0	2

* For every arms that is emboffed inftead of crefts or cyphers, add 2s.

† For every creft or cypher, which is engraved or chafed on the plates, add 9d.

EXTRA FOR PLATING THE IRON-WORK FOR A PAIR OF HARNESS.

	Plated with Silver.			Compofi- tion Metal.			Brafs.		
	£.	s.	d.	£.	s.	d.	£.	s.	d.
The collar tug-buckles — —	0	10	0	0	7	6	0	5	0
The trace-rings — —	0	14	0	0	10	6	0	7	0
Woodcock { Common eyes -	1	4	0	0	18	0	0	12	0
eyes. { Spring ditto —	1	7	0	1	0	0	0	13	6
The collar-dees ——	0	9	0	0	6	0	0	4	6
The HEAMS.									
For fmall 3-8th mouldings on the fronts — —	0	15	0	0	10	0	0	3	9
The tips and loops plated —	2	10	0	1	14	0	1	5	0
Ditto, with links plated —	3	10	0	2	6	0	1	15	0
The whole heams, loops, and links, plated — —	7	0	0	5	5	0	3	10	0
Solid loops, or dees, for the reins — —	0	12	0	0	9	0	0	3	0
The BITS, plated.									
Straight check-bit —	2	4	0	1	11	6	1	1	0
Duke's bits — —	2	8	0	2	2	0	1	9	0
Bridoon-bits —	0	12	0	0	10	6	0	8	0
Stirrups for a poftillion fad-dle —	1	6	0	1	1	0	0	18	0

Thefe are the prices to be charged, if the Iron Furniture is plated; the feparate Parts of the Furniture are comprehended under the fubject of Repairs, where the Prices, Plain and Plated, are feparately ftated.

Half price for the above extras to the furniture, if for a fingle-horfe harnefs.

CHAP.

CHAP. XI.

ON FINISHED HARNESS.

FROM the former defcription of a plain harnefs, a knowledge of the price of the other
forts is to be obtained, by adding to the plain
harnefs the feveral ornaments and conveniencies
which may be found neceffary; yet, as the information would be more compleat by a reprefentation, four of the moft ufual forts of harnefs
will be defcribed, viz. two of the breaft collar
houfing-harnefs, and two of the round-collar
faddle harnefs, the patterns of which will anfwer
for either the wheel, the leading, the poftillion,
the curricle, or the chaife harnefs, by making
fuch allowance as the difference of each requires.

The harnefs being of feveral defcriptions, the
price of each, in the following tables, will be feparately ftated, but all with one fort of furniture,
viz. the filver plated, which is the moft general
in ufe by upwards of fifty to one; as it would be
too prolix to enumerate the compofition metal
and brafs furniture in the fame tables, they are
therefore omitted; but the value of each is eafily

M 3

to

to be afcertained by referring to the former
tables, and obferving the fame rule as is laid
down in the following.

SECT. 1.

A PLAIN BREAST-COLLAR HOUSING-HARNESS.

PLATE L.

IN this pattern of a harnefs, there is nothing
more than what is neceffary, and, for common
ufe, is to be recommended ; to add more is to
burden, and reftrict the horfe in the free exer-
cife of his ftrength, fuch a harnefs is therefore
to be regarded for general ufe, in preference to
others which are more loaded with ftrappings or
fuperfluous ornaments, for it not only faves labour to the horfe, but trouble to the fervant in
cleaning, and money to the proprietor in the
purchafe.

Breaft-collar harnefs is the moft general in ufe,
in particular for coaches or chariots; they are
not fo good for draught, but are more eafy to
be put on or taken off, are alfo lighter, and of
lefs expence, than the round collars, and, if for
frequent

frequent ufe, and the draught very light, may be
recommended. Houfings are moft generally
ufed, and, where the weight is not required to
be on the back, are lefs heating, and more to be
recommended than faddles.

DESCRIPTION OF PLATE L.

A PLAIN breaft-collar harnefs, with falfe
belly-bands; the bridle plain, with bearing-reins
hung to the throat-band by throat-latch dees;
the houfing and winkers fquare, with the corners rounded, but without ornaments.

The furniture filver plated, with the corners
rounded; the buckles half fquare, of the fame
pattern; throat-latches at the throat-band; the
collar-buckles, dees, trace-rings, and bits, are
of polifhed iron as ufual.

PRICE OF THE
PLAIN BREAST-COLLAR HARNESS.

	Coach.			Chariot or large-sized Phaeton.			Middle or small-sized Phaeton.		
	£.	s.	d.	£.	s.	d.	£.	s.	d.
The wheel harnefs —	11	14	0	10	14	6	10	4	3
EXTRAS.									
A pair of falfe belly-bands —	0	12	0	0	10	0	0	10	0
A fet of throat-latch dees —	0	10	0	0	10	0	0	10	0
Total — —	12	16	0	11	14	6	11	4	3
A pair of leading harnefs, with long reins of the fame pattern	12	14	0	11	12	9	11	2	3
EXTRAS.									
Long traces, or fplinter-bars and a pole-hock — —	1	15	0	1	15	0	1	15	0
A fet of throat-latches —	0	3	0	0	8	0	0	8	0
Total — —	14	19	0	13	17	9	13	7	3
The riding or wheel poftillion harnefs — —	11	14	0	10	14	6	10	4	3
EXTRAS.									
A pair of falfe belly-bands —	0	12	0	0	10	0	0	10	0
A fet of throat-latches —	0	10	0	0	10	0	0	10	0
Total — —	12	16	0	11	14	6	11	4	3
The leading harnefs, with long traces · — —	13	9	0	12	9	6	11	19	3
EXTRAS.									
A fet of throat-latches —	0	10	0	0	10	0	0	10	0
Total — —	13	19	0	12	17	6	12	9	3

The

	£.	s.	d.
The curricle harnefs, with the bar and bearers	14	10	0

EXTRAS.

			£.	s.	d.
Falfe belly-bands	—	—	0	10	0
A fet of throat-latches	—	—	0	1	0
	Total	—	15	8	0

			£.	s.	d.
The chaife or gig harnefs	—	—	5	7	0

EXTRAS.

			£.	s.	d.
A pair of throat latches	—	—	0	4	0
	Total	—	5	11	0

SECT. 2.

PLAIN NECK, or ROUND, COLLAR HARNESS, with SADDLES instead of HOUSINGS.

PLATE LI.

THE round or neck collar harnefs for curricles or chaifes, is moft generally ufed, and is
much to be preferred, as the horfes have a
ftronger purchafe, and work with more cafe in
them than in the others; but their advantage is
difregarded from the prejudice of cuftom, and
the abfurdity prevails of ufing breaft-collars to
heavy

heavy four-wheeled carriages, and the neck-collar to light two-wheeled carriages. With hackney and stage coaches, and post-chaises, the neck-collars are, in general, used, as the proprietors are sensible of the advantages thereof; but a similar appearance to these is the principal objection many persons have to the use of them, yet, if they are neatly finished, have an appearance far before the others.

The breast-collars have a light appearance, and, if the draught is light, and the journey short, may with propriety be used; but, if otherwise, the round neck-collars are much to be preferred. Saddles were never intended but to carry weight, and, for that purpose, are always used, in particular, for chaise and curricle harness, where the weight of the fore part of the carriage rests on them, yet as the form of them is more agreeable to the eye than the housings, they are often used to harness for four-wheeled carriages, and, if made light and small, have a smart appearance.

DESCRIPTION OF PLATE LI.

THE representation more exactly describes a one-horse harness, having a saddle and a backband, with tugs for the shafts to hang by; but, except the tugs and back-band, this pattern will answer for any other. It is a plain neck-collar, saddle harness, with false belly-band; the wink-

3

ers

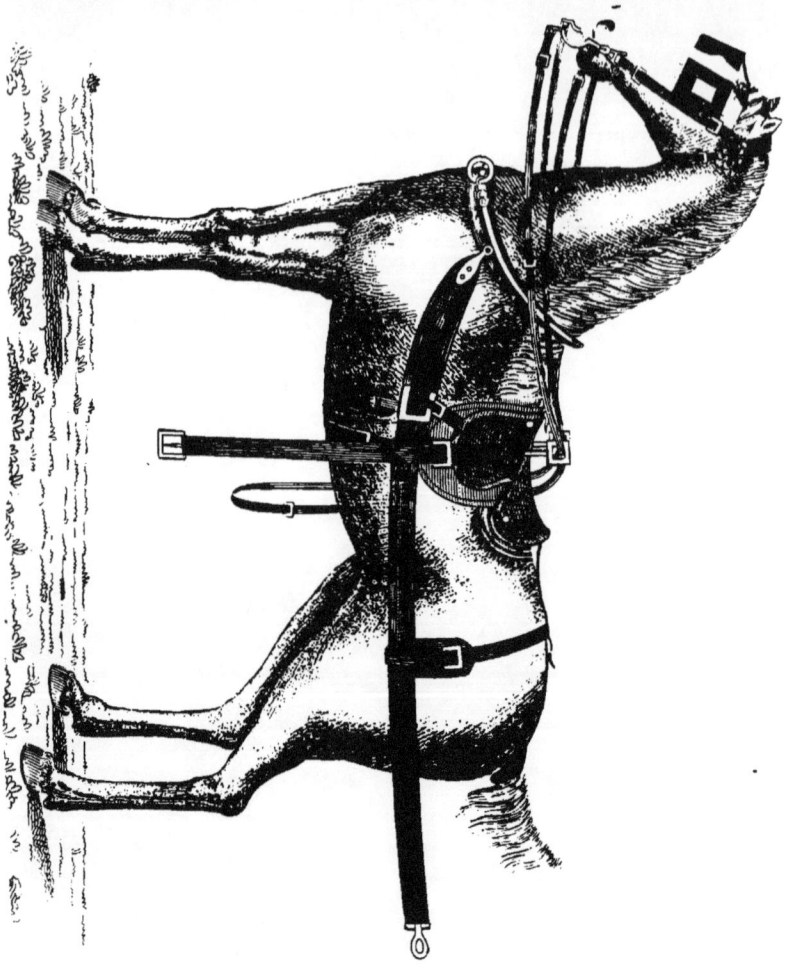

ers fquare; the faddle jockey, or double-fkirted, with a plain faddle-cloth bound round with cloth; the front lapped, and a pair of rofes; the furniture fquare, with a half-fquaré buckle; fquare plates on the winkers. The heams, bits, collar-buckles, rings, and woodcock eyes, are of polifhed iron, or covered with leather.

PRICE OF THE

PLAIN NECK, OR ROUND-COLLAR HARNESS.

	Coach.			Chariot or large-fized Phaeton.			Middle or small-fized Phaeton.		
	£.	s.	d.	£.	s.	d.	£.	s.	d.
The wheel harnefs —	11	14	0	10	14	6	10	4	3
EXTRAS.									
Saddles inftead of houfings —	1	4	c	1	1	o	1	1	o
Neck, inftead of breaft-collars -	1	5	o	1	3	c	1	3	o
Saddle-cloths, plain, bound —	o	10	o	o	10	o	o	10	o
A pair of worfted or tape rofes, and lapping the fronts —	o	8	o	o	8	o	o	8	o
A pair of falfe belly-bands —	o	12	o	o	10	o	o	10	o
A fet of winker-plates, 2¼ inches	o	9	o	o	9	c	o	9	o
Total — —	16	2	c	14	15	6	14	5	3
The leading harnefs —	12	14	6	11	14	6	11	4	3
EXTRAS									
The fame as before, except the falfe belly-bands —	3	16	o	3	11	o	3	11	o
Total — —	16	10	o	15	5	6	14	15	3

The

	Coach.			Chariot or large-sized Phaeton.			Middle or small-sized Phæton.		
	£.	s.	d.	£.	s.	d.	£.	s.	d.
The riding or poftillion wheel harnefs — —	11	14	6	10	14	6	10	0	0
EXTRAS The fame as to the other wheel harnefs, except one faddle and cloth — —	3	11	c	3	5	6	3	5	6
Total — —	15	5	6	14	0	0	13	5	6
A poftillion leading harnefs, with long traces —	13	9	c	12	9	6	11	19	6
EXTRAS The fame as to the other leading harnefs, except one faddle and cloth — —	2	19	0	2	15	6	2	15	6
Total — —	16	8	c	15	5	0	14	15	0

	£.	s.	d.
The curricle harnefs, with the bar, &c. —	14	10	0

EXTRAS.

	£.	s.	d.
The fame as to the firft fmall phaeton wheel harnefs, except the faddles — —	3	0	0
Total —	17	10	0

	£.	s.	d.
The chaife or gig harnefs — —	5	7	0

EXTRAS

	£.	s.	d.
The fame as the laft, but only half the quantity, and a falfe belly-hand excepted ——	1	5	0
Total — —	6	12	0

SECT.

SECT. 3.

A FASHIONABLE ROUND-COLLAR SADDLE HARNESS.

PLATE LII.

WHEN a carriage is ornamented in a fuperior manner, it then becomes neceffary to make the harnefs fuitable, which may be done without overloading it with ftrappings. Its neatnefs confifts chiefly in the ornaments, which are, according to the prefent fafhion, moftly lavifhed on the head. Round, neat collars, and fmall faddles, have the moft genteel appearance, in particular if the iron-work is plated. Breechings, martingales, nofe-bands, forehead-pieces, and bridoon-reins, make the harnefs look more full and compleat, but may all be regarded as unneceffary for ufe, and only for ornament.

DESCRIPTION OF PLATE LII.

A NECK collar faddle harnefs, with breechings, martingales, bridoons with double chains, front nofe-bands, forehead-pieces, filk rofes with ear-bows, faddle-cloths trimmed with two-inch lace, the winkers of a pattern fuitable to the form of the faddle. The furniture of a half oblong form;

form; the territs round, with a centre one on
each faddle; and a fly head-ring on each head-
ftall. The ornaments to the winkers are frames;
to the faddle and winkers double rims, and filver,
emboffed crefts. The loops, links, and tips of
the heams are plated: the collar-buckles and
dees, the trace-rings, or woodcock eyes, plated.

———

PRICE OF THE
FASHIONABLE ROUND - COLLAR SADDLE
HARNESS.

	Coach.			Chariot or large-fized Phaeton.			Middle or fmall-fized Phaeton.		
	£.	s.	d.	£.	s.	d.	£.	s.	d.
The wheel harnefs —	11	14	0	10	14	6	10	4	3
EXTRAS.									
A pair of breechings —	1	6	0	1	6	c	1	1	0
Neck, inftead of breaft-collars	1	5	0	1	3	0	1	3	0
Saddles. inftead of houfings —	1	4	0	1	1	c	1	1	0
A pair of fhort, or half martin-gales —	0	12	0	0	12	c	0	12	0
A pair of front nofe-bands —	0	4	0	0	4	c	0	4	0
A pair of bridoons, with double chains —	1	15	0	1	15	c	1	15	0
A pair of center territs —	0	12	0	0	12	c.	0	12	0
A pair of fly head-rings —	0	12	0	0	12	c	0	12	0
Four light 3 Sth frames to the winkers —	1	0	0	1	0	c	1	0	0
Eight 3-inch, and eight 2¼ inch rims, for the winkers and fad-dle —	1	12	0	1	12	c	1	12	0
Eight filver emboffed crefts —	2	13	4	2	13	4	2	13	4
A pair of faddle cantles —	0	8	0	0	8	c	0	8	0
Carry over —	24	17	4	23	13	4	22	17	7

A pair

Plate LII.

	Coach.			Chariot or large-sized Phaeton.			Middle or small-sized Phaeton.		
	£.	s.	d	£.	s.	d.	£.	s.	d.
Brought over —	24	17	4	23	13	4	22	17	7
A pair of faddle-cloths, trimmed with 2¼ inch lace —	0	16	0	0	16	4	0	16	4
A pair of filk rofes, with earbows, and the fronts lapped -	1	0	0	1	0	0	1	0	0
The collar-buckles and tracerings plated — —	1	4	0	1	4	0	1	4	0
Total — —	27	17	4	26	12	10	25	17	7
The leading harnefs —	12	14	0	11	14	0	11	4	3
EXTRAS									
The fame as before, except the breechings —	14	10	4	14	5	4	14	3	10
Total — —	27	11	4	26	6	10	25	16	7
The riding, or poftillion wheel harnefs — —	11	14	6	10	14	6	10	14	6
EXTRAS									
The fame as to the other wheel harnefs, except one faddle and cloth, four rims, two crefts, and a cantle for ditto —	13	15	0	13	10	0	13	5	0
Total —	25	16	6	24	11	6	24	8	0
The poftillion leading harnefs	13	9	0	12	9	6	11	19	6
EXTRAS									
The fame as the laft, but without breechings —	12	16	0	12	11	0	12	12	6
Total — —	26	5	0	25	0	6	24	12	6

The

	£.	s	d.
The curricle harnefs, with a bar, &c. —	14	10	0
The bar plated — — —	2	10	0

THE EXTRAS

The fame as to the driving wheel harnefs for the middle-fized phaeton, except the faddles	14	12	4
	£. 31	12	4

	£.	s.	d.
The chaife harnefs — —	5	7	0

THE EXTRAS

Half the price of the curricle extras —	7	6	2

SECT. 4.

A BREAST-COLLAR, HOUSING, FULL-MADE HARNESS.

PLATE LIII.

FOR town ufe, a handfome, full, breaft-collar harnefs, may, with propriety, be ufed; as the carriage runs much lighter on the ftones than it generally does on the roads, and, as the jour-nies about town are moftly fhort, no great difad-vantage in the draught can be felt from the breaft-

Plate LIII.

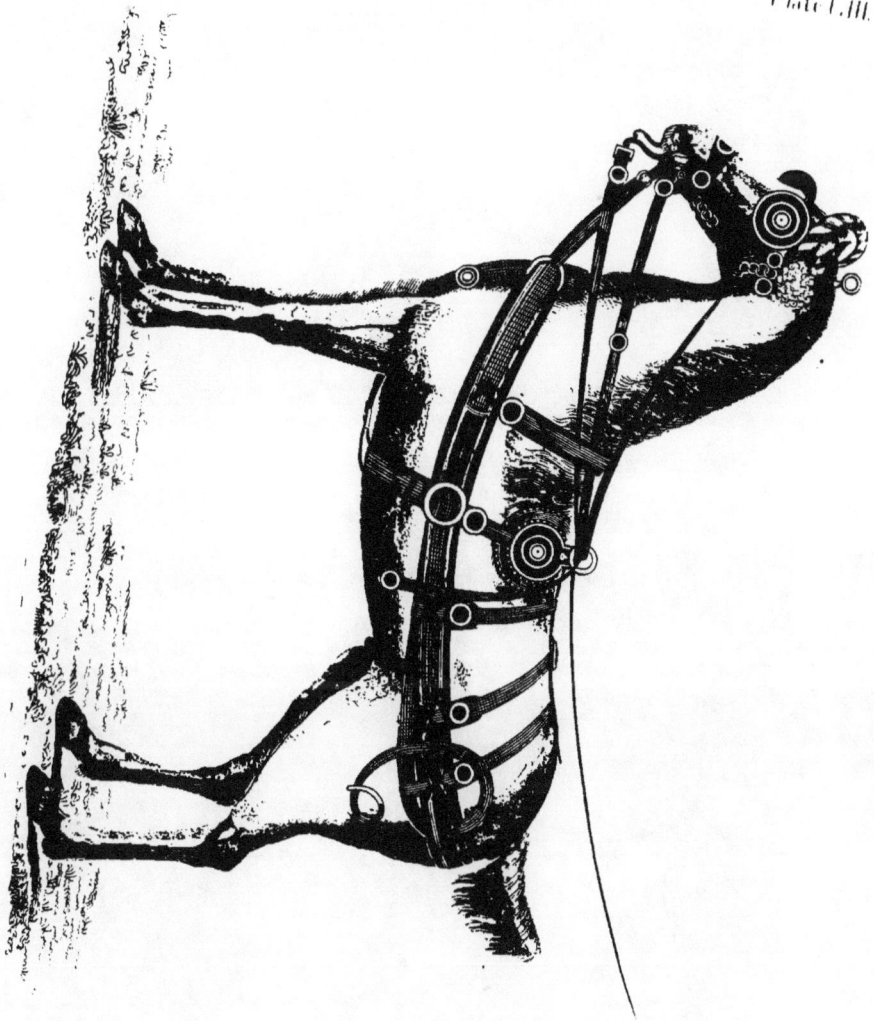

breaſt-collar, or in the weight of the harneſs, from the extra ſtrapping with which it is ornamented. To a handſome carriage, a handſome harneſs is indiſpenſable, and, for ſhew, the round furniture looks beſt, but is the moſt troubleſome to put together or take aſunder, as the rims of the buckles are too narrow for the ſtraps, which are thick and not pliable ; the ſquare buckle is much more convenient, but the half ſquare buckle is the moſt uſeful of any. Ornamenting the ſtraps with ſmall ſtuds has been much in uſe, but is now out of faſhion, except for very grand equipages, and they are beſides ſometimes decorated with ribbands, both of which are omitted in the repreſentations, being but ſeldom uſed.

DESCRIPTION OF PLATE LIII.

A BREAST-collar full-made harneſs, with houſings; breechings; two back-ſtraps ; martingales ; bridoon-heads, with double chains ; noſe-bands; forehead pieces ; roſes, and earbows; pad-cloths bound with lace.

Whole-buckle furniture ; centre and head territs; frames to the houſings and winkers ; eight $2\frac{1}{2}$ inch rims, and eight two-inch plates, on both three two-inch rims, and three $1\frac{1}{2}$ inch plates for the noſe-bands, forehead-pieces, and martin-

N   gales;

gales; the bits, collar-buckles, dees, and trace-rings, plated.

PRICE OF THE

BREAST-COLLAR HOUSING HARNESS.

	Coach.			Chariot or large-sized Phaeton.			Middle or small-sized Phaeton.		
	£.	s.	d.	£.	s.	d.	£.	s.	d.
The wheel harness —	11	14	0	10	14	6	10	4	3
EXTRAS.									
A pair of breechings —	1	6	0	1	6	0	1	1	0
Two pair of back-straps —	1	16	0	1	16	0	1	12	0
A pair of martingales —	1	0	0	1	0	0	1	0	0
A pair of forehead pieces —	0	3	0	0	3	0	0	3	0
A pair of bridoons, with double chains —	1	15	0	1	15	0	1	15	0
A pair of nose-bands —	0	6	0	0	6	0	0	6	0
A pair of silk roses, and ear-bows, and lapping the fronts	1	0	0	1	0	0	1	0	0
A pair of pad-cloths, bound with lace —	0	12	0	0	12	0	0	12	0
Two centre and two head territs	1	4	0	1	4	0	1	4	0
Two housing and four winker frames of a half-inch moulding	2	18	0	2	18	0	2	14	0
Eight 2¼-inch rims, and three two-inch ditto —	0	17	4	0	17	4	0	17	4
Eight two-inch plates, and three 1½-inch ditto —	1	0	6	1	0	6	1	0	6
A pair of duke's bits plated —	2	8	0	2	8	0	2	8	0
The bridoon bits ditto —	0	12	0	0	12	0	0	12	0
The trace-rings ditto —	0	14	0	0	14	0	0	14	0
The collar-buckles ditto —	0	10	0	0	10	0	0	10	0
The collar-dees ditto —	0	9	0	0	9	0	0	9	0
Whole buckles, instead of half to the common harness —	0	14	0	0	14	0	0	12	0
Ditto to the extra strapping —	0	7	0	0	7	0	0	6	0
Total —	31	5	10	30	16	4	29	13	7

A lead-

	Coach.			Chariot or large-fized Phaeton.			Middle or fmall-fized Phaeton.		
	£.	s.	d.	£.	s.	d.	£.	s.	d.
The leading harnefs	12	14	0	11	14	6	10	14	6
EXTRAS The fame as before, except the breechings	18	5	10	18	5	10	17	11	10
Total	30	19	10	30	0	4	28	6	4
The riding, or poftillion wheel harnefs	11	14	6	10	14	6	10	14	6
EXTRAS The fame as to the other wheel harnefs, except one territ. one frame, two rims, two plates, and one pad-cloth for the houfing	18	4	6	18	4	6	17	5	6
Total	29	19	0	28	19	0	28	0	0
The poftillion leading harnefs	13	9	0	12	9	6	11	19	6
EXTRAS The fame as the laft, excepting breechings	17	18	6	17	18	6	17	4	6
Total	31	7	6	30	8	0	29	4	0

————

	£.	s.	d.
The curricle harnefs, with the bar, &c.	14	10	0

EXTRAS.

The fame as to the fmall phaeton driving wheel harnefs, except two centre territs, and frames for the houfing	17	13	10
Total	32	3	10

The

		£.	s.	d.
The chaife or gig harnefs	— —	5	7	0

EXTRAS

Half the amount of the laft-mentioned curricle	8	14	5
Total — —	14	1	5

END OF THE SECOND VOLUME.

THE

SUPPLEMENT

TO THE

TREATISE ON CARRIAGES:

COMPREHENDING ALL THE

NECESSARY REPAIRS;

THE MODE AND TERMS FOR HIRING;

WITH INSTRUCTIONS HOW TO

PRESERVE AND PURCHASE

ALL KINDS OF

CARRIAGES AND HARNESS NOW IN USE.

CONTAINING ALSO OTHER

USEFUL INFORMATION THEREON;

WITH THE

PRICES FOR EVERY ARTICLE ANNEXED.

ADVERTISEMENT.

IT having been suggested by some Gentlemen, who have lately purchased new Carriages, and may not have occasion for another new purchase, that it would be convenient for them to have the Supplement by itself, in order to direct them in a proper manner how to preserve, or repair, the Carriage or Carriages they are already possessed of; or if their inclination should lead them to adopt the custom of hiring, that they may have the benefit of such instructions as are there given on that subject. The Author has therefore ordered an additional number of the Supplements to be published for the accommodation of such Gentlemen as wish to purchase them separately.

A 2

CONTENTS.

Hind

CHAP.

Obfervations,

SUPPLEMENTARY

OBSERVATIONS

ON

REPAIRING, PRESERVING, AND *HIRING*

CARRIAGES, &c.

TO thofe who keep carriages, nothing can be more fatisfactory, than to know what the expences thereof are likely to be for any length of time : as alfo how they may repair or preferve their carriages, or harnefs, without the rifk of incurring extravagant expences.

The expence of carriages, at the firft purchafe, has often proved comparatively fmall with the after expence for maintaining them in repairs, principally owing to the want of fuch inftructions as might

B effectually

effectually guard them againſt impoſition, and directions what was proper to be done, as well for the neceſſary repair as the preſervation.

Many perſons have denied themſelves the convenience of a carriage, by anticipating thoſe evils, which are well known to have long exiſted; and although many carriages have been kept, yet many more would have been, had the means been deviſed, whereby the expences could have been computed with any degree of certainty, and without ſo much trouble in attending to the care of them.

It is by the coachmen gentlemen are uſually biaſed in what is to be done in the repairs, or alterations of the carriage; and who, from intereſted motives, or capricious whims, often go to extravagant lengths, abuſing the implicit confidence their maſters place in them, not only to the ſacrifice of their property, but to the injury of the carriage, which often becomes a kind of property to the coachman or coachmaker, and the proprietor a dupe to one, or both of their artifices.

Coach

Coachmakers are too frequently made fubfervient to the coachmen, owing to the influence they have with their employers, and are therefore obliged to countenance the impropriety of their orders, if they wifh to preferve their cuftomer. Therefore, by ftating what the probable expence for repairs may be, for any length of time, a perfon may judge, whether or not he has been taken advantage of, by one or the other. It is in confequence of frequent and expenfive repairs, which gentlemen often experience, that they are induced rather to job or hire, than to purchafe a carriage, fuppofing this the beft way to know the extent of their expences; but in that they are frequently difappointed, by a number of charges for extras, and what are termed accidents, which often exceed the expence of their own carriage. It will, therefore, be neceffary to explain the general terms of hiring, and what the expences annexed are likely to be, fo that a perfon may decide, whether the purchafe or hire be moft eligible.

It

It is alfo effential to know, in what
manner a carriage may be beft preferved, both in ftrength and beauty; for by
neglect, or ignorance, a carriage is as
much injured as by ufe. This depends
entirely on the care of the fervant, and
is a matter of confequence to the proprietor, to examine as fcrupulously into the
merits of the coachman, refpecting his
knowledge of a carriage, as it is of his
experience among horfes, or his fkill in
driving them. A proper qualified coachman, made independent of his cuftomary
emoluments, is as valuable a fervant as
any in a gentleman's family; but, otherwife, is as likely to be one of the worft,
as his expectation of perquifites often
produces extravagant expences to his
mafter, and brings difcredit on the builder; it is proper, therefore, for a gentleman
to confider his own advantage, and make
an adequate allowance to his fervant, for
the emoluments he deprives him of,
whereby he may fecure to himfelf treble
advantages.

Many inconveniencies arife to gentlemen,

men, from not knowing the extent or manner of paying the duties; to prevent tedious refearches in the feveral acts of Parliament made thereon, an abftract will be given, which, with every other information relating to Carriages, cannot fail to be of material advantage to every proprietor of a carriage.

CHAP.

CHAP. I.

ON REPAIRS.

IT is in a carriage, as in many other mechanical
ſtruɛures, that in order to repair, the taking
to pieces and putting together coſts more than
the repair itſelf, and the charges for trifling things
appear enormous ; but in general it is taken advantage of by ſome coach-makers, who copiouſly
mention in their bills every circumſtance of the
job, almoſt to the number of turns of the ſcrews,
or blows of the hammer, with a conſtant repetition
of driving out, driving in, taking off and putting
on, unſcrewing and ſcrewing, nailing and unnail-
ing, unhanging and rehanging, &c. &c. which
by ſome is done only to countenance impoſition,
by confounding the charge for the job with ſo
many different matters, as to make it, to a gentleman, incomprehenſible. The following tables
ſhew what the ſeparate prices are, whereby they
may eaſily be collɛfed.

It may be diſputed by ſome, the probability of
fixing a regular price for repairs, on account
that they are not always executed with equal
acility ; certain it is, that ſometimes a repair will

B 4 coſt ·

coſt double the labour and time that it uſually
does, and as often may be done with half;
therefore no exception ſhould be taken on account of theſe accidental circumſtances, but a
regular average price charged for all jobs of the
ſame kind.

It is next to impoſſible to ſtate with accuracy
every repair that is done to a carriage; for an
accident may happen in ſuch way that the means
of repairing cannot even be ſurmiſed, but muſt
be left with the coach-maker to make his own
charge for the trouble and time the repairs may
coſt him.

The nature of repairs is ſo various, that it is·
neceſſary to arrange them under ſeparate heads,
that they may be collected with more eaſe; ſo
that if a number of articles of repairs are done,
and in a bill are jumbled together under one
charge, the ſeparate prices of the different articles ſhould be compared with the amount charged for the whole.

Carriages, if well looked after, ſuffer no material injury with ſtanding by, even for five or ſix
years; it is the conſtant work and frequent waſh-
ings which bring them to decay.

Driving very hard on the ſtones expoſes a carriage to many accidents, either by running againſt
others, or breaking by the violence of its uſe; the
ſprings and axletrees are moſt likely to fail in
those

thofe cafes, as the weight and ftrain lie chiefly
on them; and although the coach-maker infures
it for a time from any accident by fair ufe, yet
it ought to operate with gentlemen as a matter
where their perfonal fafety and intereft depend,
not to allow their coachman to drive fo faft, in
particular on rough ftoney ground, they would
thereby avoid danger, and preferve the carriage
from much injury.

SECT. 1.

ON GUARANTEEING OF CARRIAGES.

IT is cuftomary with the builder, to warrant
his work, for the firft fix or twelve months; but
moftly for twelve; except chaifes, and they are
feldom for more than fix, which is a fufficient
time to prove the quality of either carriage: all
failures within that time are obliged to be made
good by the builder; fuch an obligation is neceffary with fome, to make them cautious of future expences; yet accidents are unavoidable;
however cautious a tradefman may be; the worft
of which is the failure of the iron work, in particular the axletrees, as from that, the greateft
danger is to be expected. The coach maker's
infurance extends to failures which happen in
confequence

confequence of bad materials, and not what
arifes from wear by ufe; any of the *Timber* or
Iron work breaking, the *Plating* wearing through,
the *Leather* unfewing, the *Paint* or *Varnifh* flying,
except if badly ufed, are what are meant to be
made good, if faulty.

The *Wheels* are alfo included with the reft of
the carriage, as the guaranteeing as confined to
failures, only in confequence of faulty materials,
and not to fair wear; for it would be impoffible to
afford the replacing a fet of wheels, or make
good other deficiencies which arife from the ex-
ceffive ufe fome make of a carriage, though many gentlemen are diffatisfied, if charged for any
thing done in the fpace of that time, which the
carriage is warranted for, without confidering
that any part of the carriage may require mending in confequence of the wear it has had, though
it cannot be expected to be any thing very confiderable, if the work is moderate; all that may
be expected, is the lining with leather, or refitting
the wheel-boxes, if worn fo as to become loofe.

It would fave much perplexity, if a contract
could at firft be made with the builder, to maintain the carriage in repair, by the year, after
the following manner, which will prove what the
expences for repairs ought to be for any length
of time, to any fort of carriage in ufe.

SECT. 2.

THE EXPENCES COMPUTED BY THE TIME THE WHEELS WEAR.

TO prove the regular work of a carriage, is to afcertain it by the wear of the wheels, which being of three forts, muft be computed by the length of time they feparately wear; of any fort of wheels, it can only be expcéted to wear down the iron which rims them, which in general is proportioned to the wheel, and the wheel to the weight of the carriage; but whether ftraked, hooped, or patent rims, if the timbers wear as long as the iron, the wheels are equally good of their kind; but that is feldom the cafe.

The wheels being of three forts, wear different lengths of time; for example, the ftrake-rimmed wheel, on conftant work, wears out in twelve months; the hoop-rimmed wheel in fifteen months; the patent-rimmed wheel, in eighteen months. The goodnefs of the wheels may be computed by the number of miles they each run over; the calculation therefore, is on the fuppofition that each wheel runs nearly five miles per day in town, and eight in the country, which is the fhorteft time they may be expeéted to laft,

MILES.

MILES.

A ſtraked wheel, on rough ſtoney ground to run — 1825
Ditto, on ſmooth turnpike road — — 2920
A hoop-rimmed wheel, on rough ſtoney ground — 2282
A ditto, on ſmooth turnpike road — — 3660
A patent-rimmed wheel, on rough ſtoney ground — 2738
Ditto, on ſmooth turnpike road — — 4380

Light carriages, ſuch as phaetons and chaiſes, in general are uſed but half the year, and that in fair dry weather: when the roads are good, and being alſo lighter on the wheels, the wear is not ſo great on them, and of courſe may be expeĉted to run more miles than the other, by about one third; for example, a ſet of ſtrake-wheels to a coach or chariot may run 2920 miles in the country, taking the work regular all the year; a ſet of the ſame ſort of wheels, alſo in the country, to a phaeton or chaiſe, 3894, when the roads are good, and taking alſo the work to be only for the ſix ſummer months in each year. The wear of thoſe carriages, except the wheels, is the ſame in proportion to the work they do, and the expence for repairing them is proportioned to the ſame; therefore, to compute the expence for each, is to ſtate them all at four years, allowing to the coach and chariot a ſet of wheels annually; to a phaeton or chaiſe, two ſets in four years, ſuppoſing the work to be regular. This way the amount for repairs may be computed by the length of time the wheels laſt, whether it is longer or ſhorter than what is here ſtated.

EXPENCE

EXPENCE OF REPAIRS CALCULATED BY TIME OR WEAR OF THE WHEELS.

Suppofing the work to be fuch, that the ftrake wheels of a coach or chariot is worn out each year; and to a phaeton or chaife in three years.

	Coach.	Chariot.	PHAETONS. Large.	Middle.	Small.	Curricle.	Gig.	Whifk/Rev.
	£. s. d.	£. s. d.	£. s. d.	£. s. d.	£. s. d.	£. s. d.	£. s. d.	£. s. d.
First year: Repairs	3 0 0	2 10 0	2 0 0	2 0 0	2 0 0	2 0 0	1 15 0	1 10 0
Wheels	7 10 0	7 10 0	4 0 0	3 10 0	3 0 0	3 0 0	2 10 0	2 0 0
Second year. Repairs	4 10 0	7 0 0	6 12 0	5 11 0	5 0 0	4 0 0	3 2 0	2 11 0
Wheels	7 10 0	7 10 0	4 0 0	3 10 0	3 0 0	3 10 0	2 10 0	2 0 0
Third year. Repairs	7 0 0	6 12 0	3 15 0	3 2 6	3 4 6	3 4 6	3 0 0	2 6 0
Painting	7 0 0	5 10 0	5 10 0	2 0 0	2 6 0	2 6 0	3 10 0	3 0 0
Hammer-cloth, &c.	7 12 0	6 12 0	—	—	—	—	2 6 0	2 11 0
Fourth year. Wheels	7 0 0	7 0 0	—	—	—	—	2 6 0	2 6 0
Repairs	8 10 0	7 0 0	—	—	—	—	4 10 0	4 0 0
Total for Repairs	59 19 0	55 9 0	28 17 0	25 13 6	22 2 6	21 2 6	18 9 6	15 12 0
Firft coft of each	120 0 0	110 0 0	63 0 0	55 0 0	50 0 0	45 0 0	40 0 0	31 10 0
Total coft —	179 19 0	165 9 0	91 17 0	80 13 6	72 2 6	96 2 6	58 9 6	46 2 0
Value of each carriage at the four years' end	40 0 0	36 10 0	21 0 0	18 10 0	16 10 0	15 0 0	13 0 0	10 0 0
The expence for four years	139 9 0	128 19 0	70 17 0	62 3 6	55 12 6	51 2 6	45 9 6	36 2 0
The annual expence	34 17 3	32 4 9	17 14 3	15 10 9	13 18 6	17 15 6	11 7 4	9 0 6

By

By thefe ftatements any perfon may compute their expences, without being much at a lofs to know whether the purchafo or hire is preferable; this calculation is for plain fubftantial carriages, which in four years having worn out fuch a number of ftrake wheels, amount to half the expence of the original purchafe, and after that time, become an expenfive charge for repairs: the moft advifable plan then is, to difpofe of the old carriage, while the fafhion and the appearance are good, and which then may be fuppofed to be worth near one-third of its original coft, exclufive of the fuperfluous ornaments which are of no ufe to a fecond perfon at the difpofal.

By the moderate ufe fome people make of their carriages, the wheels are not worn out in four, five, or fix years; they may, therefore, compute their expence to be nearly eight pounds for repairs, for the time the ftrake wheels are in wear, ten pounds for the hoop wheel, and twelve pounds for the patent rim wheel, hammer-cloths, painting, and other additions excepted.

The expence of harnefs to be ufed with each carriage may be computed at five pounds per annum for a pair, and three pounds for a fingle harnefs.

Alluding to thofe rules, a perfon may judge of the fairnefs of his ufage, either by his coachman or coach-maker; for if the expence much exceeds this

this, the carriage muſt be badly built, or unfair
ly uſed.

———

PREPARATIONS FOR REPAIRS.

THE taking to pieces, and putting together,
as before obſerved, is a great part of the expence
of many, and the principal of ſome repairs; it is
therefore beſt, while the carriage is aſunder, to
do all that is neceſſary, as the frequent taking to
pieces does material injury, and the more there
is done at one time, the expence will, in proportion, be leſs; yet if the old timbers are perfect,
it is equally as improper to replace them with
new, as it is to let them remain if doubtful.

The expence of unhanging, taking to pieces,
putting together, and re-hanging, is the ſame in
ſmall as in large repairs, therefore the price for
unhanging, &c. will be ſeparately ſtated from that
of the repairs, ſo that to whatever extent the repairs are carried, the price for unhanging, &c.
may be added, and the whole amount obtained
with more accuracy.

It is alſo proper to obſerve under what circumſtance it is neceſſary to unhang the body, or
take the carriage to pieces, whereby thoſe expences

pences are incurred; for it is not uncommon to
do it without neceffity, and even to charge for it
when not done at all.   Painting the new timbers,
and fitting the old iron'work, are always neceffary to complete the repair, and are included in
the price; but if the failures in the iron work are
fo as to require mending, the expence is feparately charged for.

In repairing the upper carriage with any new
timber, the body muft be taken off, and if the
failure is in one of the tranfoms, or bars, that
end is obliged to be taken afunder; the iron
work muft alfo be taken off, but if the failure
lies in the perch, the carriage muft be wholly
taken to pieces.

In repairing the under or fore carriage, the
body need not be removed, the centre bolt or
pin, called the perch bolt, need only be taken
out, and the upper carriage, with the body on it,
may be fupported on a treffel, while the fore carriage is taken out, and repaired.

SECT.

SECT. 4.

NECESSARY MATTERS PREVIOUS TO REPAIRS.

Unhanging the Body,

IS the taking off the body from the carriage, in order to new paint, varnifh, japan, or to put in a new infide lining, to put in new pannels, to re-mount the body with plated or other mouldings ; to put on a new fet of braces, to re-fet or mend two or more of the fprings. All repairs to the doors, falfe linings, joints, head plates, lamps, &c. may be done without unhanging the body.

———

Unhanging the Body, and taking the Hind or Fore End to pieces,

Is taking the body from the carriage, and taking the fore or hind end framings to pieces, to put in new timbers, fuch as the hooping wings, fpring bed, tranfom, hind axletree bed, or budget bar.

C   *Unhanging*

*Unhanging the Body, and taking the Hind and Fore
End, or all the Carriage to pieces,*

Is taking off the body, and taking all the carriage to pieces, in order to put in a new perch,
new hind or fore tranfom, or fore tranfom, and
hind axletree bed, or new timber work throughout.

———•———

Taking off the Fore Carriage.

Is the taking off that part of a carriage, to
which the fore wheels are placed, for the purpofe of putting in new futchels, a fway bar, a
fore axletree bed, alfo for lining the perch bolt,
or perch bolt hole, the tranfom plate, the perch
at bottom, the fway bar, or to take out the fore
axletree.

———•———

*The Re-Hanging the Body, putting together the
Hind End, the Fore End, or both; and Re-fixing
the Fore Carriage,*

Are matters of courfe for completing the job,
and are included in the following prices, for
unhanging, &c.

PRICE

PRICE OF UNHANGING, AND TAKING TO PIECES, &c.

	£.	s.	d.
To unhanging and rehanging the body ——	o	2	6
To unhanging and rehanging the body, and taking the hind or fore end of the carriage to pieces, and putting together the fame ——	o	5	o
To unhanging and rehanging the body, taking the fore and hind end, or all the carriage, to pieces, and putting together again — —	o	7	6
To taking out the fore carriage, and putting under again —— —— ——	o	1	o
To taking off and refixing the boot ——	o	1	o
Ditto the coach-box —— ——	o	1	o

Thofe are to be charged for previous to the repairs which follow, except when the carriage-timbers are all new, and then the taking to pieces, putting together, &c. are not charged for.

———

SECT. 5.

REPAIRS OF THE TIMBER-WORK OF THE CARRIAGE AND BODY THROUGHOUT.

THE principal repairs to the timber-work are on the carriage-part, and they become neceffary either from decay, faulty wood, or being too light made; fometimes the failures are occafioned by accident, or violence, which may be

C 2 judged

judged of when taken afunder; when any of the
timbers begin to decay, the greater part may be
fuppofed to be in a fimilar flate, and failures then
become frequent; in which cafe, the whole timber-work of the carriage ought to be renewed,
in order to make the repair compleat and fubftantial, whereby expence, trouble, and danger
may be avoided, the perch being the main timber of the carriage with which the others are connected, and which fupports the weight of the
body, is frequently, from one caufe or other,
out of repair either in the plates or the timber.
It more frequently needs to be renewed, in confequence of having fettled with the weight of the
body, than from other failures, for, by its fettling, the carriage is diftorted from its proper
fhape, and thereby runs heavy.

　Repairs to bodies are lefs frequent than to
carriages, owing to their being placed in as eafy
a manner as poffible, for the accommodation of
the paffengers, and are thereby not fo much
racked or fhook about, as the carriage part una-
voidably is. The only likely repairs to bodies
is the mending the pannels or mouldings, which,
by accident, may be either bruifed or broken.
There are a variety of other repairs both in the
body and the carriage, befides the timber work,
all of which will be noticed under the feveral
fections to which the matter belongs.

　　　REPAIRS

REPAIRS TO THE TIMBER-WORK OF THE BODIES.

PANNELS, Including the Painting, without Ornaments.	Coach, Chariot, Landau, Vis-à-Vis.			Whole Pannel Phaeton, Gig, &c.			Half pannel Phaeton, G g, Chaife, & Whifkey.		
	£.	s.	d.	£.	s.	d.	£.	s.	d.
A door pannel —	1	4	0	0	15	0	0	15	0
A fide, or quarter ditto —	1	4	0	1	4	0	0	18	0
A back, or front ditto —	2	6	0	1	15	0	1	1	0
An upper back or front ditto -	2	6	0	—	—		—	—	
An upper fide, or quarter ditto	1	4	0	—	—		—	—	
To mending a pannel by battening or blocking on the infide -	0	10	6	0	10	6	0	10	6
A new fore footboard —	—	—		0	10	0	0	10	0
A pair of brackets —	—	—		0	8	0	0	8	0
One ditto —	—	—		0	5	0	0	5	0

The price for the pannels includes the painting without ornaments; but only two-thirds of the above prices are to be charged, if all the pannels are to be new painted, as the painting a pannel alone forms a material part of the expence, and, befides, feldom proves a match with the reft.

The taking up and putting down the lining are included in the expence with the pannels, as is alfo the brading, fcrewing, or otherwife putting on the old mouldings; but, if new mouldings are neceffary, they are feparately to be charged for.

MOULD.

MOULDINGS.

For every six inches or under.			£.	s.	d.
To fitting in a single piece of wood bead on the leather or mouldings	—	—	0	0	9
To fitting in a piece of moulding the breadth of the framing	—	—	0	1	6
To fitting in a piece of moulding cased round the framing	—	—	0	3	0
To a spliced end to a bottom side 18 inches long, or under	—	—	0	12	0

DOORS.

		£.	s.	d.
To easing each door	—	—	0	1	0
To fitting a piece of fencings to the lights	—	0	1	0
To a new garnishing-piece to the top of the door	0	3	0
To a ditto to the middle of ditto	—	0	5	0
To nailing the lining-boards of ditto	—	0	2	0
To a new hinge	—	—	—	0	2	0
To a new handle, silver plated	—	0	8	0
To a new spindle to the handle	—	—	0	2	6

PRICE

PRICE OF REPAIRING WITH NEW TIMBER-WORK FOUR-WHEELED CARRIAGES.

	Coach or Chariot.			Large Phaeton.			Middle-sized Phaeton.			Small Phaeton.		
	£.	s.	d	£.	s.	d	£.	s.	d.	£.	s.	d.
A straight perch —	3	3	0	3	0	0	2	13	0	2	10	0
A pair of hind hooping-wings — —	1	15	0	1	14	0	1	12	0	1	10	0
A fore hooping-piece, long or short — —	0	16	0	0	15	0	0	14	0	0	13	0
A fore transom —	1	8	0	1	6	0	1	4	0	1	2	0
A hind transom —	1	8	0	1	6	0	1	4	0	1	2	0
A budget-bar —	0	15	0	0	14	0	0	13	0	0	12	0
A hind axletree-bed —	1	8	0	1	6	0	1	4	0	1	2	0
A fore axletree-bed —	1	8	0	1	6	0	1	4	0	1	2	0
A pair of hind nunters —	0	12	0	0	11	0	0	10	0	0	9	0
A pair of futchels —	1	5	0	1	3	0	1	2	0	1	1	0
A splinter-bar —	0	16	0	0	15	0	0	14	0	0	13	0
A sway-bar —	0	9	0	0	8	0	0	7	0	0	6	0
A pole — —	0	15	0	0	14	0	0	13	0	0	12	0
A gib — —	0	1	6	0	1	3	0	1	0	0	1	0
This forms the compleat timber-work of a perch carriage, which, without the hind or fore blocks, amounts to (plain painting included) —	15	19	6	14	19	3	13	15	0	8	15	0
A perch with plated sides	4	4	0	4	0	0	3	13	0	3	10	0
One futchel	0	14	0	0	13	0	0	12	0	0	11	0
One nunter —	0	7	0	0	5	6	0	5	0	0	4	6
One hooping-wing —	0	18	0	0	17	0	0	16	0	0	15	0
A pair of fore nunters, if used —	0	15	0	0	14	0	0	13	0	0	12	0
One ditto —	0	7	6	0	7	0	0	6	6	0	6	0
A pair of wood locking stops to the fore bed -	0	4	0	0	4	0	0	4	0	0	4	0
A pair of round robbins to ditto —	0	10	0	0	10	0	0	9	0	0	8	0

For a compass perch to either carriage add one-fourth of the above price.

C 4   PERCH

PEARCH CARRIAGES.

	Coach or Chariot.	Large Phaeton.	Middle-fized Phaeton.	Small Phaeton.
	£. s. d	£. s. d.	£. s. d.	£. s. d.
The compleat new timber-work to a perch carriage, exclufive of hind or fore blocks, or coach-boxes, but includes plain painting — —	16 14 6	15 13 3	14 8 3	13 7 3

CRANE-NECK CARRIAGES.

	Coach or Chariot.	Large Phaeton.	Middle-fized Phaeton.	Small Phaeton.
	£. s. d	£. s. d	£. s d	£. s. d.
A fore tranfom —	1 15 0	1 11 6	1 10 0	1 10 0
A horn bar —	1 1 0	0 18 0	0 17 0	0 16 0
A fore bar —	0 15 0	0 14 0	0 13 0	0 12 0
A pair of fore wings —	0 16 0	0 14 0	0 13 0	0 13 0
A whole cafing to the horizontal wheel —	0 16 0	0 14 0	0 13 0	0 13 0
A pair of under felly of wheel-pieces —	0 10 0	0 10 0	0 9 0	0 9 0
A hind tranfom —	1 10 6	1 10 0	1 8 0	1 7 0
A hind axletree-bed —	1 15 0	1 11 6	1 10 0	1 8 0
A fore axletree-bed —	1 10 0	1 8 0	1 6 0	1 5 0
A pair of futchels —	1 8 0	1 6 0	1 5 0	1 4 0
A fplinter-bar —	0 16 0	0 15 0	0 14 0	0 13 0
A pole —	0 15 0	0 15 0	0 14 0	0 13 0
A gib —	0 1 6	0 1 6	0 1 0	0 1 0
Sums total for new timber-work to a crane-neck carriage, agreeable to the prefent mode of building —	13 9 0	11 9 0	11 13 0	11 4 0

A fingle

	Coach or Chariot.	Large Phaeton.	Middle-sized Phaeton.	Small Phaeton.
	£ s. d.	£ s. d.	£ s. d.	£ s. d.
A single piece of wheel casing — —	0 5 0	0 4 6	0 4 0	0 3 6
A single under felly or wheel-piece —	0 5 0	0 4 6	0 4 0	0 3 6
A single futchel —	0 16 0	0 15 0	0 14 0	0 13 0
A single fore wing —	0 9 0	0 8 0	0 7 6	0 7 0
Wood casing to the cranes throughout —	2 12 6	2 6 0	2 2 0	2 0 0

Shafts to a four-wheeled carriage, either perch or crane-neck, for one horse to draw by —		
A pair complete —	1 1 0
One shaft —	0 10 0
A bar —	0 7 6

———

PRICE OF REPAIRING TWO-WHEELED CAR-RIAGES WITH NEW TIMBER-WORK.

	Curricle.	Gig.	Whiskey.
	£. s. d.	£. s. d.	£. s. d.
A pair of shafts — —	2 14 0	2 16 0	2 18 0
A pair of hind bars —	1 10 0	1 8 0	1 4 0
A pair of fore ditto for the curricle, and one for the gig -	1 10 0	0 15 0	0 12 0
A pair of hind nunters for the gig, and a pair of fore and hind ditto for the curricle -	0 18 0	0 9 0	0 8 0
A pair of splinter-bars for the curricle, and one for the gig, &c. — — —	0 10 0	0 5 0	0 5 0
A pole for the curricle —	0 15 0		
A ladder-prop for ditto —	0 12 0		
Carry over —	8 9 0	5 13 0	5 9 0

The

	Curricle.			G'g.			Whiſkey.		
	£.	s.	d	£.	s.	d.	£.	s.	d.
Brought over —	8	9	0	5	13	0	5	7	0
The pole, the extra fore-bar, the ſplinter-bar, nunters, and the ladder-prop, to make the gig a curricle — —	—	—		2	16	0	2	16	0
A pair of ſhafts for the curricle, ſo as to be uſed with one horſe — —	1	1	0						
The timber-work for the gig curricle, or curricle gig —	9	10	0	8	9	0	8	3	0
A ſingle ſhaft to the chaiſe, or ſhaft and main ſide to the curricle — —	1	10	0	1	8	0	1	10	0
A ſingle bar — —	0	15	0	0	14	0	0	12	0
A ſingle nunter — —	0	5	0	0	5	0	0	5	0
A ſingle ſplinter —	0	5	0	0	5	0	0	5	0
A ladder-prop new ſide —	0	7	0						
A ditto new croſs-bar —	0	4	0						

SECT.

SECT. 6.

WHEELS.

WHEN new wheels are put on to old carriages, the old wheels are most frequently taken in exchange; and, to regular customers, one guinea for the set, or half a guinea for the pair, is the usual allowance, let them be good or bad; but to chance customers, the price to be given for the old wheels is in proportion to their value.

The old wheels are mostly the perquisite of the coachman, and the allowance is then given to them; but the servant can have no claim on them, unless he has been one year, or as long in his place as the wheels have been in use.

	Coach.			Chariot or large Phaeton.			Middle-sized Phaeton.			Small Phaeton.			Curricle or Gig.			Whiskey or Chair.		
	£.	s.	d.	£.	s.	d.	£.	s.	d.	£.	s.	d	£.	s.	d	£.	s.	d.
Patent	11	11	0	10	10	0	9	9	0	8	8	0	5	5	0	4	14	6
Hooped	8	18	6	8	8	0	7	7	0	6	6	0	4	4	0	3	13	6
Straked	6	16	6	6	16	6	6	6	0	5	15	6	3	10	0	3	3	0

Agreeable to the present custom, these are the general charges for new wheels put on old carriages, and which also includes the painting and boxing them with the old boxes.

The coach and chariot wheels, for those prices, have for the hind wheels fourteen, and for the fore wheels twelve spokes in each; the middle and small phaeton have ten and twelve spokes in each; the curricle or gig fourteen; and the whiskey or chair twelve.

The

The rims of the wheels are what moftly wear out firft, and are fometimes new rung with both iron and timber; the ringing is about one-third the price of new wheels, and, if the fpokes and ftocks are good, will anfwer the purpofe, but not otherwife.

A PAIR OF EIGHTS.		Patent. £. s. d.	Hooped. £. s. d.	Straked. £. s. d.
New tyre	— —	1 10 0	1 10 0	1 0 0
New fellies	— —	1 15 0	1 0 0	1 0 0
A PAIR OF TENS.				
New tyre with nails	—	1 15 0	1 15 0	1 5 0
New fellies	— —	2 0 0	1 5 0	1 5 0
A PAIR OF TWELVES.				
New tyre with nails	—	2 0 0	2 0 0	1 10 0
New fellies	— —	2 15 0	1 10 0	1 10 0
A PAIR OF FOURTEENS.				
New tyre	— —	2 5 0	1 5 0	1 15 0
New fellies	— —	2 15 0	1 15 0	1 15 0

The taking off the tyre, mending, and putting on again, with new nails to each wheel.	An Eight. £. s. d.	A ten.	A twelve.	A fourteen.
Hoop or patent rim with nails —	0 8 0	0 10 0	0 12 0	0 14 0
Ditto with bolts —	0 10 0	0 12 0	0 14 6	0 16 0
Strake rim —	0 7 6	0 9 0	0 10 0	0 13 0

Faftening

	£.	s.	d.
Faftening each end of a ftrake — —	o	1	o
Nailing a hoop, for each nail — —	o	o	6
Driving backwards or forwards the axletree or wheel-box, and tightening it in the wheel by wedges — — —	o	2	o
A clip for faftening the felly — —	o	2	o
Mending each fpoke with fpoke-plates —	o	1	o
Taking off two ftrakes, and cutting the felly fhorter at the joint, to bring the timbers to a bearing, when fhrunk with ftanding by —	o	5	o

SECT. 7.

BOOTS AND BUDGETS,

THE leather-work is what principally requires to be repaired in boots and budgets, the other parts are moftly mended with plates of iron when defective.

	£.	s.	d.
The taking off and putting on either a boot or budget	o	1	o

THE TRUNK BOOT.

	£.	s.	d.
Taking off the front plate, taking up the leather, and putting on one or two new hinges, refixing, &c. — —	o	5	o
A new faftening for the lid — —	o	2	o
A new thumb-nut or ferew for ditto —	o	1	6

A new

	£.	s.	d.
A new lid or door　—　　—　　　—	0	7	6
New piece of welting, under fix inches　—	0	0	9
For every fix inches of ditto　—　　—	0	0	9

THE PLATFORM BOOT OR BUDGET.

	Large.			Middle.			Small.		
	£.	s.	d.	£.	s.	d.	£.	s.	d.
A new cover　—　　—	2	2	0	1	15	0	1	10	0
A ditto welted　—　　—	2	10	0	2	5	0	1	15	0
A new end to the cover　—	0	12	0	0	10	0	0	8	0
Ditto welted　—　　—	0	15	0	0	12	0	0	10	0
A new leather fide　—	0	18	0	0	15	0	0	12	0

	£.	s.	d.
The leather ftripped off, and the fide iron mended, and the leather fewed on again　—	0	12	0
A new ftrap　—　　—　　　—	0	1	0
A new buckle and ftrap　—　　　—	0	2	0
Welting, under fix inches, and for every fix inches	0	0	9
A top crofs piece to fupport the cover　—	0	5	0

SECT. 8.

COACH-BOXES,

THE neceffary repairs to coach-boxes are moftly to the feat, the cradle, the footboard, or the ledge; the timber-work of the common coach-box fometimes fails, but of the others it very feldom does, and is more eafily mended

with

with plates, or bolts of iron, than with new timber; it will therefore be only neceſſary to ſtate the repair throughout of the common coach-box, which, except the fore ſtandards and ſtays, are the ſame in all.

	£.	s.	d.
The taking off the coach-box to do any repair, and re-fixing it again — — —	0	1	0
A pair of fore ſtandards — —	1	1	0
One ditto — — —	0	10	6
A pair of ſtays — — —	0	18	0
One ditto — — —	0	10	0
A fore footboard — —	0	8	0
A pair of croſs or ſtandard bars —	0	10	0
One ditto — — —	0	6	0
A footboard ledge — —	0	2	6
A ditto with ſcroll ends — —	0	5	0
A cork ledge — — —	0	2	6
The wood-work complete to the old iron-work, including painting — —	2	19	6
If ornamented brackets are uſed, the price is, for a pair of middlingly-ornamented brackets —	0	10	6
A pair of coach-box ſteps — —	0	12	0

REPAIRS TO THE SEAT AND CRADLE.

	£.	s.	d.
Taking off and refixing the ſeat —	0	1	6
A new lath for the ſeat — —	0	2	0
Covering the ſeat with new baize —	0	3	6
New ſtuffing the ſeat —	0	2	6

Two

	£.	s.	d.
Two new galling-leathers to the feat	o	2	6
One ditto	o	1	o
Lining with leather the two ends or four corners of the feat	o	2	o
Lining one end, or two corners, with leather	o	1	o
For each new thong for the hammercloth to be tied on with	o	o	3
A new loop or billet for the cradle	o	1	6
Two new feat-ftraps	o	4	o
One ditto	o	2	o

SECT. 9.

RAISED HIND AND FORE ENDS, PUMP HANDLES AND SHORT BLOCKS.

THERE are few carriages without one or other of thofe things, except phaetons or chaifes; and, when carriages are repaired, with new timber, throughout, thofe things are moftly neceffary to make them complete; therefore, to any carriage, with either fort of blocks, pump-handles, &c. add the price of them to the price of the compleat repair, as before ftated.

A pair

	Plain.			Middlingly ornamented.			Much ornamented.		
	£.	s.	d.	£.	s.	d.	£.	s.	d.
A pair of pump handles —	1	10	6	2	5	0	3	0	0
One ditto — —	0	16	0	1	4	0	1	12	0
A pair of short blocks —	1	4	0	1	16	0	2	8	0
One ditto — —	0	13	0	1	0	0	1	6	0
A whole footboard for either -	0	7	6	0	8	6	0	9	6
A half ditto — —	0	4	0	0	5	0	0	6	0
BUDGET BLOCKS, or RAISED FORE ENDS.									
A pair of side blocks —	1	0	0	1	10	0	2	0	0
One ditto — —	0	10	0	0	15	0	1	0	0
A front block —	0	10	0	0	15	0	1	0	0

HIND STANDARDS WITH FOOTMANS' CUSHIONS.

	Middlingly ornamented.		
	£.	s.	d.
A pair of hind standards, with bar and wings complete — — —	3	3	0
A pair of hind standards with a bar —	2	5	0
One standard — — —	0	15	0
A crofs bar — — —	0	15	0
A pair of wings — —	0	18	0
One wing — — —	1	1	0
A new bottom to the footman's cushion —	0	7	9
Covering the top with leather —	0	12	0
Covering with japan, or other leather, the sides and ends — — —	0	5	0
Ditto, if welted — — —	0	10	0
Covering one side or end only — —	0	2	0
Ditto, if welted — — —	0	5	0

The standards and bar are sometimes not carved, but only painted in imitation thereof, and are then only half the price of thofe stated.

D

SECT. 10.

REPAIRS TO THE IRON-WORK.

THE repairs to the iron-work are more fre-quent than to the wood-work, in particular the ſtays, plates, and bolts, which, whether to large or ſmall carriages of any deſcription, are nearly the ſame in expence either for new or repairing. The expence for taking to pieces and putting to-gether is included with the prices here ſtated.

	Coach, Chariot, or large Phaeton.			Middle or ſmall-ſized Phaeton, or Gig.		
CRANES.	£.	s.	d.	£.	s.	d.
To mending the pair if broke, or altering the form of them	3	3	0	2	12	6
To mending one if broke, or altering if ſtrained	1	15	0	1	10	0
AXLETREES, each.						
To a new axletree arm, fitting the old box, and reſetting it to the way	0	18	0	0	15	9
To a new axletree nut	0	4	0	0	3	6
To fitting the nut to the ſcrew	0	1	0	0	1	0
To ſetting the axletree to rights, or ſetting fair if ſtrained	0	8	0	0	7	0
To a ſhoulder waſher	0	1	0	0	1	0
To a dozen of lince-pins	0	2	6	0	2	6
WHEEL-BOXES, per pair.						
To a pair of new ones	0	18	0	0	16	0
To a ſingle box	0	10	0	0	9	0
To fitting the pair of old ones to the arms	0	8	0	0	7	0
To cutting ſhorter a pair to make them fit the arms	0	6		0	5	0

Taking out and putting in the boxes to the wheels are included.

SPRINGS

SMALL SPRINGS.	Coach, Chariot, or large Phaeton.			Middle or small sized Phaeton, or Gig.			Grafshopper or double el- bow fprings.		
	£.	s.	d.	£.	s.	d.	£.	s.	d.
A main or back plate —	0	15	0	0	12	0	0	12	0
A long gut plate — —	0	12	0	0	10	0	0	10	0
A fhort gut ditto — —	0	8	0	0	7	0	0	7	0
A fhackle eye only to the plate	0	5	0	0	5	0	0	5	0
An out or infide flap to the fpring	0	6	0	0	5	0	0	5	0
A hoop and rivet to ditto —	0	3	0	0	3	0	0	3	0
A rivet only — —	0	1	6	0	1	6	0	1	6
A fhackle for a fpring —	0	2	6	0	2	6	—	—	
A Jew's-harp ftaple —	—	—		—	—		0	7	6
A fide to ditto — —	—	—		—	—		0	4	0
A new fcroll iron —	—	—		—	—		0	5	0
Mending of ditto —	—	—		—	—		0	2	6
A lugg plate — —	—	—		—	—		0	2	6
Taking to pieces, cleaning, and fetting each pair of fprings to another form — —	0	12	0	0	10	6	0	10	6
Setting up or down by altering at the bearings or flap only	0	6	0	0	5	0	0	5	0

———

STAYS AND PLATES.

WITH new timber-work the fitting the plates are not to be charged for, only the mending, if broken. The following are the charges for making new, or mending old, iron-work to the carriage throughout; the fhortening or lengthening are all charged the fame price, and are each confidered under the title of mending.

D 2   STAYS.

STAYS.	New.			Mending.		
	£.	s.	d.	£.	s.	d.
A spring stay	0	4	6	0	2	0
A horn or budget bar stay	0	7	0	0	2	0
A coach-box stay	0	5	0	0	2	0
A bind standard stay	0	8	0	0	2	0
A wheel iron	0	5	0	0	1	6
A wheel iron shortened, or set in at the eye	—	—		0	0	9
A seat-iron for a coachman's seat	0	5	0	0	2	6
A bottom or main stay to a chaise or curricle	0	15	0	0	3	6

PLATES.						
A transom-plate	0	7	6	0	2	6
A whole wheel plate	1	10	0	0	7	6
A half ditto	1	0	0	0	5	0
A bottom perch plate	0	18	0	0	3	6
A bottom wearing plate	0	5	0	0	2	6
A side perch plate	1	11 -	6	0	7	0
A set of standard plates for a coach-box	0	12	0	0	6	0
A pair of ditto	0	6	0	0	3	0
A sway-bar plate	0	5	0	0	2	6
A nose or crofs-key plate	0	2	6	0	1	6
A pump-handle plate	0	2	6	0	1	6
A short-block plate	0	2	0	0	1	6

SOCKETS.						
A double socket for a curricle-gig shaft	0	10	0	0	2	0
A pair of splinter-bar sockets	0	5	0	0	2	0
A pair of ditto for a chaise, with dragon's tongues and eyes	0	3	6	0	1	0

BOLTS and NUTS.						
A bolt and nut, under six inches	0	1	0	0	0	6
A ditto, from six to twelve inches	0	1	6	0	0	6
A nut only	0	0	3	0	0	2
A perch bolt	0	3	6	0	1	6
A nut for ditto	0	1	0	0	0	6
A key for ditto	0	0	6	0	0	3
A splinter-bar roller bolt	0	2	6	0	0	9
A small T head bolt and thumb screw	0	1	0	0	0	6
A large thumb nut, or screw only, for a boot	0	1	6	0	0	6
A nut head-screw	0	0	4	0	0	6
A pole pin	0	0	9	0	0	6

RINGS, LOOPS, HOOKS, STAPLES, HOOPS, and STEPS.	New.			Mending.		
	£.	s.	d.	£.	s.	d.
A plain body loop for a coach or chariot	o	7	6	o	3	6
A ditto for chaise or phaeton ——	o	6	o	o	3	o
A check-brace ring — ——	o	1	o	o	o	6
A collar-brace ring — ——	o	1	o	o	o	6
A double ditto ——	o	3	o	o	1	o
A pole ring — — ——	o	3	o	o	1	6
A pair of breeching staples ——	o	3	o	o	1	o
A pole staple —— ——	o	1	o	o	o	6
A footman's step —— ——	o	6	o	o	2	o
A single chaise step — ——	o	7	6	o	3	o
A double ditto — ——	o	15	o	o	4	6
A pair of shaft-hooks, or tug-plates —	o	3	6	o	1	6
An axletree hoop — ——	o	2	6	o	1	3
A perch ditto —— ——	o	3	c	o	1	6

———

SECT. 11.

TRIMMINGS AND LININGS.

THE statement for repairing the lining with new trimmings are for the common $2\frac{1}{2}$ inch broad worsted lace, with flat taffels to the holders, the different value of the other forts must be referred to in Vol. I.

The lining and putting on of the holders are included in the prices stated for them.

       THE

THE TRIMMINGS.

	£.	s.	d.
A pair of infide hand holders complete	0	18	0
A pair of fwing holders	0	12	0
A fet of glafs-ftrings or holders, for either coach or chaife	0	16	0
A fet of new French ftrings	0	6	0
A fet of new rofes for a pair of hand holders	0	7	6
Mending the lining of holders or ftrings	0	1	6
Mending each button-hole of ditto	0	0	3
For every yard or lefs of new feaming lace	0	0	9
Ditto of pafting lace	0	0	9
Ditto of binding, 2½ inch broad	0	2	6
Pafting down the old lace, per yard, or lefs	0	0	3

———

THE LINING.

	£.	s.	d.
Taking up and putting down the back and two fides of either coach, chariot, phaeton, or chaife, for the infide framing to be repaired	0	3	0
Taking up and putting down a door-lining of a coach or chariot, or the front lining of a chariot, for repairing the wood work	0	2	0
Taking up the feat roll and fall, and putting them down again	0	2	0
Wet fcouring the lining	0	10	6
Dry ditto	0	7	6
Taking out the falfe lining, wafhing, and putting in again	0	12	0
Ditto, if the holders and ftrings are covered	0	16	0

Taking

	£.	s.	d.
Taking out the old ſtuffing from one long or a pair of ſhort cuſhions, quilting with the ſame, and ſtuffing them with the old ſtuffing —	0	3	6
Ditto with new tuffts — —	0	4	0
For every pound of flock ſtuffing added —	0	1	6
A new bottom carpet, bound round the edges, for a coach or chariot — —	0	10	6
Covering the two bottom ſides with new leather	0	6	0
An oil-cloth or carpet for a chaiſe —			

———

STEPS, GLASSES, BLINDS, SHUTTERS, CURTAINS, &c.

STEPS.	Double.			Treble.		
	£.	s.	d.	£.	s.	d.
New trimming the whole with new leather, carpeting the treads, and facing the front with new cloth and lace —	1	15	0	2	12	6
New carpeting only — —	0	10	6	0	15	0
New facing only — —	0	8	0	0	8	0
One leather daſh only — —	0	4	0	0	4	0
A new ſtep-board fitted in —	0	2	6	0	2	6
A new iron tread, untrimming and re-trimming —	0	7	6	0	7	6
A new main ſide, new head, and ditto -	0	9	0	0	9	0
A new rivet to the joint —	0	2	6	0	2	6
Faſtening the joint-rivets —	0	1	6	0	1	6
A ſet of new ſtops — —	0	3	0	0	3	0
One ditto — —	0	1	0	0	1	0
Faſtening the ſet of ſtops —	0	1	0	0	1	0

D 4   GLASSES.

GLASSES.

	£.	s.	d.
A new door glaſs, common ſize — —	1	10	0
A coach front ditto —	1	4	0
An oval or octagon glaſs behind — —	0	5	0
A ſet of new glaſs frames covered with new cloth	1	4	0
Ditto with new lace two inches wide —	2	2	0
For each new ſide to the frame, covered with new cloth — — —	0	4	6
Ditto with old cloth and lace — —	0	2	6
New covering the ſet of frames with new cloth	0	15	0
For each frame ditto — —	0	7	0
For each ſide ditto — —	0	2	0
Renailing on a bottom glaſs-ſtring —	0	0	6
Securing the two corners of each frame with thin plates — —	0	1	0
Silvering the ſet of old rollers — —	0	5	0

For Lamp Glaſſes, ſee Lamps.

SHUTTERS.

	£.	s.	d.
New ſtringing the ſet — —	0	5	0
A new top, bottom, or ſide — —	0	2	6
A new pannel — — —	0	3	0
A new loop only — —	0	0	9

VENETIAN BLINDS.

	£.	s.	d.
New painting and ſtringing a ſet —	1	1	0
A new lath to a blind — —	0	5	0
A new ſide, top or bottom — —	0	5	0
		Mending	

	£.	s.	d.
Mending the lock fpring	o	5	o
Eafing each glafs frame, fhutter, or blind, to flide in the grooves	o	1	o

SPRING CURTAINS,

INCLUDING THE TAKING DOWN AND PUTTING UP.

	£.	s.	d.
New filk to the four barrels	1	10	o
Turning the filk upfide down ·	o	10	o
A new curtain ftick	o	2	6
A new filk line for each curtain to run on	o	1	o
Mending the curtain barrel	o	5	o
Setting the curtain to rights when the fpring has loft its force	o	1	6

SQUABS.

	£.	s.	d
The taking down and re-fixing a pair of fquabs to a coach or chariot	o	2	o
New binding with narrow lace a fide or end	o	1	o
Putting on new loops, each	o	o	6

CHECK-STRINGS.

	£.	s.	d.
A new check ftring	o	1	o
A ditto with taffel	o	2	o
A check-ftring eye	o	o	6

SECT.

SECT. 12.

HAMMERCLOTHS and FOOTMAN-HOLDERS.

THE expence for repairing a hammercloth depends on the quantity of work done, and materials ufed, thereon at the time, which cannot even be furinifed at; thofe are for the ufual repairs to hammercloths, but further than what are ftated cannot be given.

HAMMERCLOTHS.

ALL NEW TRIMMINGS ARE TO BE CHARGED FOR AT PER YARD.

	£	s.	d.
The taking to pieces, dying, preffing, and remaking a fix-breadth hammercloth, with the old trimmings of lace only	2	2	0
Ditto with the old trimmings of lace and fringe	2	10	0
Extra for a new thick canvafs lining	0	15	0
Shortening the front by taking out a piece from the top of the fall, and replaiting it	0	7	6
Lining with leather, or ftout canvafs, the two ends or four corners	0	4	0
For each new loop	0	0	3
Sewing the lace where ripped, per yard, or under	0	0	6
Scouring a plain-trimmed hammercloth	0	7	6
Ditto a fringed-trimmed ditto	0	10	6

OIL.

OIL-SKIN HAMMERCLOTHS.

	£.	s.	d.
A new half top —— ——	0	5	0
A new end —— —— ——	0	7	0
A new back or front —— ——	0	10	0

FOOTMAN-HOLDERS.

	£	s.	d.
A new pair of footman-holders, with billets and buckles — —— ——	0	8	0
A pair of lace 2½ inch ditto with ditto —	0	12	0
For a new billet and buckle only to a footman's holder . —— — ——.	0	2	6
A new billet only to ditto — ——	0	1	6
To sewing the lace-holders if ripped, each —	0	0	9

SECT. 13.

PLATED WORK,

IF the old plating is bad, and requires to be replaced with new, a reference for the price muft be had to Vol. I.; the following are for the repairs generally done. Plating that is worn through cannot be replated but at as much expence as new would coft. The mouldings or ornaments fhanking and refixing are the

2   principal

principal of the repairs required to plated work.

	£.	s.	d.
Taking off the old moulding and putting in new shanks, and putting it on again, at per foot	0	0	6
The taking off, cleaning, and putting on six head-plates to a coach or chariot — —	0	2	6
Ditto, with new plated pins or nails ———	0	5	0
For each large plated head-plate, nail, or pin —	0	0	2
For each small ditto —— ——	0	0	1
The taking off and putting on a pair of sham joints	0	1	6
The fastening down the moulding with a plated nail or pin —— —— ——	0	0	6
A large plated knee boot button ——	0	1	3
A small ditto ——— ——	0	0	9
A large silvered ditto —— ——	0	0	6
A small dittto ——— ——	0	0	4
Painting a pair of lamps —— —	0	3	0

SECT. 14.

L A M P S.

THE repairs to lamps are very frequent, for, on account of their being so prominent, the glasses are often broken by the coachman backing in low gateways; the size of the lamp makes no difference in the price for the repairs.

A front

	£.	s.	d.
A front convex glaſs to a globe lamp	0	5	0
A front ditto to an Italian or oval ditto	0	3	6
A ſide glaſs to ditto	0	2	0
Repairing the back by ſoldering on the iron-work, and ſetting it fair	0	2	6
New ſticking or repairing the reflector	0	2	6
A new plated barrel	0	3	6
A ditto plain	0	2	6
To a new ſpring for the candle	0	1	6
A new head, plain	0	1	6
Ditto, plated	0	2	0
A new grate to either head	0	1	6
A ſtaple to the barrel for the ſtrap	0	0	9
A keeper to ditto	0	0	9
A pair of lamp-ſtraps and buckles	0	2	0
A lamp-fork	0	1	6
A new hinge or faſtener to the door	0	1	0
Faſtening the iron-work of the lamps to the body	0	0	6

SECT. 14.

PAINTING.

THE price for new painting old carriages may be known by deducting one-fourth from the prices ſtated for painting in the firſt volume; but, as that may be troubleſome to the reader, they are here briefly ſtated, with the bodies and carriages ſeparate, as alſo the prices for only japanning and varniſhing them, which, as they are often ſeparately ſo done, it will give more ready information of the whole or ſeparate prices.

3   OLD

OLD BODIES NEW PAINTED AND VARNISHED.

	Coach.			Chariot.			Large Phaeton.			Middle-fized Phaeton.			Small Phaeton, or Curricle.			Half Pan-nel.			Cane or Ribbed.		
	£.	s.	d.	£.	s.	d.	£.	s.	d.	£.	s.	d.	£.	s.	d.	£.	s.	d.	£.	s.	d.
An old body plain painted and varnished	2	5	0	1	17	6	1	10	0	1	8	6	1	4	6	1	2	6	0	13	6
Picking out the mouldings	0	10	6	0	10	6	0	7	6	0	7	6	0	7	6	0	7	6	0	7	6
Japanning the quarters of a coach and chariot, and the doors and fword-cafe of a chaife	1	17	6	1	10	0	0	8	0	0	8	0	0	8	0	0	8	0	0	8	6
Polifhing the pannels	2	10	0	2	0	0	1	5	0	0	1	5	0	5	3	0	1	1	0			
High varnifhing the pannels	5	15	0	4	4	0	3	3	0	3	3	0	3	3	0	2	10	0			

OLD CARRIAGES NEW PAINTED.

	Coach.			Chariot.			Large Phaeton.			Middle-fized Phaeton.			Small Phaeton, or Curricle.			Half Pan-nel.			Cane or Ribbed.		
	£.	s.	d.	£.	s.	d.	£.	s.	d.	£.	s.	d.	£.	s.	d.	£.	s.	d.	£.	s.	d.
An old carriage painted, the boot and budget japanned	1	11	6	1	11	6	1	4	0	1	2	0	1	0	0	0	16	0	0	16	0
Picking out the mouldings one colour	1	1	0	1	1	0	0	18	0	0	15	0	0	12	0	0	10	0	0	10	0
Ditto, two colours	1	15	0	1	15	0	1	11	6	1	10	0	1	4	0	0	18	0	0	18	0
Oil varnifhing the carriage after painting, which gives the paint a fine glofs, and very much preferves it	0	15	0	0	15	0	0	15	0	0	15	0	0	10	0	0	10	0	0	10	0

VARNISHING ONLY.

IF the ground colour of the body is good, varnifhing will fometimes do nearly as well as new painting.

VARNISHING.	Coach. £. s. d	Chariot. £. s. d.	Phaeton or Chaife. £. s. d	Ha. pannel Phaeton or Chaife. £. s. d.
The rubbing down, and once varnifhing the pannels — —	0 12 0	0 10 6	0 7 6	0 6 0
To twice ditto —	1 0 0	0 18 0	0 12 0	0 10 6
JAPANNING.				
To once japanning the upper parts of a coach or chariot, or the doors and fword-cafe of a chaife or phaeton — —	0 10 6	0 7 6	0 3 6	0 3 6
To twice doing the fame	0 18 0	0 12 0	0 5 0	0 5 0

If the body is unhung for the varnifhing, as it moftly is, 2s. 6d. muft be added for that trouble, but cannot be charged for twice under one repair.

BOOTS, &c.	A Trunk Boot. £. s. d.	A Salifbury Boot. £. s. d	A Dafhing Leather. £. s. d.	A Footman-cufhion Frame. £. s. d.
To once japanning —	0 2 6	0 3 6	0 2 0	0 2 0
To twice ditto —	0 4 0	0 5 5	0 3 6	0 3 0

PAINTING

PAINTING of ARMS, CRESTS, and MANTLES.

THESE ornaments are fometimes wifhed to be preferved, to fave the expence of new painting them ; the trouble of painting the ground colour is then greater, and increafeth the price 1s. 6d. for preferving each ornament, whether the mantle, arms, or crefts.

	£.	s.	d.
Each new mantle painted in relief, or contrafted colours —— —— ——	0	7	6
For each coat of arms ditto — —	0	7	0
For each creft ditto —— ——	0	4	0
For each cypher in gold or colours ——	0	3	0
Rubbing out the old, and laying a frefh ground in the mantle to repaint any other arms —	0	1	6

PAINTING OF WHEELS.

IF new wheels are put on, when the carriage is to be new painted, the following prices for plain painting them are to be deduted from the former prices of wheels; this will alfo fhew what the value of painting a fet, or pair, of wheels amounts to, if done alone, as they fometimes are.

Plain

	Coach, Chariot, or large Phaeton.			Middle or small sized Phaeton.			Curricle, Whiskey, or Gig.		
	£.	s.	d.	£.	s.	d.	£.	s.	d.
Plain painting the wheels —	0	12	0	0	10	6	0	6	0
Picking them out one colour —	0	4	0	0	4	0	0	2	0
Ditto, two colours —	0	6	0	0	6	0	0	3	0
The rims picked out two colours —	0	8	0	0	8	0	0	4	0
Ditto, one colour —	0	4	0	0	4	0	0	2	0

PANNELS.

THE pannels, if bruifed, are not eafily repaired, fo as to be undifcovered; as new and old colours do not eafily match, the readieft method is, if the paint is rubbed through to the wood, to fill up the blemifhed place, with a hard ftopping, level with the other furface, and then colour and varnifh it; but, if the colour is not a good one to match, the whole pannel fhould be done, preferving, at the fame time, the ornaments, if any.

	£.	s.	d.
Mending a pannel by ftopping, and painting to match — — —	0	5	0
New painting and varnifhing the whole door or fide pannel — — —	0	10	6
Ditto the back or front pannel —	0	15	0

F.

SECT.

SECT. 15.

CHAISE HEADS, WINGS, KNEE FLAPS, AND DASHING LEATHERS.

NEGLECT is the principal caufe of fome of thofe things wanting repairs, in particular the chaife heads and knee flaps, which, if not kept properly fuppled, the leather will contract and rot, and require much ftraining to bring it to its bearing ; and the front rib, or flatt, of a chaife head is what is likely to be broken thereby.

The taking off the mouldings and leather-work and putting them on again are included in the ftatements.

CHAISE HEADS.

	Round.			Square.		
	£.	s.	d.	£.	s.	d.
A new entire front flatt —	0	12	0	0	10	6
A new top or fide to ditto ——	0	8	0	0	7	0
Mending the corner joint with a plate —	0	5	0	0	5	0
A new neck-plate to the flatt ——	0	2	6	0	2	6
A new prop for the joint ——	0	2	0	0	2	0
A new joint ——	0	5	0	0	5	0
Setting ditto if ftrained, mending it if broken, fhortening or lengthening it —	0	2	0	0	2	6
A new cloth lining complete ——	4	0	6	3	0	0
A new ferge ditto — ——	2	0	0	1	10	0
A new ferge fide or back ——	0	15	0	0	10	6
A new cloth ditto — ——	1	5	0	1	0	0
A new leather back — —	1	10	6	1	5	0
A new valent ——	0	15	0	0	12	0
Mending ditto at each feam or corner —	0	1	0	0	1	0

WINGS.

WINGS.

	£.	s.	d.
Trimming the old wing-frames, with new cloth, leather, and lace	1	6	0
Covering the old frames with new neat's leather to the old trimmings	0	12	0
Ditto with bafil leather	0	9	0
Ditto with cloth and lace $2\frac{1}{2}$ inches wide	0	18	0
Ditto with cloth only	0	7	6
Ditto with lace only	0	12	0
A new plated frame	0	16	0
Setting up or down a wing that is ftrained	0	1	6
Faftening a wing with a new nut-headed fcrew	0	1	0
Ditto with a new key-bow ring	0	2	6

KNEE BOOTS, OR FLAPS.

	£.	s.	d.
A new cloth fall bound with lace	0	8	0
A new cloth lining	0	10	0
A new ferge or linen ditto	0	5	0
Two new lugs for the top to faften it up by	0	2	6
Sewing on one old lug or flap	0	0	6
A new check to the fide	0	10	6
A new bottom piece for the knee-boot, which takes off	0	5	0
For each new filver button to the top	0	0	6
For ditto for the fide	0	0	6
For lining each button-hole	0	0	6
For a piece of welting under fix inches	0	0	6

DASHING

DASHING LEATHERS.

	Large.			Small.		
	£.	s.	d.	£.	s.	d.
To ſtripping the frame, mending it, and ſewing on the leather again ———	0	7	6	0	5	0
To covering the old frame with new leather ——— ———	0	15	0	0	12	0
To a new back-ſtay — ———	0	3	6	0	3	0

SECT. 16.

B R A C E S.

NEW braces to phaetons or chaiſes are ſeldom found neceſſary; if, however, they ſhould be required, their prices may be collected from the firſt volume. The prices for mending of braces are what are principally required to be known, and whether for coach, chariot, phaeton, or chaiſe, the prices for repairing them are the ſame.

SECT.

REPAIRS TO THE BRACES.

	Main Brace.			Collar Brace.			Check Brace.			Pole Piece.		
	£.	s.	d.	£.	s.	d.	£.	s.	d.	£.	s.	d.
Splicing a piece on the wearing place —	0	1	6	0	1	0	0	0	6	0	1	0
Shortening by cutting at the buckle or point end, and making it good by sewing — —	0	2	0	0	1	0	0	0	6	0	1	0
Mending by splicing on a piece at the point, for every six inches or under — — —	0	2	6	0	1	6	0	0	9	0	1	6
To sewing in a new loop	0	0	6	0	0	4	0	0	3	0	0	4
Sewing each place where ripped — —	0	0	6	0	0	6	0	0	3	0	0	6

——

SECT. 17.

TRAVELLING REQUISITES.

IT is but seldom these things are repaired, for, when defective, new is mostly substituted; but, when done, the prices are nearly as follow:

TRUNKS.

TRUNKS.	Large.			Middle.			Small.		
	£.	s.	d.	£.	s.	d.	£.	s.	d.
A trunk new lined with paper	0	4	0	0	3	0	0	2	0
Ditto with linen ——	0	8	0	0	6	0	0	4	0
A new flap to the lid, nailed all round — —	0	5	0	0	4	0	0	3	0
Ditto front or end —	0	3	0	0	2	6	0	2	0
A new handle — —	0	1	6	0	1	3	0	1	0
A new lock and key —	0	2	6	0	2	0	0	1	9
A new key to fit the old lock	0	1	3	0	1	0	0	0	9
Mending the bottom with a batten —	0	2	0	0	1	9	0	1	6
New ftraps per foot, per pair	0	1	6	0	1	3	0	1	0
A chain-belt, per foot each —	0	2	9	0	2	9	0	2	9
Lengthening a ftrap, per foot, or under — —	0	1	0	0	0	9	0	0	6
Ditto a chain-belt, per fix inches	0	1	9	0	1	9	0	1	9

TRUNK COVERS.

	Large.			Middle.			Small.		
A new leather cover —	2	5	0	2	5	0	1	15	0
A new fide to ditto —	0	12	0	0	10	0	0	8	0
A new front, top, or back to ditto — —	0	15	0	0	14	0	0	12	0
Mending by welting, per foot	0	1	6	0	1	6	0	1	6
Oil-cloth covers —— —	0	10	6	0	7	6	0	5	0
A new end — —	0	2	6	0	2	6	0	1	6
A new front, top, or back —	0	3	0	0	2	6	0	2	0
New welting, per foot —	0	0	9	0	0	9	0	0	9
New painting the old cover -	0	2	6	0	2	0	0	2	0

IMPERIALS.

FOR A COACH.

	Whole.			Half.		
	£.	s.	d.	£.	s.	d.
A new leather roof — ——	3	3	0	2	2	0
A new fide or end — ——	0	15	0	0	12	0
A new linen lining — ——	0	15	0	0	12	0
Covering and ftuffing the bottom with new baize —— — ——	0	12	0	0	9	0

FOR

FOR A CHARIOT.

	Whole.			Half.		
	£.	s.	d	£.	s.	d.
A new roof ———	2	2	0	1	10	0
A new fide or end — ———	0	12	0	0	9	0
New lining the infide with linen ———	0	12	0	0	9	0
Covering and ftuffing the bottom with baize	0	10	0	0	8	0

For either COACH or CHARIOT IMPERIAL.

An infide girth ftrap — ———	0	2	0	0	2	0
An outfide imperial ftrap and buckle —	0	1	0	0	1	0
A leather handle — ———	0	1	6	0	1	6
A new padlock and key — ———	0	2	0	0	2	0

WELLS.

	£.	s.	d.
A new bottom to a well ——— ———	0	10	0
A new lid to ditto ——— ———	0	7	6
A new iron faftener for it to hang by ———	0	2	6
New lining the infide — ———	0	6	0

SPLINTER BARS.

	£.	s.	d.
A new main bar ——— ———	0	10	0
A ditto with the old iron-work ———	0	5	0
An end or fmall draught bar — ———	0	7	6
A ditto with the old iron-work ———	0	4	0
A new drag-chain ——— ———	0	8	0
Ditto covered with leather ———	0	10	6

E 4 SECT.

SECT. 18.

LINING AND COVERING WITH LEATHER THE PERCH-BOLT, &c.

THE lining or covering with leather thofe parts where the friction lies, is frequently neceffary, and forms a material part of the expence among the number of repairs. The expences of taking to pieces and putting together again, are included in the under-mentioned prices; and whether to a phaeton, chariot, or coach, the charges are the fame.

	£.	s.	d.
The perch-bolt hole	0	2	6
The upper or under tranfom-plate	0	5	0
The felly-piece, or fway-bar	0	1	6
The perch at the bottom	0	1	6
The pole or futchels in the chaps	0	1	0
The futchels or pole at the gib	0	1	0
The pole new ftuffed and lined at the fhoulders and hips	0	9	0
The pole half ditto at either place	0	5	0
Mending the pole-lining at either place with a fmall piece of leather	0	2	0
Each cap of the fplinter-bar roll lined	0	1	6
Each roll of ditto ditto	0	1	0
The fplinter-bar under each roll, ditto	0	1	0
A fhaft-point of a one-horfe chaife, ditto	0	2	0
A ftep-tread of ditto	0	2	0
A new gib-ftrap	0	0	9
A new pole-pin cap	0	1	0
The ftandards at bottom	0	1	6

CHAP.

CHAP. II.

REPAIRS OR ALTERATIONS TO THE HARNESS.

THE harnefs being a matter unconnected with the carriage, a feparate defcription of it, when new, is given in the former part of this work. This being for the repairs thereof, is alfo divided from the carriage, for the more ready information of the feparate expences.

From a bad harnefs, as much danger may be apprehended as from a bad carriage; and, however fkilful the driver may be, if the harnefs is not perfect, the horfes cannot be well managed. Befides, an old harnefs is always in want of repairs; and many people, from a faving notion, continue repairing, till there is fcarce a veftige of the original left, and the repairs have even coft twice the price of the harnefs when new.

That harnefs might neither be thrown away too foon, nor ufed fo long as to become expenfive and troublefome in the repairs, it will be proper to obferve the length of time it may be expected to laft, and what the expence for re-

pairing

repairing it may be, while in regular ufe. This, in a great meafure, depends upon the quality of the leather, and the fufficiency of the workman-fhip. It is neceffary to examine, at the firft, that the leather be firm, and yet pliable; and that, by pulling it, it does not contract in the width, or extend in the length, which bad leather will do, and will, befides, be ragged at the edges, and rough on the infide. Good fewing alfo tends much to the prefervation. The furniture with which the winkers and houfings are mounted, fhould be of filver, and not of plated metal, which makes but little difference in the firft expence; for they will laft with the harnefs, but otherwife are frequently obliged to be renewed.

Harnefs perifhes with hanging by; and, however moderate it may be ufed, yet, after fix years, cannot be very fit for further fervice, unlefs great care indeed has been taken to preferve it. To prove its goodnefs, is to compare it with the number of wheels worn out on the carriage with which the harnefs has been ufed, either in town or country; in town it will laft with three fets of wheels; and in the country two; or four years regular work, fuppofing the work, on the average, to be about five or fix miles a day conftant. As additions are frequently made, after the firft finifhing of a harnefs, it will be neceffary

3

to ftate what is the value of the feparate parts thereof, fo that, for any alteration the price may be known. When brafs or coloured-metal furniture is ufed, a reference muft be made to the prices ftated in the former tables. The following comprehends the filver and filver-plated, being the only fort now in general ufe.

―――

PRICES OF ORNAMENTS

With which the Houfings and Winkers are mounted, including the putting them on.

Different Sizes.			Emboffed CRESTS or CYPHERS.				PLATES or PIECES.				CIRCLES or RIMS.			
			Silver.		Plated.		Silver.		Plated.		Silver.		Plated.	
Inch.	Inch.	Inch.	s.	d.	s.	d.	s.	d.	s.	d.	s.	d.	s.	d.
4	by 3	or 3½	12	0	10	0	6	0	3	6	4	0	2	4
3½	by 3	or 3¼	11	0	9	6	5	6	3	3	3	6	2	2
3	by 3	or 3	10	0	9	0	5	0	3	0	3	3	2	0
3	by 2½	or 2¾	9	0	8	0	4	6	2	9	3	0	1	10
2½	by 2½	or 2½	8	0	7	6	4	0	2	6	2	9	1	8
2½	by 2	or 2¼	7	6	6	6	3	9	2	3	2	6	1	6
2	by 2	or 2	7	0	6	6	3	4	2	0	2	3	1	4
2	by 1½	or 1¾	6	6	5	6	3	0	1	9	2	0	1	2
1½	by 1½	or 1½	6	0	5	0	2	6	1	6	1	9	1	0
1½	by 1	or 1¼	5	6	4	6	2	0	1	3	1	6	0	10½
1	by 1	or 1	4	6	4	0	1	9	1	0	1	3	0	9
		7/8	4	0	3	6	1	6	0	10½	1	0	0	7
		5/8	3	6	3	0	1	3	0	9	0	10	0	6
		5/8	3	0	2	6	1	0	0	7½	0	8	0	5
		4/8	2	6	2	0	0	9	0	6	0	6	0	4

If the arms are emboffed, inftead of a creft or cypher, add 2s.

If

If a creſt or arms, in plated metal, is only raiſed from the back, and chaſed on the outſide, it cannot be conſidered as an emboſſing, but as a pierced creſt, and only charged after the rate of 1s. 6d. for thoſe above two inches, and 1s. for thoſe under.

For a cypher chaſed or engraved on the *plate* or *piece*, add 9d.

THE FURNITURE.

PLATED BUCKLES.	Sizes. Inch	Whole. £. s. d.			Half. £. s. d.		
	$\frac{1}{4}$	0	0	9	0	0	5
	$\frac{7}{8}$	0	0	10½	0	0	6
Buckles, dees, or bridges, for	1	0	1	1½	0	0	7½
the reins and ſtrappings,	1¼	0	1	3	0	0	10½
each	1½	0	1	6	0	1	0
	1¾	0	2	0	0	1	6

TRACE RINGS, TUG BUCKLES, &c. per pair.	Iron.			Plated.		
Collar tug buckles —	0	3	0	0	10	0
Collar dees — —	0	3	0	0	12	0
Trace rings — —	0	3	0	0	10	0
Woodcock eyes —	0	3	0	0	15	0
Spring ditto — —	0	4	6	0	18	0

BITS, each, with CURBS.	Iron.			Plated.		
A coach or chariot duke-bit —	0	8	0	1	12	0
A chaiſe ditto — —	0	7	0	1	10	0
A coach or chariot ſtraight check-bit —	0	6	0	1	8	0
A chaiſe ditto — —	0	5	0	1	6	0
A bridoon-bit with horns —	0	2	6	0	10	0
A ditto, plain —	0	2	0	0	8	0
Stirrup irons, per pair — —	0	5	0	0	18	0

HEAMS,

HEAMS, per pair.

		Large.			Small.	
		£.	s.	d.	£.	s.	d.
Plain polifhed or covered	—	—	0	10	0	0	8	0
Plated all over the outfides	—	—	4	0	0	3	18	0
Ditto, the loops only	—	—	1	15	0	1	13	0
Ditto the loops and links	—	—	2	5	0	2	3	0

Extra to the Heams.		Plated.		Iron.	
Solid loops in the heams for the reins to pafs through	—	—	0	6	0	0	3	0

HOUSING OR WINKER FRAMES.

			HOUSINGS.		WINKERS.	
	Size of the moulding. ths		Silver.	Plated.	Silver.	Plate1.
			s. d.	s. d.	s. d.	s. d.
A fquare or octagon frame for the out edges	4–8 3–8 2–8	of an inch.	18 0	8 6	12 0	6 0
			14 0	7 0	10 0	5 0
			11 0	5 6	8 0	4 0
A faddle cantle 2 or 3–8			— —		8 0	4 0

HOUSING FURNITURE.

				£.	s.	d.
A territ for a faddle or houfing	—	—		0	6	0
Ditto for the headftall	—	—		0	5	6
Ditto, with a fly	—	—		0	6	6
A fcrew for the houfing	—	—		0	1	6
A focket for either territ or fcrew	—	—		0	1	0
A fcutcheon for a fcrew or territ	—	—		0	0	6
A watering or bearing hook	—	—		0	5	0
A plate for ditto	—	—		0	1	6

BRIDOON

BRIDOON FURNITURE.

	£.	s.	d.
A throat-latch dee	0	3	c
A single chain of three links	0	1	6
For each link more than three	0	0	6
A double chain of the curb pattern, per inch	0	0	9
A swivel	0	1	9
A hook for the bridoon chain	0	2	0

THE following are the prices of the separate parts of a harnefs, both with and without the furniture, for the purpofe of fhewing what each part will coft, as it often happens that new leather-work is put to the old furniture, and fometimes new furniture to the old leather. The *Heams*, the *Collar-dees*, the *Trace-rings*, the *Tug-buckles*, and *Bits*, are confidered to be of polifhed iron : the other parts of the furniture are plated with filver, and confift of the *Half-buckles*, the *Dees*, the *Bridges*, the *Territs*, the *Hooks*, &c. But the ornaments for mounting the houfings and winkers are not included, being of fuch various patterns; therefore a reference muft be made to the table, (page 59.) wherein thefe things are all ftated.

THE BRIDLE.	With furniture.			Without furniture.		
	£.	s.	d.	£.	s.	d.
A bridle complete —	1	1	0	0	12	6
A headstall —	0	2	6	0	2	0
A throatband —	0	2	6	0	1	6
A winker —	0	3	6	0	3	6
A winker-strap —	0	1	6	0	1	6
A cheek to a winker —	0	3	6	0	2	6
A front of plain leather —	0	2	6	0	2	6
A nose-band —	0	3	0	0	2	0
A forehead-piece —	0	1	6	0	1	6

THE REINS.

	With furniture.			Without furniture.		
A set of long reins, complete, for a pair of horses —	0	18	0	0	16	0
A pair of long hand-reins only —	0	10	0	0	9	0
A pair of coupling-reins —	0	7	6	0	6	6
One ditto —	0	4	0	0	3	6
A pair of bearing-reins —	0	12	0	0	9	6
One ditto —	0	6	0	0	4	6
A chaise long hand-rein —	0	10	0	0	9	0
A bridoon complete, with chain —	0	17	6	0	9	0
A bridoon head and rein, without chain -	0	8	6	0	7	0
A bridoon-rein only —	0	5	6	0	4	0
A bridoon-strap —	0	1	0	0	0	9

COLLARS.

	With furniture.			Without furniture.		
A round or neck collar, with heams and tugs complete, for a phaeton or chaise	1	10	0	1	0	0
Ditto, for a coach or chariot —	1	11	6	1	2	0
A collar only, of neat's leather —	0	9	0	0	9	0
Ditto, of basil —	0	6	0	0	6	0
A pair of collar-tugs —	0	14	0	0	12	0
A heam-strap —	0	1	0	0	1	6
A round false collar —	0	7	6	0	7	6
A housing or cap for a round collar —	0	2	6	0	2	6
A breast-collar —	0	15	0	0	10	6
A false breast-collar —	0	8	0	0	8	0

THE BREECHING AND BELLY-BAND.

	With furniture.			Without furniture.		
A breeching for coach or chariot —	0	12	0	0	10	0
Ditto for a chaise —	0	10	0	0	8	0
A breeching-strap —	0	3	6	0	3	6
A false belly-band —	0	6	0	0	4	6

THE

THE CRUPPER.	With furniture. £. s. d.			Without furniture. £. s. d.		
A crupper, with a long turn back-strap —	0	12	0	0	10	6
Ditto, without a turn back-strap —	0	10	0	0	8	6
A crupper-dock —— —	0	2	0	0	2	0
The TRACES for a COACH and CHARIOT.						
A pair of wheel, or short leading traces, two inches wide — ——	1	0	0	0	18	0
A pair of long leading-traces, ditto —	1	18	0	1	16	0
A pair of wheel, or short leading traces, 2¼ wide —— ——	1	4	0	1	2	0
A pair of long leading-traces, ditto —	2	4	0	2	2	0
HOUSINGS.						
A housing, with its pad and belly-band complete —— ——	1	10	0	0	12	0
A pad only for a housing ——	0	5	0	0	5	0
A long side belly-band to the housing —	0	3	0	0	2	6
A short side ditto to ditto — ——	0	2	0	0	2	0
SADDLES.						
A saddle complete, with surcingle, &c. for a chaise harness — ——	1	16	0	1	0	0
A ditto, with double or jockey skirts, for a ditto —— ——	2	0	0	1	4	0
A short side of the surcingle or belly-band	0	2	0	0	2	0
A long side of ditto — ——	0	3	6	0	2	6
A new pannel put in either chaise saddle -	0	6	0	0	6	0
A back-band for a chaise saddle —	0	8	0	0	8	0
A pair of shaft-tugs for ditto —	0	8	0	0	5	0
A shaft-band to a tug — ——	0	2	0	0	2	0
A postillion-saddle, with stirrups and girths complete —— ——	2	6	0	2	2	0
A pair of worsted girths for a saddle —	0	3	6	0	2	6
A pair of new stirrup-leathers for ditto -	0	9	0	0	5	0
A new pannel for a postillion saddle —	0	8	0	0	8	0
STRAPPINGS and TUGS.						
A back or hip-strap, with tugs —	0	10	0	0	8	0
A tug for either strap — ——	0	4	0	0	3	0
A Newmarket strap — ——	0	3	0	0	2	0
A neck or wither-strap — ——	0	5	6	0	3	6
A ditto with a ley — ——	0	7	0	0	5	0

..RTINGALES.

MARTINGALES.	With furniture. £. s. d.	Without furniture. £. s. d.
A martingale from the head to the belly-band —— ——	0 15 0	0 12 0
A ditto from the collar to the belly-band or breast-piece —— ——	0 8 0	0 5 0

PAD-CLOTHS.		
A pad, or housing-cloth, bound with lace	— —	0 6 0
A saddle ditto —— ——	— —	0 8 0

ROSES, FRONTS, and EARBOWS.	Worsted.	Silk.
A pair of white or coloured roses, and lapping the old fronts — —	0 8 0	0 16 0
Ditto with a pair of new fronts ——	0 11 0	0 19 0
For lapping the old pair of earbows —	0 2 6	0 4 0
For a pair of new earbows and lapping -	0 5 0	0 7 6
A pair of new roses, and lapping the front of a one-horse chaise harness ——	0 7 6	0 15 0
Ditto, with a new front and lapped —	0 9 0	0 16 6
Ditto, with a new earbow, ditto —	0 10 6	0 18 0

F

SECT. 1.

MENDING THE HARNESS

By fplicing on new Pieces of Leąther, putting on new Billets and Loops, and fewing the Places where ripped.

For every fix inches or under.	A fplice. £. s. d.	A fewing. £. s. d.
To the trace —	0 1 6	0 0 9
To the breeching-ftrap, or ley —	0 0 9	0 0 6
To the crupper-ftrap, or ley —	0 0 8	0 0 6
To the ley of the breaft-collar or heam-tug —	0 1 0	0 0 6
To the pipe of the breaft-collar or heam-tug —	0 1 3	0 0 9
To the belly-band —	0 0 9	0 0 6
To any of the ftrapping, of $1\frac{1}{2}$ inch wide	0 0 8	0 0 6
To the reins or bridle —	0 0 6	0 0 4
Refixing a buckle, a bridge, or dee —	0 0 6	0 0 4

LOOPS and BILLETS.	A loop.	A billet.
To the ftrapping —	0 0 3	0 1 0
To the bridle or reins —	0 0 2	0 0 9

CHAP.

CHAP. III.

ON HIRED CARRIAGES.

IN order to avoid future expence and trouble, many perfons prefer hiring to keeping a carriage of their own; but, unlefs very cautious in the engagement, they fall into the fame, if not greater, inconveniences and expences, than if the carriage was their own. Gentlemen, and in particular thofe of the medical line, whofe bufinefs requires an almoft conftant ufe of their carriage, find an advantage in furnifhing themfelves this way, as the frequent repairs, and delays thereof, would expofe them to a number of inconveniencies and expences, which are, by hiring, avoided; but for thofe whofe ufe of a carriage is not fo conftant, it is by no means an advifeable plan, which may be judged of by the number of wheels that are confumed, as there are many who do not wear out their wheels in three or four years, while others wear them out in twelve or fix months. The one finds an advantage, but the other pays dear for the ufe of their carriage, if

F 2   hired.

hired. The probable expences of repairs required to a carriage are ftated in page 13; from which ftatement may be determined the preferable mode to adopt.

———

HIRING CARRIAGES BY THE YEAR.

COACHES and chariots are the fort of carriages generally hired by the year; and they are moftly built purpofely for the occupier, and finifhed agreeable to his fancy, in the fame manner as if they were to be purchafed. They are generally engaged, indeed, for fuch a time as they might reafonably be expected to laft, either with the fafhion or ftrength, which is moftly for four years. Suitable harnefs is ufually engaged with the carriage; which, together, are to be kept by the builder in wheels, and every neceffary repair, excepting only fuch as have been occafioned by accident. The painting the carriage and putting on a new hammercloth are ufually done within the time; but this depends on the agreement. Phaetons, curricles, or chaifes, if built for hire, are charged for after the rate of the whole year, although only ufed fix months; which,

3

which, being thofe of the fummer, leaves the carriage an incumbrance for the winter, and when they are not likely to fell : but the price for hiring all carriages by the year, whether coach, chariot, phaeton, curricle, or chaife, is proportioned to the value of the carriage, after the following manner.

———

SECT. 2.

THE YEARLY VALUE OF HIRE RATED.

TO afcertain the yearly value for the hire of carriages with any accuracy, is to divide the firft coft, including all fubfequent expences, by one more than the number of years for which it is engaged. The one year's dividend is fuppofed to be the worth of the carriage to the coachmaker, when returned to him at the expiration of the engagement, and the others pay for the carriage while in ufe. If the carriage is hired for four years, divide the coft by five; if for three, divide by four ; and fo on for as long or fhort a time as may be engaged for above one year.

Some builders make a rule to charge for a number of articles that are added to finifh a car-

F 3   riage

riage beyond a certain extent, making extras of
as many things as amount to one year's hire.
The faireſt method is, to compriſe them all in one
valuation, with all the future coſt, which may
eaſily be computed, and divide the total as follows : Suppoſe the value of both the carriage and
harneſs amounts to 140 guineas; the expence of
the wheels, and other repairs, for the firſt year,
is 2 guineas; the ſecond year, 10 guineas; the
third year, 12 guineas; the fourth year, 16
guineas; the fifth year, 24 guineas; and, if new
painted, or have a new hammercloth and holders, add the price thereof to the price of all the
reſt, making them into one ſum total, which divide as thus—Suppoſe the firſt coſt of the carriage, with harneſs, to be 140 guineas; the expence for repairs added, makes the full coſt 180
guineas, which are then divided by one more
than the number of years, for four years' hire,
which is five, and that gives 36 guineas for the
yearly value for hire as follows, ſuppoſing the
firſt coſt 140 guineas:

Time.	Expence for Repairs.	Total Coſt.	Divide by	Year's Hire.
For one year	– 2 gs.	142 gs.	2	– 71 gs.
For two years	– 12 —	152 —	3	– 50 —
For three years	– 24 —	164 —	4	– 41 —
For four years	– 40 —	180 —	5	– 36 —

If,

If, in the time, the carriage is once new painted, and furnifhed with a new hammercloth and
footman-holders, as it moftly is, if hired for more
than two years, then 20 guineas more, or the
value of fuch hammercloth and painting, muft be
added to the fum total, and divided as above,
the expence is then as here ftated.

Time.	Expence for Repairs, &c.	Tot. Coft.	Divided by	Yearly Value of Hire.
For three years -	44 gs.	184 gs	4 —	46 gs.
For four years -	60 —	200 — 5	—	40 —
For five years -	84 —	224 — 6	—	37 —

By this rule the value of hire for every fort of
carriage may be afcertained, if greater or lefs in
the expence; allowing the carriage, when off the
job, to be worth the price of one year's hire,
which, with what is received, makes up all the
expence of the carriage.

———

COPY OF AGREEMENT.

WHEN carriages are thus let by the year, a
formal engagement is moftly entered into, to bind
each contracting party, for the full perfecting
their feparate agreement, of which the following
is a copy:

F 4　　　　'Articles

' ARTICLES OF AGREEMENT made and entered
' into this   one thoufand feven
' hundred and   between A. B.
' gent. of the county of   on the one
' part, and C. D. coachmaker, of the county of
'   on the other, and this certifies, that the
' faid C. D. doth agree to build, and preferve
' in good and fubftantial repair, a carriage, with
' harnefs, for the ufe of the faid A. B. until the
' full expiration of   years, from the date
' hereof, after the following rate and manner :

*(Here is to be inferted the manner in which the
faid coach is to be built, with all the particu-
lars of keeping the fame in repair, the time of
new painting, hammerclothing, &c.*

' In confideration whereof, the faid A. B.
' doth agree to pay, or caufe to be paid, the
' fum of   annually, the firft year's pay-
' ment on receipt of the carriage, the fecond on
' the commencement of the fecond year, and fo
' forth, each year's hire to be paid in advance ;
' and at the expiration of the   year, the
' faid carriage, with harnefs, to be returned to
' the faid C. D. with glaffes whole, and every
' part of the faid carriage and harnefs complete,
' and whole, excepting fuch deficiency as may
' be expected from reafonable wear and tear
                                    ' while

' while in ufe : And further, the faid A. B. doth
' agree to pay for all repairs done to the faid
' carriage and harnefs, which was occafioned by
' accident, and not by fair ufe; and alfo to al-
' low the faid C. D. to do thofe and every other
' repair unto the faid carriage and harnefs, pro-
' viding the diftance and time will permit, the
' faid carriage and harnefs to be fent to the faid
' C. D. but on all and every occafion to fend
' advice, when time will permit, previous to
' having any repair executed.

' The faid carriage and harnefs, for the time
' being, to be confidered as the fole property of
' the faid A. B. and for whofe, or family's, ufe
' only, the faid carriage and harnefs are to be
' furnifhed.

' In witnefs, hereof, each party hath fepa-
'   rately fet their hands and feals, this
'   day of   17

Witnefs F. G. $\left\{ \begin{array}{l} \text{A. B.} \\ \text{C. D.} \end{array} \right.$

This agreement may be drawn on two fix-fhilling
.ftamps, by any indifferent perfon.

' In the above indenture each party may bind,
with themfelves, their executors, adminiftrators,

or

or affignees; but the following infertion would
be good, in cafe of death :

    ' That in cafe of demife of A. B. the execu-
' tors, &c. do not, for the remaining part of
' the family, chufe to continue the job, but re-
' turn it on the coachmaker's hand, the ad-
' vanced price, in proportion to the time, muft
' be allowed, after the rate before ftated; but in
' cafe of demife or failure of the coachmaker,
' and no one chufe to continue the engagement,
' the coach, &c. may be returned, without any
' further confideration than that at firft entered
' upon.'

    The return of the carriage cannot be demand-
ed before the expiration of the period for which
the advanced price has been paid, being, for that
time, confidered as the fole property of the gentleman who occupies it, and by whom the duty
is always paid.

SECT.

SECT. 3.

THE HIRING FOR A SHORT PERIOD RATED.

IF a carriage be hired by the day, week, or month, or for lefs than a year, the jobber pays the duty. The accuftomed price for carriages, whether of two or four wheels, is 4s. per day, except Sunday, which is 5s.; 24s. per week; and 4 guineas per month; the carriage to be return-ed on the fame day of the week or month on which it was engaged, or may, in ftriftnefs, be fubjefted to pay for another day, week, or month fo entered on.

Phaetons, and other forts of open carriages, pay more, in proportion to their value, than the others, as the whole year's duty muft be paid for them, though they can only be ufed a few months, and are, the remainder of the year, an incumbrance.

When coaches or chariots are let by the week or month, the harnefs is not ufually let with them; but to a two-wheeled or a one-horfe car-riage, harnefs is included. The reafon, if any befides cuftom, is, that where a pair of horfes is ufed, it is alfo expefted they have been accuftom-ed to a regular pair of harnefs: but one-horfe chaifes are frequently drawn by horfes ufed for

imme-

carts, and other general purpofes, the owners of which feldom have harnefs adapted for chaife-work : but if a pair of harnefs is hired with a four-wheeled carriage, a charge of 5s. per week, and 1s. per day, is ufually made, above what is here ftated. Thofe hired carriages are expected to be turned out, cleaned, greafed, and fit for immediate ufe ; and they fhould be fuch as may be depended upon for fafety and eafe, which is but feldom the cafe, as they confift moftly of old, left-off carriages, which are much decayed, and wherein there can be but little dependance. A very unfair advantage is alfo taken by fome job-bers, who charge to the hirer for whatever is broken of the carriage while in ufe; although the damage may be occafioned by infufficiency, yet he charges for it as if it were by accident, though it ought to fubject him to a profecution for the danger the perfon who hired the carriage was expofed to. Not that it is meant to infinuate this as a general practice, as there are many re-fpectable jobbers, whofe character is above an artifice of this fort; but that it is practifed, many gentlemen, who have been in the habit of hiring carriages by the day or week, have expe-rienced. The jobber fhould always be made ac-quainted with the intended route, and the time likely to be engaged for, as by that means he has no excufe in not giving a fufficient carriage.

Carriages

Carriages failing while on hire, if at a diſtance from the jobber, ſhould be repaired at the option of the occupier, and the bill paid for the repair ſhould be deduɛted from the jobber's account, on producing a certificate that the failure was not occaſioned by violence.

When a carriage is hired by a ſtranger for a ſhort time, he ſhould pay the whole or half the amount of the engagement.

CHAP.

CHAP. IV.

CARE AND PRESERVATION.

TO preferve is certainly better than to mend; for, befides the expence of repairs, it is, at the beft, but a patch; and the injury done to the carriage, by taking to pieces and putting together, is a circumftance which ought to command every attention againft accident or neglect, whereby a carriage may foon be fpoiled in its beauty, and injured in its ftrength.

The credit of the builder and the beauty of the carriage are never fo well preferved as when the carriage is kept under the daily infpection of its proprietor, which the want of a coach-houfe adjacent to his dwelling often prevents, and the carriage thereby materially fuffers from neglect.

Gentlemen, who job their horfes, are moftly furnifhed by the jobber with a coachman, and fubmit to have their carriage ftand in the livery-yard, where it is often fo neglected as foon to become fpoiled.

The gentleman ufually boards the fervant, and furnifhes him with livery; and the hackneyman

pays

pays the falary: it is the pay and the dependance on the hackneyman that command the
greateft influence. It fhould be recommended
to gentlemen, who are thus furnifhed with horfes,
to engage their own coachman, and, if any way
convenient, to have their coach-houfe and ftabl-
ing where they can readily infpect the fervant's
conduct. The hackneyman fhould, in this cafe,
make an allowance at the rate of 10l. per annum
for a coach-houfe and two-ftall ftable, fo found
by the gentleman.

SECT. 1.

COACHMAN'S TOOLS.

IT is very impolitic in many people not to
furnifh their fervants with proper conveniencies,
for want of which they frequently incur treble
the expence in one year as would fupply, for
many, all the neceffary requifites for the coachman's ufe, with which he might employ many of
thofe leifure hours, while the carriage is unem-
ployed, equally to the improvement of himfelf,
and the benefit of his mafter.

The requifites whereby a fervant can make
himfelf ufeful, ought not to be denied him. The
principal of thefe are, a fetter-prop, a hammer,
a pair

a pair of pinchers, an iron chiffel, a fcrew-wrench, two leather fkins, two fponges, and two glafs-cloths; fome old or other ftout leather, for wafhers; fome twopenny and fourpenny clout-nails; a brufh for the lining; two water-brufhes for the carriage, the one broad and the other nar-row, called a fpoke-brufh; an oil-kettle and brufh; a rag-mop and pail; greafe, and lince pins.

Thefe are the general conveniencies given; but, excepting thofe for wafhing and cleaning, are feldom allowed, and the coachmaker is ufually applied to for the moft trifling job, which the fervant might do, if furnifhed as above. The coachmaker, and fometimes the fadler, fur-nifhes thofe conveniencies, the prices of which generally are for

	£.	s.	d.
A fetter-prop	o	16	o
A fcrew-wrench, middle fize	o	7	o
A pair of pinchers	o	2	o
A hammer	o	2	o
An iron chiffel	o	1	o
A leather fkin or difhclout	o	1	6
A glafs-cloth	o	1	o
A water-brufh	o	2	o
A fpoke ditto	o	1	6
A lining-brufh	o	2	6
Two-penny nails, per 100	o	o	6
Three-penny ditto	o	o	9
Four-penny ditto	o	1	o
A rag mop	o	1	o
A yard of ftout leather for wafhers	o	2	6

SECT.

SECT. 2.

ON DRIVING.

EXPERTNESS in driving is the principal qualification of a coachman ; but to know how to drive, fo as to preferve the carriage from the injury it is likely to receive by violent jolts or twiftings, is a merit of no lefs value. If a carriage is driven on uneven pavement, it requires fome attention to keep it always on a level, as it may receive more injury from inattention to this caution, although of only one mile's fpace, than it would otherwife do by a week's fair and moderate ufe. Befides, the rifk of breaking the axletree or fprings, and the probable danger thereby to be apprehended, ought to operate as an additional caution in this refpect.

The paces fhould be regulated according to the roughnefs of the ground, and the turnings according to the room ; for, if not turned fair acrofs a channel, it twifts the perch, or cranes, according to the defcent, as the one wheel falls when the other, on the oppofite angle, is on the rife ; and frequently by this the main, or perchbolt, is broken ; and, befides the ftrain it gives to other parts of the carriage, does it a material injury, in particular, when going faft. The ·

G　　　　　　fame

fame frequently happens in roads where the ruts
are deep, by fhifting of fides; the fore wheels
fhould always be fo directed as to roll on an even
furface, and the hind ones, of courfe, will follow
the fame tract.

SECT. 3.

ON BRACING.

NEW braces always ftretch in proportion to
the weight of the body, and to the fubftance and
quality of the leather; they are ufually buckled
at the point-holes, when firft turned out from the
builder: other holes are made for the allowance of taking up when ftretched; which is
done by putting a reft-ftick under the bottom
of the body, on that fide which is to be taken up
firft, fo as to relieve the weight from the brace
while fhifting; before the main braces are taken
up, the collar and check-braces muft be let out.
They feldom ftretch fo as to require taking up
above two holes, unlefs it be owing to the perch
fettling, whereby the body comes fo clofe to the
fprings as to afford but little room for it to fwing.
When the braces, by being taken up, become fo
long at the points as to look ill, the fuperfluous
part

part may be cut off, or buckled down. Thofe
braces, which check or ftay the body, fhould
not be tightened more than will prevent it ftriking againft the wheels or coach-box; for the
more room the body has to fwing, the eafier is
the riding to the paffengers; the collar-braces,
in particular, fhould not be too much tightened,
as the fudden check the body of the carriage receives, renders the feat uncomfortable.

Shifting the braces from the bearings is effential to preferve them, as that part on which the
weight refts is deprived of the moifture, or greafe,
which preferves the leather; the brace then becomes dry, and fufceptible of the wet and dirt,
which there lodges, and that part is foon cracked
and broke, while the reft is quite good and frefh;
therefore, to change the fituation of the brace,
however little, once a month, or lefs, will prevent the frequent neceffity of lining, cutting, and
fplicing, to repair it, and which is alfo a great
eye-fore. By this care the braces will look well,
and laft a longer time than they otherwife would
do. The fame to be obferved in pole-pieces, &c.

SECT. 4.

HAMMERCLOTHS.

THE hammercloths ſhould always be turned up after uſe, except when wet with rain, for, if prevented from drying, it will rot. After a duſty journey, let it be well bruſhed, for, if neglected till it gets wet, the beauty of it will be ſpoiled, by having the duſt and rain combined. The lace and fringe harbour much duſt, and therefore require to be well looked after to preſerve it clean.

The hammercloth ſhould always be ſecurely fixed to the ſeat by the loops, for, if not well confined, it will ſhift, and wear very faſt through the lining. When the ſeat gets ſo hollow that the hammercloth lies under the coachman's feet, the cradle muſt be tightened, or a piece ſloped out from the top of the front breadth of the cloth, and retrimmed as before. If at the top the cloth begins to rip from the ſeam, let it be immediately ſewed, as the great weight of the cloth and trimmings, hanging only by the ſewing, will ſoon extend much further, if neglected. The oilcloth covers ſhould be as little folded or handled as poſſible, being very careful, when mounting the coach-box, not to lay hold thereof, as the

ſlighteſt

flighteft touch will tear them; let them alfo be
fecurely fixed to the corners and middle of the
other feat with rings and tapes.

————

SECT. 5.

L I N I N G.

LET the carpet be often cleaned and reverfed,
fo that the wear may not always be in one place.
Let the powder be well brufhed from the cloth
after ufe, and often change the cufhions of a
coach to the oppofite fides; if to ftand by any
time, turn them; and place a flat, broad piece
of wood in the hand-holders, to preferve their
fhape. The blinds ought always to be put up,
to keep out duft or vermin. The fhutters of the
doors, and the front lights, if made of cedar,
will prevent moths harbouring; if not, a few
cedar fhavings in a bag, laid on the feats, will
anfwer the purpofe. If foiled, ufe a little pipe-
clay with the brufh till it comes out, but not fo
much as to let it come off on the clothes of the
paffengers. When the narrow lace about the
lights and doors rifes, place it down with a little
fhoemaker's pafte.

G 3   SECT.

SECT. 6.

D O O R S.

A DIFFICULTY is often experienced in opening or fhutting the doors; and frequent application to the coachmaker is made to eafe them, which is done by planing away the fides, and giving more room; but in dry weather, after fuch eafing, the vacancy is often fo great as to be quite unpleafant, frequently miffing the ravets, and letting in both light and air, for which there is but little remedy. The fwelling of the doors is occafioned by a moift or damp air, which operates on the timber as on a barometer. As, in moift air it fwells, fo, in dry, it fhrinks; although the timber, when ufed, may be perfectly well feafoned. When this occurs, rub the fhutting edges, or ravets, with foap, which moft likely will eafe the obftructions; and, if not very troublefome, bear a little with the inconvenience, rather than admit of too great a reduction of the doors, which is doing them an injury paft remedy. In fhutting the door, care fhould be taken not to force it with fudden violence, whereby the glafs is fometimes broken: the lock-bolt ought to be fufficiently turned back, that it may not ftrike againft the pannels in fhutting. In opening the

door,

door, it fhould not be thrown back with violence, as the hinges may likely be ftrained or broken. If the hinges are a little ftiff, fweet oil or greafe is good. The lock fpindle is eafily twifted by the handle being forcibly ftrained, and then it lies in a direftion fo as to make it doubtful if the door be faftened. Glaffes and fhutters are fometimes obftrufted in the fliding; to remedy which, rub the grooves on which they flide moderately with foap, fo as not to foil the cloth which covers the frames : wet weather contributes much towards this; therefore, after being expofed to the rain, let the glafs-frames remain up to dry.

SECT. 7.

S T E P S.

BE particularly careful that thofe ftops, or iron fupports, againft which the fteps ftrike in falling, are neither of them removed, fo that the preffure may not injure the mouldings, or the ftep be ftrained for want of an equal bearing. If moved or loofened, put in a ftout fourpenny nail, with the point cut acrofs to prevent its fplitting the wood; and fcrew the nut tight, but fo as not to confine the joint, or prevent the free aftion of

G 4 the

the ſtep.   If the joints are ſtiff, a drop of ſweet
oil, worked in, will eaſe them.   If the top joints
are too looſe, ſo that the ſtep is ready to fall, on
opening the door, tighten the under nuts; and
if the other joints are looſe, whereby the ſtep
ſhakes on the inſide, tighten the rivets, by holding the head of one hammer on the head of the
rivet, and with the tail of another, ſpread the
rivet on the inſide: about a dozen light blows on
each will do it.

SECT. 8.

COACH-BOX-SEAT AND CRADLE.

THIS often gets looſe by the ſhaking of the
carriage, and the weight of the coachman; to remedy which, let the ſeat-ſtraps be unnailed and
untwiſted from the ſtandards, and then tightened
as much as poſſible by the moſt forcible purchaſe;
the hammer handle is a good inſtrument for that
purpoſe: let it then again be twiſted round the
ſtandard, and nailed as before.   Thoſe cradles
are the beſt which are made to buckle, ſo
that, without taking off the ſeat, they may be
taken up or let down at pleaſure.   For the other,
the ſeat muſt be removed, and the ſtraps, which
ſupport the cradle at one end, unnailed from the

1   top

top of the ftandard. Thofe ftraps are twifted round an iron ring in the cradle end, and round the loop end of the feat-iron; and likewife twift-ed round the feat-iron itfelf, fo as to bring the ends of the ftrap back to the top of the ftandard, where it is nailed, and is, by this means, let down or taken up at pleafure.

———————

SECT. 9.

SCREWING THE BOLTS.

THE fhaking of the carriage frequently loofens the bolts and nuts; and, if not attended to in time, the timber, or iron-work, thereby confined, fuffers a material injury; and, though a fimple matter to fecure, the coachmaker is often fent for to do what the coachman himfelf might eafily do. The fcrew-wrench is here particular-ly ufeful, as it can be adapted to all the fizes of the nuts. A carriage in conftant work fhould have the bolts or nuts tried once a fortnight; but, in fcrewing them tight, no violence fhould be ufed, whereby the threads of the nut may be ftrained, or the bolts broken. Be particularly careful not to injure the paint with the wrench:

thofe

thofe nuts which are in fight ought not to be touched, unlefs loofe, on that account.

—◆—

W H E E L S.

WHEELS fuffer much by hard driving on rough ground. It refts with the proprietor to guard againft this, whofe option alone can dictate. The common principle of wheel-boxes fhould, while in regular ufe, contain the greafe one week, unlefs travelling hard, or going poft, then twice or thrice a week is needful. By letting the wheels have much room on the axletree, the carriage is made to run lighter, as it takes away the friction on the furface of the back and front fhoulders, but prevents the greafe from being fo long retained, and gives more play, whereby the boxes are fooner worn out. When both (or either) of the extremities of the wheelnave are worn by friction, a leather-wafher, or two, according to the neceffity, cut fo as to fit exactly to the axletree, muft be applied, and fhould be placed at the fore, or lince, end, and tightened by the nut againft the wheel, as forcing it back towards the fhoulder helps to fit the

box

box tighter to the arms. When it gets too roomy, it muſt be taken out, and fitted by the coachmaker. The nuts, when looſe on the ſcrew, make an unpleaſant rattling; to remedy which, wind a little tow round the ſcrew, which will prevent noiſe, till the nut can be altered.

SECT. 11.

WHEEL-IRONS.

THOSE things are never tight longer than the ſplinter-bar is on the ſtrain; and, when looſe, will make an unpleaſant, rattling noiſe; to remedy which, the hooks muſt be turned further down, which ſhortens the irons, and ſtrains the ſplinter-bar ſo as to keep them tight; but, as the ſplinter-bar, in a little time, ſettles to the ſtrain, the irons ſhould be but as ſeldom and as little ſhortened as poſſible; for, by too frequently ſhortening the wheel-irons, they contract the ſplinter-bar ſo far round as to touch the wheel, which is injurious and unſightly. To prevent ſhortening, let the neck of the hook be lined with hard leather, and place alſo a piece of leather in the eye of the ſplinter-bar ſocket. If the eye of the wheel-iron, which is placed on the axletree, is got too large, let it be refitted, or

place

place a wafher fo cut as to fill the internal part, and fupply the defeft. A piece of lay-cord wrapped round the ring of the eye will anfwer the purpofe.

———

P O L E S.

WHEN the pole has too much room in the futchel-chaps, whereby it fhakes about, two thin pieces of leather fhould be nailed to the fides, before and behind. If it requires to be raifed, a piece fhould be nailed on at the bottom in front, and at the top behind. If the gib has too much room, a piece of leather, nailed on its bottom, or on the top of each futchel, helps to tighten and fit it to the ftaple. A piece of leather, like a wafher, or ring, placed between the pole-pin head and timber, will much preferve the futchel at the pole, as the working of the pin deftroys the timber. The pin fhould always be moderately tight in the hole; when loofe, fupply the room with a piece of leather: and it fhould be drove out with another pin of a fmaller fize, as the hammering againft the timber bruifes it much, and often occafions the neceffity of a new futchel.

futchel. To prevent the horfes gnawing the pole, let it be cafed with tin.

———

SECT. 13.

RATTLING.

RATTLING is very unpleafant, and is a fure fign of fomething being loofe about the carriage, which requires to be tightened, or lined with leather. Where iron works upon iron, if a thin piece of leather can be introduced between them, the rattling will be ftopped. The fqueaking of any part is to be remedied by a little greafe or oil: it frequently happens in the bolts of the fprings, or the fhackles, where the wet has got in, and rufted; but it generally proceeds from fome loofe bolt or nut.

———

SECT. 14.

CLEANING.

A CARRIAGE ought always to be cleaned, if poffible, immediately after ufe, before the dirt dries on it; but when that cannot be effected, and the dirt is ftiff, fluice it well, and give the water time to loofen it, as, by rubbing it, when dry, the
fand

fand and gravel in the dirt will fcratch the paint, and particularly injure the varnifh on the pannels. In placing the fetter, to clean and raife the wheels, care fhould be taken that it does not prefs on, or rub againft, any part; but that the bearing may reft on the pin only, as frequently the timbers are much bruifed by this inattention. Soft water is preferable, if to be obtained: fea water is a great hurt to the paint, as the falt penetrates through the colour; which on the iron-work it totally deftroys the paint, and leaves the iron bare and rufty. The iron-work fhould always be wiped perfectly dry, particularly the fprings, as the wet, or damp, gets between the plates, which occafions them to ruft, and to blifter out at the edges. A carriage cannot have too much care taken in the cleaning, as by that it is much preferved.

SECT. 15.

TO PRESERVE WHILE STANDING BY.

A COVER is here very needful, as it keeps the pannels and braces from moulding by the damp. The hammercloth fhould be taken off, and put in the body. Once every month the carriage fhould be taken out; the leather braces wiped over with a greafy rag; the pannels and

japan

japan wiped over with a foft, woollen cloth, damped with a little fweet oil, and dried off with another foft cloth, fprinkled with a little flour; the doors fhould be opened to let out the mufty or foul air ; the timber wetted by fluicing a quantity of water over it, particularly the wheels; and if dry weather, and the carriage is likely to ftand long, a hay-band fhould be wrapped round the fpokes at the bottom againft the nave, and wetted thoroughly ; to prevent it from fhrinking, change the bearing of the wheels oppofite, when put in again.

SECT. 16.

TO PRESERVE THE PAINT OR VARNISH.

TO preferve the original luftre of varnifh, is to maintain the beauty of carriages, which may, in a great meafure, be effected by a little attention and care. The paint being coated with varnifh, is preferved thereby. The principal objects are the varnifhed pannels and the japanning. The wheel, or carriage part, is only once varnifhed, to affift the glofs on the firft painting ; and being fo fubject to rub in wearing, it cannot be fuppofed to maintain its original beauty long, though much may be done by keeping it free from

from dirt or greafe of any kind, and not to rub it, in cleaning, with any thing coarfe, but to ufe foap with warm water, if much tarnifhed by ftanding long, and to put it always by in a dry ftate, in particular the iron-work.

SECT. 17.

COMMON VARNISHED PANNELS.

THE luftre of thefe is not fo high, nor the furface fo fmooth as on the polifhed pannels; but, by attention, will likely wear better and longer, as the quantity is not fo great, which is the principal caufe of its failure. The japan and varnifh are much of a quality, and the treatment fhould be the fame. A carriage, when firft painted, fhould have every poffible care to preferve it from fpotting with dirt, in particular with chalk or clay foil, as the body of colour and varnifh takes a confiderable time to harden fufficiently to refift the penetrating damp of the dirt or clay, which, if allowed to dry, or remain any time on, leaves a ftain which fometimes cannot be effaced but by time and air; in fome colours, particularly verdigrife greens, thofe fpots cannot be effaced, or at leaft for a confiderable time. Therefore, fo foon as a carriage, newly painted,

comes

comes in from work, and is any way fpotted, fluice the dirt from the pannels, and with a wet leather-fkin, or fponge, rub them well all over. Stains will alfo appear where the rain has run for any length of time: for this obferve the fame rule; but if it fhould not be effaced by thefe means, let it remain a day or two, and then rub the pannels all over with a foft baize and a little fweet oil, fo as juft to damp them; then rub the ftained places with a little more ftrength than the other parts of the pannels; dry off the damp of the oil with another piece of baize; then, with a third piece, and a little flour, wipe or rub the pannels very dry; and, if the ftain has not then difappeared, rub it hard with the palm of a dry, foft hand, drawing it fmartly down, which is only known to be fufficiently done when it creates a fqueaking found by the rubbing. This will probably clear the ftains; if not, leave it fome time longer, and again ufe the fame experiment: if then it cannot be cleared, the colour, or paint, beneath the varnifh, is fure to be injured, and nothing but time will effect a change. Rubbing thofe common varnifhed bodies rather ftrong with a foft fkin, and drying them well with another, helps to increafe the luftre of the varnifh; and a common varnifhed body, well kept, and often cleaned, frequently improves in its luftre.

H   SECT.

HIGH VARNISHED, OR POLISHED PANNELS.

THE clear brightnefs of this polifhed furface fhews every little blemifh to a difadvantage ; and, though likely to be ftained from the fame caufes as the other, yet the colour is not fo apt to be affected, as it is much thicker coated with varnifh, and the refiftance ftronger, but, for which, ufe the fame experiment as before noticed. Thefe bodies, in cleaning, are to be dealt with lightly. Be very careful not to rub them with any thing hard ; fponge the dirt well off, and wipe them very dry with a foft baize. While the pannels are wet, they muft not be expofed to the fun, which indeed, at all times, ought to be avoided as much as poffible, as nothing affects the varnifh more. When the pannels are warm with the fun, do not immediately wafh them, but let the carriage remain in a fhade till they are cool : if dufty with the road duft, let it be brufhed off, as wiping it with a cloth may fcratch or rub the varnifh.

SECT. 19.

TO RESTORE THE LUSTRE OF VARNISH.

THE caufe of varnifh looking dull, ftriking in, or cracking, as often arifes from the badnefs of its own quality, as from any improper treatment in the cleaning, or effect of the weather; the high varnifh, in particular, on account of the extra quantity, which, if not good, produces a change much fooner than the common varnifh, the latter being much thinner. When the varnifh appears to crack, it can only be remedied by the painter, who fhould be immediately applied to; but if the varnifh ftrikes in, and looks dull, as is often the cafe from the weather, ufe the following means: Get a quarter of a pound of rotten ftone, or Tripoly powder, from a colour-fhop, which muft be ground with water, and ufed of the confiftency of pafte in the following manner: double a piece of woollen cloth, and, with the flat part, rub each pannel, with a gentle force, for about a quarter of an hour, taking care to rub it equally all over; wafh off the fubftance, and, with the hand free of corns, and damped with a foft leather, which is held in the other, rub it fmartly downwards, till, by the friction, it makes a fhrieking noife, as before

H 2   noticed.

noticed.   If this does not fufficiently polifh,
which feldom fails, the rubbing with rotten-ftone
and the hand fhould be again repeated.   Much
depends upon the hand rubbing clean off the
pannels and mouldings, as before directed, with
foft baize, oil, and flour. If well managed, the
body will look nearly as well as if new painted,
particularly with common varnifhed bodies, they
having never gone through the procefs before.

Thus, with one or two days trouble, and for
about one fhilling, the expence of new painting
may fometimes be faved.

Polifhed bodies fhew the leaft blemifh ; but,
if not fcratched, may eafily be cleared off, by a
little rotten-ftone, and rubbing that part only,
as before mentioned: but if, by rubbing, it
looks brighter than the reft, do it all over.   A
fcratched pannel, where the injury has not pene-
trated to the colour, may be polifhed out, rubbing it firft with a little fine-powdered pumice-
ftone, with a cloth and water, the fame as with
rotten-ftone ; but care muft be taken not to rub
it hard or long, as it is a fharp and penetrating
powder, and ought only to be ufed when the
other is not effectual, and with a careful hand.

A little colour, the fame as that with which
the carriage is painted, fhould always be kept in
referve, as the change, by time, occafions a difficulty in matching it. This would be convenient,

3   alfo,

alfo, in touching the blemifhed places, particularly the mouldings, or *carriage* part, &c. About as much as will fill a fmall gallipot of each colour will be fufficient; which, to preferve good and moift, muft be kept in a pan of water, taking care that it never be fuffered to dry. The brufh or pencils muft alfo be kept in the water. A little varnifh, alfo, in a clean phial, kept clofely corked, may fometimes be found convenient. The whole amount of the expence cannot exceed three or four fhillings.

H 3   CHAP.

CHAP. V.

PURCHASING OF SECOND-HAND CARRIAGES.

THOSE who are inclined to purchafe fecond-hand carriages, ought to be very cautious in their dealing, as the impofitions practifed in this bufinefs are not inferior to thofe ufed by horfe-dealers.

The great demand, within thefe twenty years, for fecond-hand carriages, for foreign and home ufe, has induced many unfkilful perfons to commence dealers, who call themfelves *Brokers*, and pretend to buy for the purpofe of breaking up, and difpofing of the old materials, but who, in general, inftead of breaking, vamp up, and refell fuch carriages at an exorbitant price, impofing thereby both on the public and the trade. The profit which thofe dealers realize on an old carriage of 50 or 6ol. price, is commonly greater than the builder's originally was, when new, and often exceeds the half of what it is fold for; yet many people imagine, if the price is about one-half

half the original value, the purchafe is reafonable, when, in faƐt, it is not worth one quarter,
or even an eighth.

The means whereby thofe people are enabled
to fell their carriages, is by giving to them a good
appearance, and imitating, as much as poſſible,
the faſhion. This they do by ornamenting them,
in particular with plated work, new painting, putting in a new lining, with fome ſhowey lace, new
wheels, or ringing them with new iron, to give
them the appearance of new, adding new lamps,
&c. All the materials ufed for this purpofe are
of the cheapeſt fort, manufaƐtured on purpofe;
but which, to a perfon ūnacquainted, look, for
the moment, as well as the beſt. The expence,
in fitting up, is chiefly beſtowed in ornament,
without, in the leaſt, attending to the fubſtance
of the carriage, which is feldom worth one-half,
for ufe, of what is thus beſtowed upon it in ornament.

SECT. 1.

REPOSITORIES.

BROKERS, or dealers, find a great convenience in Repofitories, now eſtabliſhed in numbers; as they can there vend their carriages, with-

II 4   out

out being queſtioned as to their quality, which
might otherwiſe deteƐ the impoſition; others,
who are of the trade, ſometimes make a convenience of a Repoſitory, for the ſame reaſon
as the brokers; as they may there vend what, in
their own ſhops, they would be aſhamed of.
From the apparent advantage of purchaſing from
thoſe Repoſitories, people are induced to buy
from them, in preference to dealing with a private trader: but every perſon attending thoſe
places ought to aƐ with double caution, as the
principal ſtock belongs to the brokers, or dealers
in ſecond-hand carriages, who take care to fur-
niſh thoſe places with a variety of all ſorts. It
is therefore the intereſt of the Repoſitory-keep-
ers to recommend the carriages of brokers, in
preference to thoſe belonging to ſtrangers, which
not only ſerves the brokers, but themſelves; for,
from frequent ſelling, and being again immediately ſupplied by the ſame parties, nothing is loſt
by the rent for ſtanding, and much gained by
commiſſion; while a ſtranger who has but one
carriage to ſell, the longer it remains unſold, and
at rent, the better; when, at laſt, the proprietor,
wearied with waiting, and having the expence
increaſed, and the carriage prejudiced by long
ſtanding, is induced to accept the broker's price,
who moſtly becomes the purchaſer.

Another

Another great difadvantage attending thofe
places is, that as a communication is feldom ad-
mitted between the buyer and the feller, théy are
both liable to be impofed upon, by exacting of
the buyer more, and paying to the feller lefs than
the carriage was fold for; fo that a confiderably
greater profit than that arifing from the commif-
fion and ftanding, may be derived by the Re-
pofitory-keeper, without adding any thing to the
value of the carriage thus fold.

As there are fuch rifks, it is to be recommended that no perfon will purchafe from thofe
places, but under the direction of fome fufficient tradefman, who may be competent to judge
of the real value of carriages in every ftate; for,
although a carriage may look fair, by being dif-
guifed with paint and putty, which is artfully
laid on, yet the carriage may be nearly rotten,
and ought rather to be broken up than made ufe
of.

SECT.

SECT. 2.

DIRECTIONS for PURCHASING CARRIAGES.

THE moſt obvious way to prevent being im-
poſed upon, in the purchaſe of ſecond-hand carriages, is to expoſe ſome of the moſt general artifices made uſe of by the ſellers; and, by attending to the few inſtructions here given, a perſon
may purchaſe with tolerable ſecurity. It is uſual,
in order to promote the ſale of a carriage, to pretend it belonged to ſome perſon of credit, who
has parted with it only becauſe one of another
kind was more convenient ; or that the parties are
dead, gone abroad, &c. It may alſo be noticed,
that on the pannels are uſually ſome fictitious
arms, creſts, or coronets, and the name of a perſon, of whom they have once bought or exchang-
ed a carriage, is made uſe of to ſell twenty by.
They always pretend the carriage to have been
but lately built, having then only its firſt or ſecond wheels on; but, as a carriage bears no
mark, like a horſe, whereby its age may be known
to any certainty, yet, by minute inſpection, it
may be nearly aſcertained, if the perſon has any
experience, and who always ſhould make the following obſervations :   .

SECT.

SECT. 3.

OBSERVATIONS.

FIRST, obferve the fhape of the body, keep-ing in mind the time when fuch a pattern was in vogue, and compare it with the prefent; and then examine the materials, in particular the tim-bers of the carriage, for, although well puttied, yet, in fome particular parts, its infirmity may be very vifible : if old, the futchels in the chaps, at the pole-bolt hole, and at the top where the gib is placed, are rough, and patched with leather; the pole, if the original one, on the fides and top which go into the futchels, is like-wife worn and patched, and near the top, unlefs hid with a tin covering, fee if it is reduced by the horfes gnawing it; look alfo to the tranfom-plates, if they are flat, thick, and clean, and that, by pufhing againft the coach-box or fprings, the upper carriage does not rock on them; fee that the fore axletree-bed, and tranfom at the middle, where the perch-bolt is placed, are found, and that about the perch-bolt hole there is not much patching with leather; that the ends of the tranfom, where the fprings and coach-box are placed, look clean and found : the fplinter-bar, if much worn, has the moulding towards

the

the ends nearly effaced; the fway-bar, and that
part of the bottom plate of the perch againft
which it wears, after much ufe, is gulled, and
the defeft is made up with leather patched on it;
the ends of the hind tranfom, in particular where
the fetter is placed, if old, are much gulled.
Look on thofe parts of the hind axletree-bed
where the fpring-ftays reft, which, if much in-
dented, is old: the hind footboard in the middle,
and the fore footboard-ledge, being worn hollow, are always proofs of the carriage having
been much ufed.

As to the body part, examine principally the
bottom fides, at the ends where the loops are
placed, and in the corners of the rabbits, under
the door bottoms, where the ftanding pillars are
framed, if very old, they will be rotten and appear rough.   The mortices of the door-locks, if
gulled, and the bolts of the locks, if loofe on the
fpindles, are proofs of their being old; and fo it
is, if the leather, which covers the roof of the
quarters and boot, appears to have been much
mended at the welts, or if it has drawn from the
fewings or nailing: the braces fhould be fupple
and clean, free from patches, or cracks at the
bearings; the fteps, if ricketty at the joints, and,
when down, if the treads drop under, and the
leather with which they are trimmed is dingy, and
torn at the joint-knuckles, fhew them to have
                                        been

been much ufed : the leather alfo which covers
the bottom fides, at the entrance of the doors,
if old, is rough, and has the grain worn or torn
on the outfide; the mahogany fhutters, or Ve-
netian-blind frames, when old, have their colour
difcharged by the weather, and look of a dingy
brown, the glafs-frames in particular; the front
ones are, when old, loofe at the corners, the
fides of the grooves loofened, and held together
only by the cloth which covers them.

Nothing is a better proof than the mouldings of
the framings, and the fcroll ends, or finifhes of
the timber, for if much filled with paint, or de-
faced, is a certain proof of the carriage having
been often painted, and, of courfe, old; the
paint will, with a flight knock, if not newly done,
fly off in fcales, particularly from the iron-work.
Examine well thofe places in the body round the
edges, if the framing, where the wet has been
likely to lodge, has not been rotten, and that the
furface is not made up with putty, or been cafed
on the outfide with new pieces of wood moulding,
which may be feen, if looked clofely into. In
examining the cloth of the lining, obferve the
fides and back, againft which the fhoulders rub,
that the cloth is not thread-bare, and that it is
free from moth-holes in every part. Of the lace
trimmings, notice the glafs-ftrings, the hand-
                                          holders,

holders, and pafting lace, particularly the fmall
lace which is round the lights or windows.

If the carriage has a coach box, examine the
condition of the feat under the hammercloth, alfo
the hammercloth at the ends and corners on
the infide, and, if it has been much ufed, it will
be ragged and worn through in many places.

In examining the wheels, look only to the outfide edge of the iron which rims them, for
their ftrength; look alfo to the fpokes at the
nave, that they are not ftarted, and that the
wheels are firm on the axletrees: thefe are the general rules to be obferved when examining a fecond-hand carriage, without having the opinion
of a perfon who is experienced, unlefs the perfon
of whom the carriage is bought can be depended
on for fair dealing, which is hardly to be expected from thofe peddling dealers, of whom it is recommended, as a caution, never to buy, without
advice from fome fkilful perfon, capable of knowing or detecting thofe impofitions fo frequently
practifed on the unwary.

SECT.

SECT. 4.

ON PURCHASING SECOND-HAND HARNESS.

IN buying old harnefs, fome caution is alfo neceffary, though the impofition therein is not likely to be fo great as on a carriage, yet little good may be expected therefrom ; there are many harneffes made up anew for fale by thofe brokers and dealers, but be cautious to buy of them, as they are compofed of the moft inferior materials to fell cheap, which many are induced to believe are bargains, knowing that they have paid a much greater price, without fuppofing them to be fo materially different in their quality : a good, found fecond-hand harnefs is much to be preferred to them, in chufing of which, obferve the condition of the leather, which if mellow, foft, and pliable, is good ; but if dry, ftiff, and harfh, is old. See alfo if the grain is cracked, or if the fewings are gummed up with greafe; and that the vained marks on the edges are not effaced ; and that all the leathers at the buckling and looped parts are whole and perfect; the trace ends, the collars, the cruppers, the belly-bands, and billets, fhow beft at the buckling parts how much the harnefs has been ufed.

The

The furniture, except the ornaments, ufually remains longer perfeᐸ, on account of the manner of plating them, than the leather does; but look to the corners of the buckles, and rings of the territs, through which the reins pafs, and to the ornaments; likewife the infide winker-pieces, and the head chains; thefe are the likelieft parts to look to for a proof of the furniture: but the leather is the beft guide, for if the pipes and ley of the collars, the traces at the points, and the breeching at the ftraps, are perfeᐸ, the harnefs is likely to be a good one, though it feldom proves, after the expence for alterations and changing the ornaments, which neceffarily muft be done before it can be ufed, to be much cheaper than a new one.

CHAP.

CHAP. VI.

THE DUTIES ON CARRIAGES.

CARRIAGES, regarding them as luxuries, are proper objects of taxation; in particular, as the proprietors thereof are persons supposed better able than others to contribute an extraordinary share to the support of the state. Yet many, however affluent in circumstances, are unwilling to subject themselves to the extraordinary duties, which are so contrived, as to increase very considerably upon every additional carriage that is kept; and, to save so great an increase of expence, keep only one or two carriages, who would otherwise keep three or four, were the duties made to lessen in the same proportion in the number as they are made to advance, many more carriages would be kept than are. An addition would thereby be made to the revenue, and the trade of coach-making would be materially benefited. Gentlemen would likewise have much greater scope for indulging their different fancies than at present, as they certainly restrain

I　　　　　　them·

themfelves from keeping more carriages, merely
to fave the great increafe of annual expence in
the duties. The following is an abftract of the
feveral acts of parliament on the duties to this
date, fhewing what the increafe of duty upon
every carriage is, including the new additional
ten per cent.

FOUR-WHEELED CARRIAGES.

EVERY perfon who keeps a carriage with four
wheels, by whatfoever name it is called, pays for
the firft 8l. 16s. for the fecond 9l. 18s. and if three
or more are kept, pays for each, after the firft, 11l.
which makes after the rate of 8l. 16s. for the firft,
9l. 18s. for the fecond, and 12l. for the third, as
the advance of 11l. is on the fecond if a third is
kept; which is the reafon many keep only two
carriages that would otherwife keep three.

TWO-WHEELED CARRIAGES.

TWO or three-wheeled carriages, of every defcription, however many are kept, are exempt
from any advance in the duty, and pay only 3l. 17s.
a year for each, of whatever denomination, drawn
by one or more horfes.

TAXED

TAXED CARTS.

BY a late act of parliament, the 35th of Geo. III. every carriage with lefs than four wheels, drawn by one horfe and no more, to be ufed in the affairs of hufbandry, or for the pur-pofe of carrying goods in the way of trade, but which fhall be occafionally ufed for the convey-ance of perfons, pays only the yearly tax of 12s. providing it is built as under defcribed, and does not exceed the value of 12l. including any fub-fequent alterations.

To be built only of wood and iron, without any lining whatever *.   To have no other fort of co-vering than a tilt, and to have no fprings.

This carriage is to be diftinguifhed from others by having the owner's chriftian and furname, and place of abode, with the words, " A Taxed Cart " painted, in black and white colours, on the back, or fome other confpicuous place, in Roman let-ters, of one inch in length, and breadth in pro-portion.   But no carriage, however built, fhall come within the meaning of this act, where the

* A portable fpring cufhion is a convenience which no perfon need deny themfelves the ufe of with this fort of carriage, it be-ing intended as well for others, as it cannot be confidered as belonging only thereto.

I 2   firft

firft, or after alterations make the value exceed
12l. the proof of which fhall lie on the owner;
and if it fhall be built in any refpeft contrary to
the provifions of this aft, or fhall not be fo mark-
ed as aforefaid; or if fuch perfons fhall refufe or
negleft, upon demand, to produce the fame for
examination, as aforefaid, he fhall be liable to
the duty of 3l. 17s. as on other two-wheeled carriages.

———

NEW CARRIAGE DUTY.

BESIDES the before-mentioned annual duties, there is alfo another, called the New Duty,
charged on, and paid by, the coachmaker to the
Excife, but is furcharged by the coachmaker on
the proprietor of the carriage; this is, for every
four-wheeled carriage, twenty fhillings; and for
every two-wheeled carriage, ten fhillings—the
common taxed cart excepted.

———

HOW THE DUTIES ARE ASSESSED.

THE duties on carriages are collefted by the
fame officers as are appointed to colleft the houfe

3   and

and window tax, and are under the same affeffor, furveyor, and commiffioner, to whom all refer- ence and appeals are to be made.

The affeffors are, within fourteen days after their appointment, to give or leave, at the dwell- ing-houfe of every perfon, within his limits, keeping any carriage liable to the faid duties, no- tice in writing, requiring them to produce, with- in fourteen days next enfuing, lifts, in writing, of the greateft number of carriages kept and ufed by him, and alfo the greateft number kept and ufed by a lodger, or inmate, in the courfe of the year, ending on the 5th of April preceding fuch notice; and to exprefs the denomination of each carriage, and its number of wheels, dif- tinguifhing, alfo, which are kept for private ufe, which to be let out for hire, and which are ufed as public ftage coaches. And if any carriages are kept in more diftricts than one, it fhall be fpeci- fied, in a lift or declaration, the particular pa- rifh wherein that carriage is meant to be paid for; and if any perfons are affeffed in one diftrict, and fhall again be affeffed in another, the commiffion- ers within fuch latter diftrict, on application for that purpofe, are required to alter fuch affeffment, on proof being given that fuch perfons have paid the duty in another place.

THE

THE PENALTIES.

ANY perſon who ſhall neglect or refuſe to return the liſts when called for, within fourteen days
after notice left, ſhall forfeit 10l. and the aſſeſſor
ſhall, on the beſt information he can obtain, make
an aſſeſſment upon ſuch perſon keeping ſuch carriages as are liable to the ſaid duties; and ſuch
aſſeſſment ſhall be final and concluſive on the perſons thereby charged, who ſhall not be at liberty
to appeal therefrom, unleſs ſuch perſon ſhall
prove he was not at his dwelling-houſe at the
time of delivery, nor between that day and the
time limited for delivering ſuch liſt to the aſſeſ-
ſors, or ſhall allege ſuch other excuſe as the
commiſſioners ſhall be ſatisfied with.

If any perſon omit to return in the liſt an entry
of any carriage, they ſhall be ſurcharged for the
ſame double the duty ſo omitted, one-half whereof to go to ſuch perſon making the ſurcharge.

The inhabitant houſeholder of any houſe where
there are any lodgers or inmates, ſhall, within a
week after required, by notice, in writing, left at
his houſe, by any aſſeſſor or ſurveyor, deliver to,
or leave for, ſuch aſſeſſor, a liſt, in writing, of
every lodger or inmate who ſhall keep any carriage, to the beſt of his knowledge; and if he ſhall
refuſe to deliver ſuch liſt, wilfully omit, or miſ-
repreſent,

reprefent, any defcription which ought to be con-
tained therein, he fhall forfeit 20l.

Families wifhing to keep two, three, or more,
carriages, may fave the increafed duty by allowing their relatives to enter them feparately as
lodgers or inmates.

F I N I S.

GLOSSARY and INDEX.

A.

ARMS. The diftinction of families, which are moftly painted on the pannels. Vol. 1, p. 195.

Axletree. A piece of wrought iron work, fixed to the under part of the carriage, on which the wheels are placed. p. 81.

Axletree Arm. That part of the axletree which paffes through the centre of the wheel, and on which it turns. Vol. 1, p. 81.

Axletree Bed. The timber, in which the axletree is let or bedded. Vol. 1, p. 47, 50.

Axletree Boxes. Iron tubes fitted to the arms of the axletree, fixed firm in the wheel's ftock, and which contains the greafe or oil. Vol. 1, p. 82.

Axletree Hoop. An iron hoop, which fixes the axletree to the timber or bed on which it refts. Vol. 1, p. 102.

Axletree Nut. An iron fcrew, with a large furface fixed to the fore or hind end of the axletree, for the purpofe of keeping on the wheels. Vol. 1, p. 81.

Axletree Wafher. An iron collar or fhoulder, fitted to the body or large end of the axletree, againft which the back of the wheel wears, for the purpofe of keeping in the greafe. Vol. 1, p. 81.

B.

Back Band. Part of a one horfe chaife harnefs, which croffes the faddle, and fupports the fhafts. Vol. 2. p. 140.

O   *Back Strap.*

Back Strap. A part of the harnefs looped on the crupper, and buckled to a loop or tug to keep up the traces. Vol. 2, p. 134.

Bars. Timbers of various forts, particularly deferibed in alphabetical order.

Battens. Strips of wood, which are fixed on the outfide of the pannels to form the framing, and are then moulded; but when fixed on the infide of the pannels, are to mend or ftrengthen them. Vol. 1, p. 18, 21.

Beads. The mouldings which ornament the carriage. Vol. 1. p. 167.

Bearing Rein. The rein which holds up the horfe's head. Vol. 2. p. 138.

Belly Band. A leather which buckles round the horfe's belly, and fixes on the pad or houfing. Vol. 2, p. 135.

Bit. An iron inftrument, which is put into the mouth of the horfe, by which he is governed. Vol. 2, p. 146.

Blinds. Such as Venetian and fpring blinds, fee each in their order.

Blocks. Wooden raifers to the fprings of phaetons; foot-boards, budgets, fhafts, &c. moftly ornamented by carving, and are deferibed by what is raifed upon them, fuch as budget blocks, &c. Vol. 1. p. 120.

Body. That part of the carriage, which contains the paffengers. Vol. 1. p. 5.

Body Loops. Strong iron loops, ferewed or bolted to the bottom corners of the body, and by which it hangs. Vol. 1, p. 32.

Bolts. Iron pins of various lengths, headed at the one end, and ferewed at the other, and are in general about half an inch thick. Vol. 1. p. 103.

Boots and Budgets. Large leathered boxes, fixed on the fore part of the carriage, and diftinguifhed by the various names of Salifbury, platform, or trunk boots and budgets. Vol. 1, p. 115.

Boodge or Sword-cafe. A prominence from the back of the body, to carry parcels in. Vol. 1, p. 15.

Bottom or Pannel Bars. The bottom end framings of the body, on which the end pannels reft. Vol. 1, p. 12.

Bottom Boards. Boards which form the bottom of the body. Vol. 1, p. 16.

Boxes. See axletree box, feat box, coach box, driving box, cap box, &c.

Box Locks. Are the locks ufed for the doors of the body. Vol. 1, p. 161.

Braces. The leathers by which the bodies are hung, or checked Vol. 1, p. 210.

Brackets. Parts of the framing of the body, which support the foot-board, and also the carved ornaments, fixed on each side the top of the coach box foot-board. Vol. 1, p. 31, 55.

Brass Bead Edgings. Brass plates, which are screwed to the side of doors for them to shut on. Vol. 1, p. 160.

Breast Collar. A part of the harness which is placed round the horse's breast, by which he draws. Vol. 2, p. 133.

Breeching. That part of the harness which goes round the breech of the horse. Vol. 2, p. 134.

Bridle. That part of the harness which is put on the head of the horse, by which he is managed. Vol. 2, p. 136.

Bridge. Part of the furniture of the harness, mostly made in the shape of the buckle, but has no tongue, only two cross bars or bridges, round which the strapping is looped. Vol. 2. p. 165.

Bridoon. An additional temporary bridle, made similar to a riding or watering bridle. Vol. 2. p. 141.

Bridoon Bit. The bit which is used to the bridoon bridle. Vol. 2, p. 146.

Bridoon Chain, or Links. Small ornaments, through which the bridoon reins run. Vol. 2, p. 146.

Budget Boot and Horn Bar. The inner cross bar to the front of the carriage, on which the fore spring stay and budget rest. Vol. 1, p. 48.

Buggy. A small phaeton or chaise, made only to carry one person; Vol. 2, p. 121.

Buttons. Nails or screws with large brass heads, for the purpose of hitching on the straps, mostly silvered, but sometimes plated. Vol. 1, p. 163.

Button Hangers. Small ornamented tassels, which are placed on the fringe. Vol. 1. p. 136.

C.

Cabriole. A two wheel carriage, with the body somewhat like a chariot, built and used mostly in France

O 2

Cap Box,

GLOSSARY AND INDEX.

Cap Box. A long leather cafe, ufed for the purpofe of carrying ladies head dreffes. Vol. 1, p. 224.

Caps. Small pieces of leather, ufed to confine temporary pins or bolts, fuch as pole pin caps, &c.

Carriage. That part, on which the body is placed, and to which the wheels are united. Vol. 1. p. 39.

Carpeting. Covering the bottom of the body or ftep treads with carpet.

Chain Belt. A thin-wire chain, covered with leather, made in the form, and to anfwer the ufe of a ftrap, for the purpofe of fecuring trunks, &c. behind a carriage. Vol. 1, p. 217.

Chair. A light chaife without pannels, for the ufe of parks, gardens, &c. a name commonly applied to all light chaifes. Vol. 2, p. 121.

Check Brace. A fingle ftrip of leather, which is looped through a ring at the corners of the body, to check it from fwinging too much endways. Vol. 1, p. 211.

Check Ring. An iron ring fcrewed into the corner pillars of the body for the check braces. Vol. 1, p. 106.

Check String. A worfted line, by which the coachman has notice to ftop.

Coach Box. The fixture on which the driver fits. Vol. 1, p. 125.

Collar. That part of the harnefs, by which the horfe draws; it is of two forts, the breaft and the heam, alfo a fhoulder or middle to an iron ftay or bolt. Vol. 2, p. 133, 139.

Collar Bolt. A bolt with two nuts, and a collar in the middle. Vol. 1, p. 104.

Collar Brace. A ftrong leather ftrap, fixed under the body, to check it from fwinging fideways. Vol. 1, p. 211.

Collar Brace Ring. An iron ring, through which the collar brace is looped. Vol. 1, p. 106.

Cork Ledge. A long ftripe of cork, nailed on the coachman's footboard, againft which his feet are placed.

Corner Pillars. The corner framings of bodies. Vol. 1, p. 10.

Cornice Rails. The top framing of the body of a coach or chariot, called roof rails. Vol. 1, p. 13.

Counter Sunk Bolt. A bolt, the head of which is let in level with the furface of the plate it fixes

Coupling

Coupling Reins. The reins which couple the horfes together. Vol. 2, p. 137.

Cradle. A leather convenience fixed to oppofite bearings, for any thing to be carried fafe, and the coachman to ride eafy upon. Vol. 1. p. 130.

Cranes. Strong iron bars, which form the fides of the upper carriage, and unite the back and fore timbers, fhaped like a crane's neck, for the purpofe of the fore wheels to pafs under. Vol. 1, p. 94.

Crane Neck Carriage. A carriage that is made with cranes. Vol. 1, p. 53.

Crane Shaft. Wood inftead of iron, for the fame purpofe. Vol. 2, p. 83.

Crown Piece. That part of the bridle which lies on the horfe's head. Vol. 2, p. 137.

Curb. The fmall chain which goes round the horfe's jaw, and hooks to the bit.

Curb Hook. A hook which the curb is hitched to.

Curricle. A two wheel carriage, drawn by two horfes abreaft. Vol. 2, p. 95.

Curtuers or Cuttos. Projections left at the end of the axletree bed, which lie over the back part of the wheel to fhelter the axletree from gravel or other dirt. Vol. 1, p. 48.

D.

Dafhing or Splafhing Leather. A large iron frame, covered with leather, preventing the dirt from fplafhing againft the paffengers or pannels. Vol. 1, p. 206.

Dee. A ring in the fhape of a D. for a ftrap to loop through. Vol. 2, p. 145.

Door Pillars. The fide framings of the doors. Vol. 1, p. 14.

Door Styles or Middle Rails. The middle framing of the doors. Vol. 1. p. 14.

Dovetail Ketch. A fmall iron ketch, fixed on the fide of the door, to prevent it fettling. Vol. 1, p. 162.

Duke's Bit. A bit of a peculiar form on the outfide. Vol. 2. p. 146.

Drag Chain. A ftrong chain, with a large hook to hitch on the hind

hind wheel, and keep it from turning when defcending a hill, Vol. 1. p. 221.

Drag Staff. A fhort pole, which is fixed under the hind part of the carriage, and to be let down when afcending a hill, to give the horfe more cafe, by occafionally refting. Vol. 1, p. 221.

Driving Cufhion. A deep cufhion, made purpofely for the driver to fit on.

Driving Box. A portable box, on which a cufhion is placed, to raife the driver. Vol. 1, p. 149.

Drop Bottom. The bottom of a coach, chariot, or chaife body, when funk deeper than the furface of the framing, to give more room. Vol. 1, p. 15.

Drop Seat Box. A box which is made to hang between the feat rails, to carry luggage.

E.

Ear Bows. Leathers bent acrofs the horfe's ears, lapped with tape, the fame as the fronts and rofes. Vol. 2, p. 148.

Elbow Cafe. A cavity in the infide of the body, at the elbow part, for bottles, &c. feldom ufed but to travelling carriages.

Elbow Rails. The middle part of the framing to a coach or chariot, and the upper part to a chaife or phaeton body, on which the elbow refts. Infide elbows are projections within the body, for the elbow to reft cn. Vol. 1, p. 12.

Elbow Springs. Are thofe that rife in an oblique direction from their bearings, moftly ufed to one horfe, or phaeton carriages. Vol. 1. p. 76.

Emboffing. A method of raifing the crefts, &c. in filver or plated metals, &c. the fame as in relievo. Vol. 1, p. 172.

Englifh Pole Pieces. The pole pieces that are fixed to the pole-end. Vol. 1, p. 212.

F.

Falls. That part of the lining, which hang   e feat rails.

Falfe Collars. Thofe that are occafionally added under the others, to
prevent

prevent the horfe from being galled by friction. Vol. 2, p. 139.

Falfe Belly Bands. A leather ftrap, which buckles on each fide of the collar to keep it down, fo as to fave the ufe of a breeching. Vol. 2, p. 159.

Falfe Lining. A linen cover, to preferve the cloth lining clean. Vol. 1. p. 149.

Felly. A divided part of the rim of a wheel, alfo a fmall part of a circle which is fixed on the futchells, and forms a bearing for the whole or half wheel front. Vol. 1, p. 110.

Fence. A rabbet round the edges of the lights, to prevent the weather getting between it, and the glafs or fhutter frame.

Fillet. A narrow painted border, not exceeding one inch broad. Vol. 1, p. 198.

Foot Boards. Are what the feet of the fervant or driver reft on. Vol. 1, p. 31, 55.

Foot Board Ledge. A fmall piece of timber fixed on the footboard, againft which the coachman's feet are placed. Vol. 1, p. 55.

Footman Cufhion. A wooden frame ftuffed, and covered with ftout leather, to eafe and elevate the fervant behind the carriage. Vol. 1, p. 123.

Footman Holders. Lace, with taffels, hung to the back of the body, by which the footman holds. Vol. 1, p. 143.

Footman Step. An iron ftep, fixed to the hind part of the carriage, for the fervant to mount by. Vol. 1, p. 108.

Fore Bar or Block. A bar framed in the front of a carriage. Vol. 1, p. 49, 62.

Fore Carriage. The under part, or conductor of a four wheel carriage, to which the fore wheels are placed. Vol. 1, p. 49.

Forehead Piece. An ornament, which hangs loofely on the forehead of the horfe. Vol. 2. p. 142.

Fore Pillars. That part of the framing in a chariot, on which the doors hang, and which forms the front fweep. Vol. 1, p. 11.

Fore Rails. The crofs framing rails to the fore end of a body. Vol. 1. p. 15.

Fore Tranfom. The timber which croffes the perch, on which the fprings are placed, and through which the centre pin, or perck bolt, paffes to the fore carriage. Vol. 1, p. 46.

Frame Heads. The head of a chaife or phaeton, made on an iron frame, for the purpofe of taking off occafionally. Vol. 1, p. 98.

French

French Pole Pieces. Pole pieces which are made double, fo as to be taken off occafionally. Vol. 1, p. 212.

French Reins. Long coupling reins, which buckle at the upper part of the long hand reins.

Front. A broad ftripe to the front of the bridle, moftly covered with taping to match the rofes. Vol. 2, p. 137.

Futchells. The timbers of the under carriage, in which the pole is fixed. Vol. 1, p. 50.

G.

Galling Leather. A broad ftrip of leather, fewed under that part of the harnefs, where there is a buckle to prevent it from galling the horfe, or placed under the coachman's feat.

Gib. A fmall half-round wedge, which keeps the pole from rifing. Vol. 1, p. 52.

Gib Straps. Two ftraps nailed to the gib, to confine it in its places Vol. 1, p. 52.

Gig. A one horfe chaife built in a fanciful ftyle. Vol. 2, p. 96.

Glafs Rollers. A brafs machine, which eafes the weight of the glafs when drawing up. Vol. 1, p. 162.

Glafs Strings or Holders. The lace which is nailed to the frames, to draw up the glaffes by. Vol. 1, p. 142.

Globe Lamp. A lamp, the body of which is of a globular form. Vol. 1. p. 182.

Grafhopper Spring. A peculiar formed fpring, which fixes under the fhaft of a one horfe chaife to the axletree. Vol. 1, p. 76.

H.

Hammer Cloth. An ornamented covering to the coachman's feat. Vol. 1, p. 153.

Hand Reins. The reins which the driver holds, and by which the horfes are guided. Vol. 2, p. 137.

Hanging and Unhanging. Is taking the body from the carriage for any material repair, and re-fixing it when done.

Head Plates. Metal ornaments, placed at the upper parts of bodies. Vol. 1, p. 171.

Head Plate Pins. Small nails, with plated heads, to faften the head plates with.

Head Ring, or Head Territ. A ring, placed on the top of the bridle of the wheel harnefs, through which the leading reins pafs, when four horfes are drove in hand, and fometimes ufed for ornament only. Vol. 2, p. 148.

Heads. The top or cover of a phaeton, chaife, &c. or the top of the bridle. Vol. 1, p. 202.

Head Stall. The bridle without the bit or reins, and fometimes means the crown piece only. Vol. 2, p. 137.

Heam Collar. A padded or ftuffed collar, which goes round the horfe's neck, and by which he draws. Vol. 2, p. 146.

Heams. Two compaffed irons, with links at one end, and loops to buckle at the other, fitted to the neck collar, by which the draught is taken. Vol. 2, p. 146.

Heam Links. The links, which unite the heams at the bottom. Vol. 2, p. 147.

Heam Strap. A fmall ftrap, which confines the heams at the top. Vol. 2, p. 147.

Heam Tugs. A part of the harnefs rivetted to the heams, to which the traces are faftened or buckled. Vol. 2, p. 139.

Heel Boards, or Heel Leathers. Boards or leathers nailed under the feat, to fhelter the legs from the cold. Vol. 2, p. 127.

Hedge Hog. A leather ftuck full of nails, to buckle on the pole with the points upward, to prevent the horfes gnawing it.

Hind Standards. An ornamented platform, on which the footman ftands behind the carriage. Vol. 1, p. 123.

Hip Straps. A part of the harnefs, which lies on the hips of the horfe, and buckles to the breeching tugs, which it fupports. Vol. 2, p. 133.

Holders. Broad lace with taffels, by which the perfon in the carriage holds, or draws the glaffes up by. Vol. 1, p. 136.

Horn Bar. Same as budget or boot bar.

Hoop Sticks. Thin compaffed rails, which form the roof. Vol. 1, p. 31.

Hoops. Iron rims, which are tightly drove on, to ftrengthen or unite two things together. Vol. 1, p. 102.

Hooped Wheel. The wheel whereof the iron rim is one entire piece. Vol. 1, p. 111.

Hooping

Hooping Piece. A ſtrong timber, which unites the perch to the fore end of the carriage. Vol. 1, p. 46.

Hooping Wings. Two extending timbers, which unite the perch to the fore end of the carriage. Vol. 1. p. 46.

Houſing. A ſmall ſquare pad, which lies on the horſe's back, to which moſt of the harneſs is fixed. Vol. 2, p. 132.

Houſing Cuſhion. The ſoft ſtuffed under part of the houſing. Vol. 2, p. 133

I.

Imperial. A leathered caſe, which is placed occaſionally on the roof of the body, for the purpoſe of carrying cloaths, &c. ſafe. Vol. 1, p. 218.

Italian Lamps. A lamp of an oblong or cylindrical round form. Vol. 1, p. 182.

J.

Jack. A ſmall machine, in which the brace is fixed, to be let out or taken in by. Vol. 1, p. 78.

Japanning. Painting, with a black gloſſy preparation, the leather-, ed part of the body and carriage. Vol. 1, p. 206.

Jew's Harp Staple. An iron ſtaple, in the ſhape of a Jew's harp, and a connected part of the graſshopper ſpring, which it raiſes from the axletree. Vol. 1, p. 76.

Jointing. The cleaning of the mouldings, and levelling the joints of the framing, previous to new painting.

Joints. The irons, by which the heads of chaiſes or landaus are let up and down. Vol. 1, p. 107.

Joint Props. What the joints are placed on.

K.

Knee Boot or Knee Flap. The leather which covers the knees, when ſitting in an open carriage. Vol. 1, p. 205.

Knee

Knee Boot Cheeks. The flaps on the sides of the knee boots. Vol. 1, p. 205.

Knee Boot Fall. The strip of cloth, which covers the top of the knee boot, made of the same materials as the lining is.

Knee Boot Strap. What fastens the knee boot down, when out of use.

L.

Lamp Barrel. That part which contains the candle. Vol. 1, p. 182.

Lamp Fork or Prop. A small iron fixture, which keeps the lamp barrel steady. Vol. 1, p. 182.

Lamp Irons. Are what the lamps are fixed by to the body. Vol. 1, p. 182.

Lamp Spring. A spiral wire, placed in the lamp barrel, which forces the candle to rife as it consumes. Vol. 1, p. 182.

Lamp Straps. Small straps, which buckle round the barrels. Vol. 1, p. 185.

Landau. A carriage built in the manner of a coach, but with the upper part of the body to open at pleasure. Vol. 2. p. 38.

Landaulet. A chariot made the same as above. Vol. 2, p. 57.

Lays. A strip of leather, which is sewed on the top of another that is broader, for the purpose of additional strength, or to confine a smaller buckle; also particular stripes in the lace, which are always of silk, called silk lays.

Leading Harnefs, or parts thereof. Are what belong to the fore horses, when more than the ordinary number are used, commonly called leaders. Vol. 2, p. 152.

Linch Pin. A small iron pin, which goes through the axletree point, and fecures the nut to keep the wheel on.

Lining. Covering the wood work on the infide of the body with cloth, &c. or repairing any part that is worn. Vol. 1, p. 154.

Lights. The windows of the body, such as door, front, fide, or back lights.

Locking Plates. Short, thick iron plates, fixed to the fides of the perch, to preferve it from injury, by the wheel rubbing againft it when the carriage is turning.

Locking Stop. A piece of timber fixed to the fore bed, to prevent the wheel ftriking at all againft the perch.

Loops.

Loops. See body loops or running loops.

Luggage Boot. A boot with a loose cover, convenient to carry luggage. Vol. 1, p. 116.

Luggage Irons. The iron frames, of which those boots are made. Vol. 1, p. 97

Lugg Plate. An iron plate, with a part branching from the side, to unite or hang two things by.

M.

Main Braces. The strong leathers, by which the body hangs. Vol. 1, p. 210.

Mantle. A painted ornament, in form of a curtain, in which the arms, crest, or cyphers are placed. Vol. 1, p. 197.

Martingale. A temporary addition to the bridle, placed so as to prevent the horse throwing his head back, sometimes used as an ornament. Vol. 2, p. 140.

Middle Pillar, or Partition Piece. That which divides the front windows into two. Vol. 1, p. 15.

Middle Rails. The middle framing of the body. Vol. 1, p. 12.

Mortoise. A square hole, made in one timber, to receive the end of another, called a tennon, for the framings to be fastened by.

N.

Nave. The centre or stock of the wheels, in which all the spokes are fixed, and through which the axletree arms go. Vol. 1, p. 112.

Neck, or Wither Strap. A part of the harness, which crosses the withers of a horse, and supports the breast collar. Vol. 2, p. 135.

Neck Plates. Thin iron plates, fixed on the flats or wood work of chaise heads, which move by means thereof. Vol. 1, p. 107.

Newmarket Strap. A part of the harness, which buckles together the housing and collar. Vol. 2, p. 135.

Net. A convenience placed across the roof, on the inside of a coach or chariot. Vol. 1, p. 145.

Nose Band. A leather, which crosses the nose of the horse, and buckles to the cheek of the bridle. Vol. 2, p. 142.

Nose

Nose Plate. A short iron plate, fixed acrofs the chops or nose of the futchells to keep them faft, and on which the pole refts. Vol. 1, p. 100.

Nunters. Are fhort timbers, framed acrofs the beds, or tranfoms of the carriage, to ftrengthen them. Vol. 1, p. 49.

Nuts. Square pieces of iron, which are fcrewed on the bottom of the bolt. Vol. 1, p. 104.

O.

Oil Skin. Linen dreffed with oil, ufed as covers for hammer cloths, &c.

Oil Skin Patent. Woollen cloth, prepared in a peculiar manner, for the fame ufe as the linen, but is more durable.

Octagon, or Oval Light. The fmall window at the back of the body.

P.

Pad Cloth. A cloth ufually bound with lace, and put under the pad or houfing on the horfe's back. Vol. 2, p. 149.

Pannels. Are what fills the framing of the body, and are called door, fide, quarter, or back pannels. Vol. 1, p. 20.

Pafting Lace. A narrow lace, which is nailed and pafted over the nailed edges of the cloth. Vol. 1, p. 142.

Perch. The long or main timber of a carriage, which unites the hind and fore end together. Vol. 1, p. 44.

Perch Bolt. A ftrong round iron pin, on which the fore carriage turns. Vol. 1, p. 103.

Perch Carriage. The carriage made with a perch. Vol. 1, p. 43.

Perch Bolt Hole. The hole in the timber through which this pin paffes.

Perch Bolt Key, or Cotterell. Is a thin piece of iron, fixed through the eye of the perch bolt, to keep it from rifing.

Perch Bolt Nut. An iron fcrew, fixed on the perch bolt, for the purpofe of additional fecurity. Vol. 1, p. 103.

Perch

Perch Hoop. The hoop that unites the other timbers to the perch.
Vol. 1, p. 102.

Picking out. The painting with various colours the mouldings, &c.
Vol. 1, p. 193.

Pinning. The nailing with small headed iron nails, called pins,
used only to the leather or lining.

Pipe Box. See axletree box.

Plated. The strengthening the timber with iron plates, or covering
the furniture of either carriage or harnefs, superficially with
silver or other metal.

Point Straps. Small straps, which buckle down the points of the
main braces.

Pole. The long leaver, by which the carriage is conducted.
Vol. 1, p. 51.

Pole Pin. A round iron pin, which passes through the futchell ends
and pole, to keep it from coming forward.

Pole Pin Cap. A leather, which secures the pole pin. Vol. 1, p. 104.

Pole Pieces. Strong leather straps, which fasten the horses to the pole
end. Vol. 1, p. 212.

Pole Ring. A ring fixed on the pole end, with loops for the pole
pieces to be fastened to. Vol. 1, p. 102.

Pole Staple. A staple drove into the back end of the pole, with
which it is fastened by a gib. Vol. 1, p. 106.

Portfmouth Bit. A bit made of a peculiar form, for hard mouthed
horses.

Private Locks. Those fixed in the standing pillars, by which the
doors are occasionally locked up. Vol. 1, p. 161.

Props. The iron fixtures, on which the joints of chaise or landau
heads are fixed. Vol. 1, p. 107.

Pump or Plow Handles. The long projecting timbers, on the hind
part of the carriage, on which the foot-board is placed. Vol.
1, p. 121.

Q.

Quarters. The sides of a coach, divided by the middle rails into
four parts; in a chariot, only into two: the sides within the
body are also called quarters. Vol. 1, p. 16.

Rabbit

R.

Rabbet. An edge of the timber funk below the surface, for others to be lapped in.

Raifer. A fmall pillar or block, for any other thing to reft on. Vol. 1, p. 63.

Raifed Hind or Fore End. Is when the budget or footboard is raifed on blocks, for the ornament of the carriage. Vol. 1, p. 120.

Rims. Narrow ftripes of leather, of various forts, which are buckled to the bridle to manage the horfe by.

Rein rings and Hook. Are conveniencies for the reins to run in, or be hung by. Supplement, p. 69.

Rockers. The flat pieces of timber fixed within the bottom fide, on which the bottom boards are nailed, for the purpofe of finking the bottom, to give more height within the body. Vol. 1, p. 15.

Rollers. See glafs and fplinter bar rollers.

Roof Rails. The top framing of a coach or chariot body, on which the roof is fixed. Vol. 1, p. 13.

Rofes. Round ornaments for a horfe's head, moftly made up of filk or worfted ribbons, alfo a fmall trimming, through which the hand holders are fixed. Vol. 2, p. 148.

Round Robbins. Broad rims fixed to the ends of the axletree bed, to cover the back of the fore wheel, and for preventing dirt falling in to injure the arms of the axletree.

Running Loops. Leather loops, which flide on the reins to keep the points down.

S.

Safe Braces. Braces, which are placed fo, as to fupport the body, if by accident, its other fupporters fhould break. Vol. 1, p. 212.

Salifbury Box or Boot. A coach box of a peculiar form, imitating thofe originally made to the Salifbury ftages. Vol. 1, p. 126.

Screwing a Bolt. Mending the thread of it, when injured by ruft, or a bruife.

Screwing.

Screwing up the Bolt. Is the tightening the nuts to keep the work firm.

Scroll. An ornament, carved at the end of the timber.

Seaming Lace. A round lace, which is sewed in the corners, and round the edges of the linings. Vol. 1, p. 142.

Seat Boards. The boards, nailed to the seat rails, on which are placed the cushions.

Seat Box. A box, which slides under the seat of the body. Vol. 1, p. 149.

Seat Fall. A piece of cloth, nailed on the edge of the seat, trimmed with lace, and placed for ornament, and also to cover the vacant space.

Seat-Irons. Strong irons made in the form of a T, with loops at the end for the cradle to be fixed to, on which the coachman's seat is placed. Vol. 1, p. 97.

Seat Rails. The cross framing, on which the seat boards are nailed Vol. 1, p. 15.

Seat Rolls. A strip of cloth, nailed along the front of the seat, and stuffed in form of a roll, to keep the cushions in their place.

Shutter String. A tape nailed on the shutter, by which it is pulled up or down.

Shafts. The long timbers, in which the horse is placed, to a two-wheeled chaise.

Shaft Tug. Part of a chaise harness, in which the shafts of a one horse chaise are hung. Vol. 2, p. 140.

Slatt. The wooden ribs of a chaise or landau head. Vol. 1, p. 31.

Sliding Seat. A seat, which occasionally moves higher or lower, to accommodate ladies in their head dress, also a small seat that draws out to accommodate a third person to sit on.

Scroll Springs or Scroll Loops. Are springs and loops, when bent round in the form of a scroll. Vol. 1, p. 75.

Splinter Bar. The fore bar, which the horses are fastened to, and draw by. Vol. 1, p. 50, 62.

Splinter Bar Sockets. Iron ferrules, for the splinter bar ends. Vol. 1, p. 101.

Splinter Bar Rolls, or Roller Bolts. Are strong bolts, with large round flat heads, and thick rollers, round which the traces are fastened. Vol. 1, p. 104.

Shackle.

Shackle. A square iron loop, which is hung on the top of the springs, for the braces to hang by. Vol. 1, p. 106.

Spokes. The timbers, which support the rim of the wheel from the centre. Vol. 1, p. 112.

Spring Curtain. A silk curtain, which draws down over the lights or windows, and instantly rises on pulling the trigger, by means of a concealed spring. Vol. 1, p. 146.

Spring Plate. One of the members of a spring. Vol. 1, p. 71.

Spring Back Plate. The outside, or main plate of a spring.

Spring Gut Plate. The inside plate of the spring.

Spring Bars, Beds, or Transoms. The timbers, on which the springs are placed. Vol. 1. p. 46.

Spring Hoop. The hoop which confines the plates. Vol. 1, p. 71.

Spring Stay. The irons which support the springs. Vol. 1, p. 73.

Standard. The principal part of the coach box, or the perpendicular framings in other parts, such as the fore and hind standards. Vol. 1, p. 55, 123.

Standard Plates or Irons. The iron work, which fixes the standards in their place. Vol. 1, p. 100.

Standing Pillar. An upright part of the framing of the body, which supports the roof, on which the doors hang, and shut against. Vol. 1, p. 11.

Stays. The iron work, which supports or strengthens any separate article, such as the horn bar stay, the spring stay, &c. Vol. 1, p. 96.

Step Piece Body. The name of a peculiar formed chaise body. Pl. 33.

Step Plates. Thin iron plates, for the joints of the steps to wear on, and to preserve the timber.

Step Stops. Small iron fixtures, against which the folding steps rest, when let down.

Strake. The short pieces of iron, with which the ordinary wheel is shod or rung. Vol. 1, p. 112.

Strake Nails. Long strong nails, with which the strakes are fastened to the wheel.

Surcingle. A leather strap and buckle, sewed to a chaise saddle, the same as a belly band to a housing.

Swa Bar. A compassed timber, fixed on the futchell, which keeps the fore carriage steady. Vol. 1, p. 51.

P

Swa

Swa Bar Plate. A plate fcrewed on the fwa bar to ftrengthen it. Vol. 1, p. 100.

Squabs or Sleeping Cuſhions. Soft thin cuſhions, hung on the infide of the body, for the ſhoulders and head to lean againſt. Vol. 1, p. 145.

Sword Caſe. The fame as a boodge.

Sulkcy. The name of a charlot, which can hold only one perfon. Vol. 2, p. 66.

Scutcheons. Small plates, fixed between the leather, and the ſhoulders of the territts, &c.

T.

Tandum. The manner of driving two horfes in a team. Vol. 2, p. 120

Territts. Tne harnefs furniture, through which the reins are conducted. Vol. 2, p. 144.

Throat Band or Throat Latch. A ſtrap which buckles on each fide of the bridle, placed under the throat. Vol. 2, p. 138.

Throat Band Dee. A D. fixed on the throat band, to contract the bearing reins. Vol. 2, p. 145.

Thimble Hooks and Eyes. Are the iron work, on which the ſhafts for one horfe phaetons are hung. Vol. 1, p. 104.

Thumb Nut or Screw. A nut with lugs, to be fcrewed on with the finger and thumb. Vol. 1, p. 104.

Trace. That part of the harnefs, by which the horfe draws. Vol. 2, p. 153.

Trunk Faſteners. Small iron fcrews with fquare heads, by which the trunk is kept ſteady. Vol. 1, p. 105.

Tranſoms. The timbers of the carriage, which are framed acrofs the perch, on which the fprings are fixed. Vol. 1, p. 46.

Tread. Part of a ſtep or flat place, referved for the foot to be placed cn, when getting in.

Trimming. The covering with lace, cloth, leather, &c. the infide or outfide of a carriage.

Trunk Straps. Straps, by which the trunk is faſtened. Vol. 1, p. 217.

Tub Bottom Body. A body, with a roundiſh formed bottom.

Tug Plate. A plate, fixed on the ſhafts, in which the tugs of a one horfe harnefs is placed.

Tugs.

Tugs. Part of the harnefs, which fupports the bearings, fuch as collar or breeching tugs, &c. Vol. 2, p. 139, 140.

Tyre. The iron which rims the wheels.

V.

Vallens. The top rows of broad} lace, to the infide of a coach or chariot body, and the front ftrips of leather, ufed to the head of a one horfe chaife, &c. Vol. 1, p. 203.

Varnifhing. The covering with a glutinous tranfparent liquid, which gives luftre to, and preferves the paint. Vol. 1, p. 193.

Venetian Blind. A blind, for the purpofe of letting in the air, and fhading from the fun, which ferves alfo as a fhutter when clofed. Vol. 1, p. 148.

Vis-à-Vis. A fmall body, of a coach form, meant only to contain two paffengers, fronting each other. Vol. 2, p. 48.

Under Carriage. The fore carriage, which conducts the other. Vol. 1, p. 49.

W.

Webb Lace. A thick coarfe kind of lace, moftly ufed for footman holders. Vol. 1, p. 137.

Wheel Fore End. Is when the front of an upper carriage, has a whole or half circular plate, placed horizontally, for the more fteady bearing, when the carriage locks or turns. Vol. 1, p. 54.

Wheel Irons. Strong irons, which hook or bolt on the end of the fplinter bar fockets, and go on to the end of the fore axletree arm, between the wheel ftock and nut, in order to ftay and ftrengthen the fplinter bar, and affift the coachman in mounting. Vol. 1, p. 97.

Wheel Plate. The circular iron flat plate, on the fore end of the carriage. Vol. 1, p. 96.

Well. A ftrong box, conveniently placed at the bottom of the body, to carry luggage. Vol. 1, p. 220.

Welting,

Welting. Is the fewing a narrow ftrip of leather over the corner feams of that part which covers the upper part of a body, or boot of a carriage, and which forms a round moulding, and keeps out the wet.

Whiſkey. A lighter fort of a one horfe chaife than ufual. Vol. 2, p. 134.

Wings. The extended timbers of a carriage, alfo what is fixed to the fides of a chaife or phaeton body for the elbows to reft on. Vol. 1, p. 46, 204.

Wither Strap. A part of the harnefs, which goes round the withers of the horfe to hold up the collar.

Woodcock Eye. A fmall iron inftrument, fixed to the end of a trace, which hooks on the fplinter bar end for drawing by.

Worm Spring. A narrow fteel plate, twifted round in a fpiral form, fixed in the double of the main brace, to affift it in giving eafe. Vol. 1, p. 78.

F I N I S.

ERRATA TO VOL. II.

	£.	s.	d.
Page 28. 17th line, 2d column for 1l. 5s. read	2	5	0
Page 29. A new fpoke to any wheel -	0	5	0
A new felly to ditto -	0	5	0

Taking off and putting on the iron to the hoop wheel muft be added.

www.ingramcontent.com/pod-product-compliance
Lightning Source LLC
Chambersburg PA
CBHW032316280326
41932CB00009B/834